Blake, Deleuzian Aesthetics, and the Digital

Claire Colebrook

Continuum Literary Studies

continuum

Continuum International Publishing Group

The Tower Building
11 York Road
London SE1 7NX

80 Maiden Lane
Suite 704
New York NY 10038

www.continuumbooks.com

British Library Cataloguing-in-Publication Data

A catalogue record for this book is available from the British Library.

ISBN: HB: 978-1-4411-5533-7

Library of Congress Cataloging-in-Publication Data

Colebrook, Claire.
Blake, Deleuzian aesthetics and the digital/Claire Colebrook.
p. cm. – (Continuum literary studies)
Includes bibliographical references and index.
ISBN 978-1-4411-5533-7 (hardcover)
1. Blake, William, 1757-1827–Aesthetics. 2. Deleuze, Gilles, 1925-1995–Aesthetics.
3. Literature and technology. 4. Digital media. I. Title.
PR4148.A35C65 2012
821'.7–dc23 2011040985

Typeset by Deanta Global Publishing Services, Chennai, India
Printed and bound in Great Britain

This book is dedicated to Andrea Gregg.

Contents

List of Abbreviations

***Blake: Complete Writings*. Ed Geoffrey Keynes**	
Oxford: Oxford University Press, 1971.	**K**
The Complete Poetry and Prose of William Blake. 2nd ed.	
Ed. David Erdman, with Harold Bloom	
University of California Press, 2008.	**E**
There is No Natural Religion	**NNR**
Milton	**M**
Jerusalem	**J**
Songs Of Experience	**SOE**
The First Book of Urizen	**U**
The Marriage of Heaven and Hell	**MHH**
Visions of the Daughters of Albion	**VDA**
The Book of Los	**BL**
The Four Zoas	**FZ**
All Religions Are One	**ARO**
A Vision of the Last Judgment	**VLJ**

Preface

Blake and Digital Aesthetics

> If it were not for the Poetic or Prophetic character, the Philosophic and Experimental would soon be at the ratio of all things and stand still, unable to do other than repeat the same dull round over again.
>
> (NNR[b], E: 3; K: 97)

The problem of aesthetics has always been intertwined with the problem of the digital (both the digit as the counting/organizing human hand, and the digit as that which allows forms to be repeated and circulated). All problems of aesthetics are problems of the digital, or the relation between what is intuited (*aesthesis*) and the formalized systems that allow for intuitions to be given form and repeatability.[1] How is it that what is received or given to the senses is experienced as this or that identifiable form? How does sensation in its temporal complexity and openness take on a body that can be repeated, circulated, copied, and simulated? How is the fluidity and temporal richness of intuition organized into distinction? How does the flux of sensation become a world of determined, repeatable, ordered, and *synthesized* objects?

The passage from aesthesis to synthesis, from sensation to sense, becomes a problem for 'aesthetics' (or a problem of art and visual pleasure) in modernity. The great gesture of the enlightenment is to refuse any already-given synthesizing system and instead to question the genesis of system. Kant explicitly set the project of critique against the Platonic 'flight' into some higher world of already present forms and instead asked about the emergence of forms (Kant 1998, 395 [CPR A313/B370]). It is also in Kant that the problem of the aesthetic, or the synthesizing of forms, becomes apparent in the experience of beauty. Encountering a world that is not yet conceptualized but appears as if it were offering itself *to be formed,* the ordering subject feels himself to be a synthesizing power. Art is not itself ethical, but its capacity to draw the subject back to the feeling of giving the world form prepares the way for an ethical awareness that there is no law given to the world other than that which emerges from the subject. Art becomes the means by which the subject recognizes herself as the origin of form, even if that origin is transcendental (that is, not emerging from the subject as a worldly individual but as the ground from which all appearances are formed.)[2] Modernity or enlightenment is a form of maturity or 'freedom from imposed tutelage.' Art is not morality, because beauty does not offer us the form of the good; instead, art prepares the way for morality because one feels, in aesthetic pleasure, the coming into form of forms (Lyotard 1994). Morality is possible only when the singularity of the present or the given can be recognized as an occasion for a universal ruling – such that I can act *as if* my decision in this case would be made by any free will in any such circumstance.

As the post-Kantian tradition recognized, there is something necessarily communicable in morality. If something ought to be the case, then it should take the form of a law that would be articulated and agreed upon *in general.* This emphasis on communicability will increasingly be identified as '*the' political.* If there is no such thing as a private and singular ethical act this is because acting out of duty is acting *as if* one were any subject whatever, not tied to the pathology of one's own tastes and desires. For post-Kantian ethics, including liberalism and discourse ethics, one must go beyond Kant's subjectivism: one can only act ethically, or recognize the universal rule in a singular case, because there is something like a formal system that has (beyond the subject's own powers) already given the world determinable form (Habermas 1993). But if this is so, enlightenment is no longer a simple break with the transcendence of pre-modern ethics. It can no longer be the case that the subject takes over and internalizes, or recognizes as his own, the systems through which he thinks. One can no longer chart a continuous genesis of forms and systems from the subject's forming power. Something of a Platonism remains: the subject can only speak, conceptualize or act if there is already, in advance, some system of relations through which he can affect himself, return to himself and recognize himself. One way of understanding this condition of subjectivity is to see language as a privileged formal system through which the subject represents himself to himself. Another – the one explored by both William Blake and Gilles Deleuze – is to see language as possible only because there is a potential for formation that enables language to emerge. This potentiality can be understood as the virtual. The virtual cannot be located within chronological time precisely because synthesized and ordered time has as its precondition something like the potentiality for formation. It cannot be a question of the subject simply looking into the powers of his own reasoning in order to discover the emergence of order. The 'aesthetic' would not be – as it was for Kant – an experience of the human or individual forming of form so much as an experience of the universality, eternity or inhumanity of forms.

The 'reversed Platonism' considered in this book needs to be distinguished from a straightforward negation of Platonism. Forms, the eternal and the transcendental do not exist in some distinct or transcendent third realm: forms are immanent (Collingwood 1976, 71). More accurately we might say that any transcendence – any posited realm beyond the subject – emerges from the subject, but that any subject (or any supposed immanence) is made possible by forms and forces not its own (Taylor 2007, 205). Phenomenology uses the phrase 'transcendence in immanence' to capture this co-implication (Husserl 2006, 59; Byers 2002, 182). Life in this actual world harbors powers or potentialities that are fully real but virtual. It is possible, for example, to have the actualized mathematical system of number because the actual world can be counted. It is possible to have this specific organic body because life has the potentiality to create formed bodies. These potentialities are not stable essences, not already determined and decided entities; they are tendencies or potentialities for variation. If we are given this actual world, already formed and enumerated, then it is possible to consider the transcendental powers from which this world was generated; but these transcendental powers are not located in a transcendent, external or other-worldly domain. For this reason, it is art, or the variation and forming of forms, which enables us to intuit the virtual (Deleuze and Guattari 1994, 194).

Consider the standard Platonic statement of the problem: how is it that the world of chaotic sensations is lived as a meaningful world of sense? For Plato this is because the shadowy world appears only through the giving of forms. There is some condition that is transcendent to the actual and lived world that allows that world to be lived; the viewed world of shadowy types is illuminated by an other-worldly origin towards which we ought to direct our attention (Deleuze and Guattari 1994, 16). Forms or Ideas are what make the viewed viewable, and these forms can only be known by turning away from the noise of mere conversation and appearances.

Hannah Arendt has argued that this Platonic submission to inhuman forms marks a waning of practical politics (a politics of collective discussion and decision) in favor of a transcendent logic. It is not surprising that Arendt's political philosophy, and her problematising of totalitarianism, has such widespread resonance today. If 'the political' is the domain through which systems and formalizing structures emerge, how is it that we forget or repress this genesis? How do we lose sight of the coming into being of the political? Although Arendt does not accord undue privilege to the work of art, the problem of returning political thought to its practical genesis, especially by way of the Greek origin (Villa 1996, 33), has marked many twentieth-century discussions of the importance of the artwork. Giorgio Agamben's general project of 'returning thought to its practical calling' ties the meditation on the Greek origin of modern distinctions to the current problem of the work of art (Agamben 1998, 5). There was a time, Agamben argues, when the work of art emerged from a common praxis of world disclosure (Agamben 1999, 68). What Arendt referred to as a 'speaking in common' that generated the world is described by Agamben as the once collective production of the artwork that passed from praxis into poiesis. Today, Agamben argues, that disclosure of the genesis of the political has been lost, and this is because art no longer refers back to collective formation but is valued as art only through the single artist's signature. The work does not reveal a collective formation of a world in common. Art has now narrowed to being nothing more than 'a' Warhol. In the case of Duchamp's 'ready-mades' what makes the artwork an artwork is the individual gesture and its reference back to a system of signature, rather than what the art work brings to presence. The artist, in turn, is then set over and against a society reduced to mere spectatorship where images circulate as so many already-formed units.

The problem of modernity – as loss of political formation and reduction to passive consumption – therefore ties aesthetics with digitalism and synthesis, and already brings the history of art into its heart. How can we be modern? How can we live the forms and systems through which we speak as our own rather than as rules from some mysterious and frozen past?

For Deleuze, this means that the aim of all art is a retrieval of an analog language, a way of thinking beyond the digit: beyond the units that the counting and measuring hand (aligned with the reckoning eye) have used to determine the world:

> Analogical language would be a language of relations, which consists of expressive movements, paralinguistic signs, breaths and screams, and so on. One can question whether or not this is a language properly speaking. But there is no doubt, for example, that Artaud's theater elevated scream-breaths to the state of language. More generally, painting elevates colors and lines to the state of language, and it is an analogical language.

> One might even wonder if painting has not always been the analogical language par excellence (Deleuze 2005, 79—80).

The artist arrives at a canvas that is already populated with figures, and this is because the world has already been synthesized (Deleuze 2005, 62). Art must at once work with and yet de-form these figures. In doing so, however, it does not return the process of synthesis *back* to the hand of 'man' but connects with inhuman and inorganic forces of the future. In this respect Deleuze regards his work as a *reversal* of Platonism, for there remains a commitment to powers or events that are not those of man, and that have a force beyond the lived time of chronology:

> Events are ideational singularities which communicate in one and the same Event. They have therefore an eternal truth, and their time is never the present which realizes them and makes them exist. Rather, it is the unlimited Aion, the Infinitive in which they subsist and insist. Events are the only idealities. To reverse Platonism is first and foremost to remove essences and to substitute events in their place, as jets of singularities (Deleuze 64).

Once the hand is freed from the syntheses of the organism – once the hand is no longer a set of digits – then a genuine relation to powers that are not those of the body might emerge (Deleuze 2005, 326). The hand reaches out to the forces of eternity (or Aion). Whereas Platonism will argue for the eternal sameness of forms, Deleuze's emphasis on synthesis focuses on the capacity of the eternal to create difference. It is in the opening to the forces of the cosmos that the digits or units of quantitification are requalified (or counter-actualized). The *problem* of Platonism, for Deleuze, remains: the reversal of Platonism entails a move away from judging appearances according to their capacity to fulfil the ideal form, and instead adopting a general differential calculus (assessing the relations among powers):

> That is why the metaphysics of differential calculus finds its true signification when it escapes the antinomy of the finite and the infinite in representation to appear in the Idea as the first principle of the theory of problems. '*Perplication*' is what we call this state of Problem-Ideas, with their multiplicities and coexistent varieties, their determination of elements, their distribution of mobile singularities and their formation of ideal series around these singularities (Deleuze 2004B, 351).

Rather than see the actual world as deriving from static forms, the actual world comes into being by contracting all the potential differential relations (which are eternal and exist on the virtual plane). The world we know and live in is composed of actual relations among differences, but it is possible to intuit the virtual differential forces from which actuality has been contracted. Deleuze's method of intuition considers both the potential decomposition that would imagine the forces that entered into relation to produce the quantities of this world (counter-actualization) and what variation of differential powers would produce new relations. In some respects this is still a mode of Platonism insofar as it maintains the Platonic problematic of the emergence of differentiated quantities, the actualization of ideal forms in matters and the production of substances as formed matters.

Platonism (both traditionally and in its reversed Deleuzian mode) concerns the problem of incarnation: every body in this world takes on a form that allows it to pass from the virtual to the actual. Further, every expression or sense of that incarnated body must also take on some form of material support (whether that be voice, writing or gesture). It is therefore not surprising that the Christian tradition will be able to add to these two modes of incarnation (bodily incarnation and linguistic incarnation) a third sense of the passing into humanity of the divine spirit, a divine spirit which has as its essence nothing other than the power of coming into existence. It is for this reason, also, that Christianity (like Platonism) will harbor the tendency towards immanence and secularism (Deleuze 2005, 7). If the bodies of this world are made possible by forms that transcend actuality, it is nevertheless the case that forms only have their being in the actualizing world they make possible. If divine spirit can take on a living body then it is possible to see bodily life as itself divine. Certain tensions or seeming contradictions in Blake's work, though played out in a unique manner, need to be understood within this history that is (as Whitehead noted) a series of footnotes to Plato (Whitehead 1978, 39). This series of footnotes does not occur by way of textual influence or the transmission of sources so much as the intensification of a problem of emanation and incarnation. The body's form is not its own, and any body possesses not only the singularity of its incarnation but also the eternity of its distinction. In Blake's terms 'everything that lives is holy': every thing that lives already intimates a divinity beyond itself, and yet holiness is only given in the things that live: 'He who sees the Infinite in all things sees God' (NNR[b], E: 3; K: 98). Platonism therefore already partakes of two tendencies, for there is at once the need to account for actualized beings in terms of eternal ideas, as well as the recognition that the appearing of the eternal occurs through incarnation.

Reversed Platonism

In Martin Heidegger's reading of the cave allegory from *The Republic* the passage from viewing projected shadows to viewing the source of light typifies the Platonic 'decision' to turn away from what is already presented to the source that enables the presence of the present (Heidegger 1998A, 155). (There is the assumption that the world derives from a *logos* or reason that exists in advance and determines all that *is*. Heidegger strove to show that any *logos* or 'ratio' or 'logic' must have come into presencing – the presencing of the present – and that this coming forth into presence must have had its origin in a 'speaking about' [*legein*] that brought the world into the light of both revealing and concealing.) The cave allegory in *The Republic* places the world of sensations as secondary to the stable order of sense: there can only be the appearing of a certain thing if there is some Idea (*Eidos*) of the thing, something that determines *what it is*. For Plato, in the beginning is the full presence and full being of the Eidos from which distinct and temporally disclosed beings are possible. The revealing or appearing of beings occurs *after*, and depends upon, the stable forms that allow a world of shadowy flux to be illuminated. What Plato leaves unstated or unthematized, according to Heidegger, is the process both of the coming into appearance of forms, and the turn of the viewer away from the illuminated appearances to the ground or origin of appearing. This constitutes the 'forgetting' that enables something like Being – whether it be in the form of Ideas, God, Substance or Subject – to seem as though it exists as fully present, with the appearing of beings as a dependent contingency. What is never questioned is how beings appear as disclosures of Being, and how the soul focused on appearances comes to turn towards the source of all appearing. For Heidegger it is the *not* asking of this question that distinguishes the Western metaphysics of presence, or the privileging of the *logos*. Everything that appears is determined or synthesized in advance from some prior ground. For Plato this ground or source of appearing, or what allowed sensation to make sense, was the *logos*, or that which could be said of anything, that which would remain the same. For Heidegger this onto-theological forgetting marks Western thought with three features: it is mathematical (pertaining to mathemata, or what can be known in advance); it is logocentric (because the *act* of speaking becomes determined as a 'logic' or the system through which the sensed world is known); and it inaugurates a history of humanism (because man is the rational animal who can be trained in the practices of logic) (Heidegger 1998B, 239–76).

It is in this tradition – a tradition that is at once Platonic in its commitment to being and yet a reversal of Platonism in its questioning of the coming into being of being – that Deleuze will insist on the importance of the aesthetics of analog to digital. If in the late twentieth century digital synthesizers could create new qualities from new relations among quantities, this was because the actual world of measure has always been a result of a synthesis among not yet digitized (not yet differentiated quantities) (Deleuze 2005, 81; Deleuze and Guattari 2004, 121, 379). This known world of qualities has come into being from processes of what Deleuze refers to as differen*c*iation. If *differenciation* is the distribution of actual qualities, this is only possible because of differen*t*iation, the pure forces of quantities that produce encounters and relations that can then be experienced, actualized or presented as differences among distinct terms: 'Whereas differen*t*iation determines the virtual content of the Idea as problem, differen*c*iation expresses the actualization of this virtual and the constitution of solutions' (Deleuze 2004B, 261). The reversal of Platonism occurs with the questioning of Being: there is no longer a posited, already present logic from which this actual world emanates, for the actual world is a contraction from a 'swarm' of powers or forces to differ.

When Heidegger criticizes Western thought as a forgetting of the coming into presence of Being he continues a tradition of immanence that begins, at least, with Kant and that aims to *justify* any logic or system. By what right have we subordinated the difference and complexity of intuition into a world of bounded concepts? We can only justify reason, not by appealing – as Plato did – to assumed and already-present forms, but by arguing that experience is only possible because the synthesizing forms of time and space order the world into a coherent, communicable, and present whole. Thinking is only possible if there is something like reason as ratio, as an ordering power.

Kant acknowledged that the very categories that enable true experience will also lead reasoning into internal illusions. We cannot experience a *world,* a domain of present objects other than ourselves, without some sense of causal order, some sense of spatial distribution, some sense of a temporal continuity, and series; and yet these organizing forms lead to paralyzing questions. Is there a beginning to time? How can there be free subjectivity in a world of causation? Is the universe an object with a spatial location, and if so what is the border or limit of that space? Blake, too, recognized the nightmarish impossibility of such questions that would enclose the self in doubt and despair:

> To cast off the idiot Questioner who is always questioning,
> But never capable of answering: who sits with a sly grin
> Silently plotting when to question, like a thief in a cave:
> Who publishes doubt & calls it knowledge: whose Science is Despair
> (M 41, 13–16; K: 533; E: 142)

Kant's solution was to separate the subject – as a free, ordering and therefore non-objective power – from the experienced and objectified world. Certain Ideas (of freedom, the infinite or God) could be thought, but not known. We can only *know* what we have ordered and synthesized. Blake's response is slightly different, but is part of the response to the modern problem of synthesis. The world is experienced as ordered, but how is this system justified? Blake acknowledges the necessity of forming and synthesizing, but whereas Kant had argued for essential, necessary, and universal forms that are conditional for all experience, Blake's epics describe the continual historical creation and destruction of the figures that enable us to make sense of this world. Whereas Kant's aesthetic is oriented to a *sensus communis,* such that the subject experiences the world *as if* it were oriented towards the forming power of humanity in general, Blake's aesthetic is oriented to fragmentation. Systems that enable perception and life can take on a rigidity and seeming universality that must be destroyed; only with the influx and threat of chaos can the creative and binding power revive:

> And this is the manner of the Sons of Albion in their strength
> They take the Two Contraries which are calld Qualities, with which
> Every Substance is clothed, they name them Good & Evil
> From them they make an Abstract which is a Negation
> Not only of the Substance from which it is derived
> A murderer of its own Body: but also a murderer
> Of every Divine Member: it is the Reasoning Power
> An Abstract objecting power, that Negates everything
> This is the Spectre of Man; the Holy Reasoning Power
> And in its Holiness is closed the Abomination of Desolation
> (J 10, 8–17, B: 629; E: 153).

In his early work Blake writes of the 'enlarg'd and numerous senses' of an original perception that is then enslaved by the systems of the priest. In his later work he emphasizes the active creation of systems: 'I must create a system or be enslaved by another man's.'

Blake's work is at once part of, and yet resistant to, a tradition of rigorous philosophical immanence. Like the enlightenment thinkers whom he often denounced, Blake was critical of the logic of priesthood whereby one body within the world claims exceptional transcendent authority. Instead, he insisted that 'all deities reside in the human breast.' At the same time, Blake also rejected any reductive materialism that would reduce the world to its already enumerated powers. His critical aesthetics drew activity and sense back to the human hand and body, but also opened that very body to the powers of the infinite; there were, after all, deities in the human breast: 'for in brain and heart and loins/Gates open behind Satan's Seat to the City of Golgonooza/Which is the spirtual fourfold London, in the loins of Albion' (M 20. 38–40, B: 502, E: 114).

If one could only approach the world through inscription and marking, avoiding the nightmare of chaos and blind immanence, then one would also need to avoid any simple digitalism that would accept the already inscribed systems of the world. Between the Scylla of rigid systems and the Charybdis of mute chaos lies the dynamic of Blake's poetry. Blake's project of immanence was also therefore a radical Platonism and a reversal of Platonism. He resisted the world's reduction to the mere circulation of already articulated elements: the nightmare of atomism lay in its myopic restriction to the already marked, to the 'same dull round.' In this respect Blake was prophetic rather than Sophistical; there could always be a break or rupture with the domain of communication and the readily figured. And yet, Blake also continually reversed Platonism, opening the infinite from a grain of sand and other inorganic elements. In this respect, Blake's work might then be coupled with the post-enlightenment projects of immanence that drew the transcendent back into the world to account for its genesis. What renders Blake's work *post*-enlightenment is that he maintains immanence as a problem; the very power or event that will destroy the proliferation of tyrannizing specters can itself appear as one more external and governing power:

The hand of Vengeance found the bed
To which the Purple Tyrant fled;
The iron hand crush'd the Tyrant's head
And became a Tyrant in his stead (B: 431; E: 490).

This is the problem of any destruction of system: that destructive power itself can take on the form of one more system. If a power can act and have force in the world, it can also take on a form that can destroy the very generating ground from which it emerged. As in Deleuze's later interpretation, Heidegger's reading of Plato indicates what Jacques Derrida and Bernard Stiegler have referred to as a *pharmacology*: the very extension or possibility of knowing (the speaking through which the world is given) is *also* something that threatens thought from within (Stiegler 1998). Thought is always already technical – made possible by systems of spacing and difference that are never fully its own. Plato gives the *Ideas* as the ground of knowledge and if he rejects poetry or art he does so only to the degree to which it doubles or simulates the pure *logos* or pure seeing of the Ideas. Such a supposedly pure and self-present seeing is (as Heidegger and Derrida will show) already a logic. That is, in order to see the world not merely as a flux of sensations but *as* a synthesized world of sense there must be some ordering power that enables the sense of the world but that cannot itself be sensed.

Blake was even more emphatic about this double bind of writing, which is at once act and logic. On the one hand, true thinking and life cannot be the mere repetition of shadows and symbols (what Plato referred to as the shadows on the walls of the cave, what Heidegger denounced as 'idle chatter' and what Blake described as 'the same dull round'). Thinking is neither digitalization nor logic: neither mere calculation nor the circulation of already present and actualized units. On the other hand, there can be no thinking or retention without some logic or communication. For Heidegger, and especially those who follow his argument against subjectivism, we have a world that can be lived as present only because we experience it *as* this or that determined thing. It is always a world *for* some living being, and therefore must be disclosed *as* something that makes sense as part of a broader and ongoing 'lifeworld.' Heidegger rejects the notion of an already present system through which the world is known (such as Plato's 'logic'), just as Blake before him argued that before there was a system there must have been an event of perception by the 'enlarg'd and numerous senses.' Yet thinking is not without some form; thought requires some ongoing retention of sameness. Without bound or limit what is received could never be experienced *as* some being that is other than me; without form there could be no sense of that which transcends me and exists with a consistency of is own.

In many ways Blake's early relation of contrary states between innocence and experience articulates the two errors that follow from failing to see the need *both* for the bounds of form and for the openness of innocence. The very concepts of innocence and experience – for all their seeming opposition – contain the potentiality of each other, and this is why Blake could publish the same poem in both sets of songs. The relation between the two is not dialectical, for they are not opposites or negations of each other. Rather, they are contrary tendencies: the same synthetic or creative process of life must at once be open to what is not itself, and yet also have a sense of limit between itself and what it objectifies. Experience is suggestive of the brute facts of empiricism, but also of ordering and system: experience is at once a reductive immediacy (the world as a simple 'this'), and a world that is marked, catalogued, judged and enumerated. In 'London,' for example we hear both the immediacy of first-person observation ('I wander…'; 'I meet…' 'I hear') along with the 'marking' or taking note of what is seen, but also the reduction of what is seen to some generality: "every cry of every man …every infant's cry of fear… every voice." Experience is the voice of enclosed and despairing judgment:

> Thou Mother of my Mortal part.
> With Cruelty didst mould my Heart.
> And with false self-decieving tears,
> Didst bind my Nostrils Eyes and Ears.
> Didst close my Tongue in senseless clay
> And me to Mortal Life betray (SOE B: 220; E: 30)

Innocence, by contrast, suggests a child-like newness or openness to the world, at the same time as it also expresses a submissive trust in a benevolent order or paternalistic divinity. In 'The Divine Image' there is at once a sense of the world as always and already familiar, human, and one's own (in contrast to the reductive alienation of experience): 'For all must love the human form,/In heathen Turk or Jew'. And yet that trusting belief in a common humanity – the sense of a benevolent and unified world – is achieved by imagining humans as *signs of* a transcendent divinity: 'For Mercy, Pity, Peace and Love/Is God, our father dear/And Mercy, Pity, Peace and Love/Is man, His child and care' (B: 117, E: 13). By implication, if the virtues of mercy and peace are those of 'our father' then humanity itself requires some redemptive force beyond itself. If experience suffers from being alienated from a godless universe, innocence is cocooned in a trusting infantilism. Both innocence and experience imply each other; they are contraries rather than negations. It is only possible for a body to be open to the newness of life if it has marked itself out as a body, if it is already somehow other than an absolutely pure innocence. At the same time, the process of ordering, judging, marking, and predicting could only occur if there were some influx of a potentiality *for* difference that is not yet differentiated. If innocence is an openness to the world with a sense of its transcendent divinity, experience is the despair that follows from being enclosed in the systems that make self and world possible.

One could articulate these two tendencies in terms of the passage from analog to digital, or what Bernard Stiegler refers to as the pharmacological nature of grammatization: if there were only already articulated units then we would remain within a closed system, but if something like sense is to occur, then the system must be a system *of* some outside (Stiegler 2010, 43). Life must have the form of what Deleuze and Guattari refer to as 'stratification': one side turned towards efficient articulated distinctions, another towards a chaotic, 'smooth' and not yet fully formalized movement of disturbance. There must be at once the possibility of marking, inscribing, repeating, recognizing, and determining in advance (an experienced world that makes sense) and an openness, unstructured receptiveness, and an almost amnesiac capacity to encounter the world anew. If both of these are not in play at the same time one is left with the 'eternal winter' of experience or the blind faith of innocence. The latter is the less frequently noticed problem both in Blake criticism, where innocence is regarded as a desirable but necessarily lost condition, and in theory more generally where the overcoming of limits and rigid systems appears as a prima facie revolutionary good. But neither in Blake's aesthetics, nor in the modern tradition of theory more generally, is there a simple affirmation of the destruction of limits. There always remains a *reversed* Platonism: if forms or transcendent powers beyond this world are destroyed in order to pay heed once again to this world of life, there is also a due reverence paid to powers perceived within the world that are not yet formalized, systematized or actualized. That is, there cannot be a simple, immediate and fully self-present turn to life. There is an infinite that opens from within the world, pulverizing any closed or mechanistic world of already quantified units. It would be a mistake, then, to celebrate the simple destruction of limits and opening to the unlimited, for there is an equally important genetic power of what Deleuze refers to as 'pure predicates', the potentialities from which this world of actualized qualities emerges (Deleuze 2004A, 110). In Blake's terms these powers from which bodies are formed are not only given various names and topographies – such as the 'zoas' that compose the giant Albion, or the specters and emanations that emerge from the self, or the grains of sand, fleas, worms, fibres, roses and pebbles that populate Blake's poems. His poetic method grants a certain autonomy to matters that are not yet formalized; words often seem to have a power to stand alone, not so much as signs or vehicles of sense but as 'sonorous matters' (Deleuze and Parnet 2007, 164). Blake's visual scenes are at once highly figured and inscribed, in their use of iconography and letter script, while at the same time introducing mutation and variation, so that letters trail off to become parts of borders, and borders and frames interweave with floral and bodily figures.

One needs to be wary, then, of taking certain moments in the early Blake – such as *The Marriage of Heaven and Hell*'s railing against systems – as a straightforward Romantic reaction against system. In Blake's later work the problem appears to tend in the other direction, almost as though there is a valorization of forming, binding, marking, uniting, weaving, and proleptic vision against a horror of indistinction, chaos, formlessness and the perpetual present of the 'moony shades'; of Beulah (M 30, 5, B: 518; E: 129). There could be historical reasons for this transition from a radical destructiveness to an emphasis on form, such as the often-narrated distinction between an early revolutionary Romanticism favoring the overthrow of limits followed by a later, wiser, disenchanted Romanticism that recognizes the need for order (Abrams 1963). However, as Jerome McGann (1983) has argued, the received notion of Romanticism as a retreat from revolutionary striving towards aesthetic order depends upon a distinct narration and canonization. In the case of Blake's works it would allow certain double tendencies – towards destruction of limits *and* the binding of forms – to be rendered into opposites (negations rather than contraries). If it is possible to chart a temporal transition from a revolutionary, destructive and 'open' Romanticism towards a resignation to a humanist, communitarian, and limiting poetics, this is because neither mode would be sustainable or thinkable in isolation.

Romanticism itself is more than a literary period and can be better understood as a style of problem. Lyotard has already made this point about modernity: the idea of giving a law and system to oneself, in opposition to the heteronomy of the past, could never be contained *within* historical time (Lyotard 1993). The very sense of history as narrative understanding relies upon an increasing internalization and overcoming of the past. Deleuze understood the baroque in a similar manner, less as a historical period than as a way of interweaving aesthetic forms with questions of being. In its musical mode of composition, baroque counterpoint enables a single bass to be expressed in a number of melodic lines developing in their own mode – just as each monad in the universe opens its own infinite and yet remains in accord with the whole. The baroque, for Deleuze, was a problem regarding the relations among individuals that nevertheless sing from the same cosmic harmony, even if their melodic lines are distinct (Deleuze 2006B). The baroque is not so much a period as a problem, brought to the fore in a historical aesthetic: if the individual is what it is (in its unique singularity), and this individuation includes all its perceptions and affections, how do individuals compose one world? Romanticism *as a problem* might appear to be captured in the received historical narration of an initially post-enlightenment reaction against universalizing systems – the reduction of the world to so many units determined in advance – followed by a recognition that the imagination's violence and chaos requires some forming of limits. Writing in reference to musical Romanticism, Deleuze and Guattari mark a difference from classicism: whereas the latter is a commitment to the universality of forms, Romanticism concerns itself with the coming into being or genesis of relations. If classicism imposed order on chaos – form over content – Romanticism occupies itself with the 'earth', or the powers *to differentiate*. The artist encounters these forces, and far from imposing mastery, remains closely affected by energies not his own:

> If we attempt [a] definition of Romanticism, we see that everything is clearly different. A new cry resounds: the Earth, the territory and the Earth! With Romanticism the artist abandons the ambition of de jure universality and his or her status as creator: the artist territorializes, enters a territorial assemblage. The seasons are now territorialized. The earth is certainly not the same thing as a territory. The earth is the intense point at the deepest level of the territory or is projected outside it like a focal point, where all the forces draw together in a close embrace. The earth is no longer one force among others, nor is it a substance endowed with form or a coded milieu, with bounds and an apportioned share. The earth has become that close embrace of all forces, those of the earth as well as of other substances, so that the artist no longer confronts chaos, but hell and the subterranean, the groundless. The artist no longer risks dissipation in the milieus but rather sinking too deeply into the earth: Empedocles. The artist no longer identifies with Creation but with the ground or foundation, the foundation has become creative. The artist is no longer God but the hero who defies God: Found, Found instead of create (Deleuze and Guattari 2004, 373).

If the artist encounters the earth, rather than territory, then she does not face a localized space of order, nor passive or undifferentiated matter to be ordered, but – rather – she confronts forces that lie beyond ordering. Such powers take perception and affection beyond 'man' as God's good image. One can think here of Blake's figure of the poet–prophet who pours acid onto plates to reveal the infinite, who takes bodies and molds them into form, who writes and walks through eternity after being invaded by the spirit of Milton, and who encounters all the concrete and plastic arts that emphasize the resistance and positivity of materials. The Romantic model of art as an encounter with the 'depths' is possible as a historical period only because of a deeper and trans-temporal aesthetic potentiality for a transition from pure potentialities to actualized forms, from the productive chaos to formed matters (Dimock 2003). Art history is not a series of disconnected 'worldviews' but, like Deleuze and Guattari's 'universal history of capitalism,' a coming into the foreground of the problem of the differential.[3] Just as all life is made possible through the interactions of force that produce distinct quantities (with this process becoming apparent in late capitalism), so art has always been a struggle with the forces of matter and formed figures. That is, it is not the case that the world is already ordered, nor that man imposes order on chaos: there are powers of difference that enter into relation. Art history comes ever closer to its various materials' potential to produce forms; in the same manner capitalism progressively discloses social forms as the effects of relations among forces of varying quantities.

Deleuze's work on Francis Bacon appears to be, on the one hand, a meditation on the problem of a specific artist: Bacon's negotiation of the already given figures that populate any artist's canvas (so installed are we in art history), and the ability to paint the emergence or genesis of figures (Deleuze 2005, 41). In Bacon the formal problem of the relation between ground and figure expresses a deeper aesthetic problem: the passage from analog to digital, and for Deleuze it is this potentiality of life that comes to the fore in different ways in every aesthetic event. The problem of art *in general* is that of an analog language, of somehow breaking from the already digitized systems of measure and once again witnessing the emergence of measure. But that specific aesthetic problem expresses a deeper potentiality of life. In organic life there must at once be a marking out of limits, a distinction between interior and exterior and a general organization. The eye that sees masters the mouth that speaks and the hand that counts (the hand of measuring, quantifying digits):

> There are several aspects in the value of the hand that must be distinguished from each other: the digital, the tactile, the manual proper, and the haptic. The digital seems to mark the maximum subordination of the hand to the eye: vision is internalized, and the hand is reduced to the finger; that is, it intervenes only in order to choose the units that correspond

> to pure visual forms. The more the hand is subordinated in this way, the more sight develops an "ideal" optical space, and tends to grasp its forms through an optical code (Deleuze 2005, 108).

For Deleuze the digital has always been at the heart of aesthetics, both aesthetics as the sense of art *and* aesthetics as 'aesthesis' or what it is to pass from sensation to sense. At the same time, and alongside this passage towards sense and ideality, organic life must also partake in a necessary destruction or disorganization; if the organism were to remain within itself in complete integrity it would be without world and without life. Some openness to what is not determined in advance allows for an influx of the not yet formed, enabling an ongoing synthesis. Deleuze and Guattari expressed this logic of life – not organic life but a 'body without organs' that would come to be organized – through the concepts of stratification and territorialization. Each relatively stable form is at once the forming of some not yet organized matter, while matter is at once that which takes on consistency but that also bears the capacity to disturb and rupture the forms through which it is expressed. In Blake's terms one might say that there is both the art of marking, tracing, sculpting, and binding (or experience's world of repeated, already-known and fully actualized matters) and the destruction of any system with an influx of pure powers (or the openness of innocence).

In the problematization of aesthetics as a philosophical discourse, Kant's work makes this clear. First, experience of beauty is an experience of the process of formalization or discretization: one does not perceive beauty as this or that already organized and subsumed form but as an intuition conducive to conceptualization. Beauty tends towards distinction *and,* crucially, repeatability: the experience of the beautiful is an experience of what *would be* similarly formalizable for others, as though nature as beautiful seemed to offer itself for the subject's organizing (digitizing) powers. The subject then feels her capacity not simply to be affected but to render the influx of intuition into some differentiated and repeatable form. Kant also marks the beauty of the artwork as bearing a relation to the hand *as digit* rather than as manual labor: 'The characterization of the human being as a rational animal is already present in the form and organization of his *hand,* his *fingers,* and *fingertips*; partly through their structure, partly through their sensitive feeling. By this means nature has made the human being not suited for one way of manipulating things but underdetermined for every way, consequently suited for the use of reason; and thereby has indicated the technical predisposition, or the predisposition of skill, of his species as a *rational* animal' (Kant 2007, 418). As long as the work is functional or practical, or serves to further the organic needs of man, it is not art; the object as extension of the working and life-serving hand is mere craft. But if the artwork is released from the needs of life then the creating hand becomes digital, a means of formalization or idealization of materials, now expressive of a spirit freed from localized interests: 'For fine art must be free art in a double sense: it must be free in the sense of not being a mercenary occupation and hence a kind of labor, whose magnitude can be judged, exacted, or paid for according to a determinate standard; but fine art must also be free in the sense that, though the mind is occupying itself, yet it feels satisfied and aroused (independently of any pay) without looking to some other purpose' (Kant 1987, 190).

Well before Kant, and well beyond Kantian aesthetics into our own time, it is possible to note the persistence of the problem of the digital. In Plato's *Symposium,* Socrates's questions regarding the beauty of the beautiful seek to draw attention away from the desired thing to that which renders any object desirable; one passes from the beautiful observed to beauty itself. This *eidos* of beauty would be that which could be seen and repeated beyond the singular instance. Kant's aesthetics does not accept the pre-existence of the form of the beautiful but deduces, transcendentally, the sense of the beautiful: how it is that the subject can perceive in particularity that which would also be perceived by any subject whatever? Beauty is not a form that exists in advance, expressed by this or that thing, for beauty occurs in the subject's awareness of the intuition's capacity to be formalized. What is it, in the object, that offers itself for repetition? The Platonic/Socratic discourse on the beautiful was oriented towards a perception of the inhuman – moving from what is perceived as beautiful to beauty itself, and this 'beauty itself' could only be that which gives form and distinction in general. Ultimately one desires that which renders beautiful things beautiful, but this would then lead to that which would be desired *per se* – not the goodness or desirability of this or that object, but the good itself. In this respect Platonism begins with a rupture between sensation and sense, but then closes that gap by establishing true perception as a teleology. One turns from visible things towards that which allows for visibility in general, from beautiful things to beauty itself, and this then leads to the turning of the soul towards that which would be sought *as such and unconditionally* – beauty and sensation find their end in the good. Kant seeks to ground beauty not in a transcendent form but in the experience, by the subject, of that which he feels to be transcendent to his specific subjectivity but is nevertheless indicative of subjectivity in general. One feels, in beauty, the subjective power as such, the power to synthesize.

It is this relation between a Platonic sense of the inhuman transcendence of beauty *and* a Kantian sense of the genesis of beauty from synthesis that marks Gilles Deleuze's insistence on the importance of the relation between analog and digital. For Deleuze the problem of synthesis, which is also the problem of aesthetics or the apprehension of matters as substances, is also the problem of the relation between analog and digital. Deleuze's inverted Platonism, much the same as Kant's transcendental idealism, is not a rejection of ideality so much as a deduction: what is the genesis of the 'pure predicate'? How does the artwork present that which is not only there for me, now, but there for all time? How does the artwork create percepts that are *not* perceptions? In his book on Francis Bacon, and elsewhere, Deleuze ties this problem to the history of Western art, synthesis, and digitalism. The difference in music between analog and digital synthesizers can help us to approach this problem. The analog synthesizer begins from the sounds of this world and introduces further variation, releasing the potentialities for difference and becoming in given matters. Digital synthesizers operate from formal units that are then composed and combined to create varying sounds:

> *Analogical* synthesizers are "modular": they establish an immediate connection between heterogeneous elements, they introduce a literally unlimited possibility of connection between these elements, on a field of presence or finite plane whose movements are all actual and sensible. *Digital* synthesizers, however, are 'integral': their operation passes through a codification, through a homogenization and binarization of data, which is produced on a separate plane, infinite in principle, and whose sound will only be produced as the result of a conversion-translation (Deleuze 2005, 137).

For Deleuze the problem of digital-analog creation – a problem made evident in the synthesizers of the twentieth century – is a problem of art and life in general: 'Painting is the analogical art *par excellence*' (Deleuze 2005, 138). Deleuze sees Francis Bacon as trying to wrest an analog language from the digital: how does an artist begin with the already established units and figures of creation and create new lines and forms? Art is not recombination, not the rearrangement of already given units; it is not digital. It neither remains with the figured distinctions of the history of visual forms *nor* does it approach the visual field digitally – as though the hand were a set of 'digits' subordinated to the measuring eye of man. If every painter repeats the history of art she does so because she passes from analog to digital, destroying the figures that already populate the canvas, refiguring the genesis or synthesis of matters.

At one end of the spectrum Deleuze locates an aesthetics of abstraction, a cerebral mode concerned directly with pure forms; at the other is a *manual* aesthetic – where the hand is no longer a set of digits but acts directly on matters. (One could think here, in terms of the cerebral, of the geometrical forms of Kandinsky; the aesthetic of manualism in visual arts, by contrast, is readily exemplified by the Australian painter Pro Hart whose canvases were composed from thrown and splashed paint. In music one can go from the mathematical variations of a Stockhausen and the serialism of Schoenberg to Berio's use of the voice as cry, laugh or scream. In popular music one can note a formal abstraction in electro-trance where simple chord progressions foreground diatonic modulations and key changes, and an aggressively manual aesthetic where musical instruments are hit, cut or smashed – as in the frequent 1970s rebellious gestures of attacking a piano with an axe or pulverizing electric guitars by slamming them onto the stage.) There is a potential, in all arts, for pure forms whereby matter is nothing more than an almost substrate-neutral medium for repeating an ideality that is abstracted from any specific matter, and also a potential for the force of matter itself – as though matter were directly destructive of form and could exist only as singular and unrepeatable. But digitalism as a *problem* is given in a mode of art that installs itself between these two tendencies of (physical-bodily) hand and (abstract) idea. Deleuze refers to this approach as haptic. This art is neither digital – rendering matter into equivalent and repeatable forms – nor manual, proceeding directly from the hand:

> The *digital* seems to mark the maximum subordination of the hand to the eye: vision is internalized, and the hand is reduced to the finger; that is, it intervenes only in order to choose the units that correspond to pure visual forms. The more the hand is subordinated in this way, the more sight develops an ideal optical space, and tends to grasp its forms through an optical code. But this optical space, at least in its early stages, still presents manual referents with which it is connected. We will call these virtual referents (such as depth, contour, relief, and so on) *tactile* referents. This relaxed subordination of the hand to the eye, in turn, can give way to a veritable insubordination of the hand: the painting remains a visual reality, but what is imposed on sight is a space without form and a movement without rest, which the eye can barely follow, and which dismantles the optical. We will call this reversed relationship the *manual.* Finally, we will

> speak of the haptic whenever there is no longer a strict subordination in either direction, but when sight discovers in itself a specific function of touch that is uniquely its own, distinct from its optical function (108).

In the haptic, the forming of matters is itself sensed, as though sensation had the capacity to pass from the hand that feels to the hand that writes. The eye that views such a work is neither oriented to the cerebral subordination of the hand to a set of enumerating digits, nor is the eye overtaken completely by the hand. Neither the domination of matters by the abstraction of the intellect (a body organized by the mapping brain), nor a destruction of order by the immediacy of the body as a series of parts: the haptic aesthetic encounters the passage from force to form. The ear can *hear* the back of the violin bow hitting the gut of the string across the wood of the instrument; the eye can *feel* the scratching of the engraver's stylus on the plate; it is as though the organs that had been organized by the measuring eye and speaking voice expand to meet the affects of the body's largest and most distributed organ – the tactility of the skin.

In the haptic aesthetic, which Deleuze and Guattari describe as an aesthetic of 'close range', the viewing eye feels the sensation of the genesis of figures from matters (Deleuze and Guattari 2004B, 544). In Blake's plates, for example, the scarring or scratching of the plate, along with the increasing thickness of overlaid color, become visible, as though Blake's work activated the 'enlarged and numerous senses' that he claimed were once possessed by a godlike vision before priesthood. For Deleuze this aesthetic problem of the digital, or the transition from an analog intensity of infinitely small distances to a discrete series of digits, is also the problem of the inhuman. How is it that man is formed as an organism: as a seeing eye that views a world to be measured by the counting manipulating hand, expressed by the voice of reason? Kant, too, had asked about the genesis and synthesis of 'man': how is the self that thinks organized with the body that feels and the mind that counts and orders? For Kant these faculties – thinking, feeling, desiring – were ultimately harmonious by way of reflection. Kant opposed the Platonic identification of beauty with the good, and was also critical of the notion that one might simply elevate oneself from natural beauty, to the Idea of beauty and then ultimately to the Idea of the desirable as such – the Good. Such a harmonious equivalence could only lead to paralyzing contradictions: one cannot simply *extend* the insight one gains of the material world of cause and effect and then arrive at the supersensible world of freedom and the good. If the good or reason were continuous with the causal world of time and space then morality and logic – the good and the true – would suffer from the vagaries of opinion, for we would see them now in this light, now in another. For Kant it is only by marking a distinction among the truths of reason (*not* derived from sensation), the duties of a pure will (liberated from the pathologies of the bodily self) and the intuitions of a conceptualized world that one can bring accord to the faculties.

In many respects, then, Kant's enlightenment is already post-enlightenment, for critique begins with a constitutive break between the world that can be known theoretically (systematized and unified by concepts) and the world that can be thought. The world that one can imagine – either by acting *as if* one were a pure will or by feeling sensations *as if* the world were in accord with one's conceptual powers – is not the world reduced to calculation. In perceiving the beauty of nature the subject feels herself as an organizing power. This helps to evidence a relation between reason (a pure faculty capable of thinking *beyond* experience to Ideas such as freedom, God and the infinite) and the understanding, which can only know such forms as given in this world of time, space, and finitude. It is by separating these faculties, knowing their specific domain, that one achieves harmony. The perception of beauty prepares the way for the subject to feel that he is not merely a thing of this world but a forming power. From there, one can imagine oneself as a being capable of thinking of oneself as law-giving rather than law-bound (and this would yield the subject of morality); and one can also reign in any temptation to try and locate pure Ideas in this world: one could not *know* the subject of morality, God or freedom.

It may be the case that we can only know this world digitally, mediated through some formed system that orders series and synthesizes bounded forms. But such digitalization has a genesis, and it is this genesis that is felt (but neither known nor presented) in art. When Deleuze writes on Kant and (with Guattari) on the relation among the faculties he asks by what right we have assumed that one ought to harmonize these powers. If thinking can take these diverse paths, and can operate at once to think beyond this concrete world *and* to experience the singular concreteness of this world *and* to think of this world as organized into discrete and repeatable function, then why would one reduce the artwork to an indication of the faculties' harmony? And why should the harmony of the faculties be centered on the man who views the world as calculable, and who regards art as an indication of his own organizing power, and allows aesthetic response to provide a prelude to being able to judge the world as a purely moral being? For Deleuze the importance of Kant's work lies both in the discordance of the faculties and in the problem of synthesis. Kant indicates internal conflicts of synthesis, or reason's inevitable illusions: there is an infinite world of pure Ideas, a world ordered into temporal and spatial unity, and a world of the future in which one acts as if one were *not* a representative of general humanity but something closer to a 'people to come.' For Deleuze and Guattari philosophy would not be, as it was for Kant, a resolution of conflicts among the faculties, but an intuition of distinctions. Philosophy would create concepts that were not extensive. Such concepts would not generalize the good or the beautiful from its many actual instances – gathering examples into a generality; rather, concepts would be intensive. Concepts are intensive in their creation of orientations or tendencies: the concept of 'art' in modernity, for example, intertwines shock, destruction, spectatorship, radicalism, and anti-commodification with the figure of 'the' artist. Concepts are not created when we simply label already existing sets of probabilities (if, for example, I were to define art by everything that happens to be collected in the Louvre.) Philosophy creates concepts that rupture the organism's boundedness, no longer organizing the world as though it were reducible to life's bodily needs and interests. Philosophy manages to create concepts that *think beyond the actual* – inhuman concepts such as the thought of the future, of the cosmos or of the image. Deleuze and Guattari's concept of art does not generalize from what art is, but intensifies art's potentiality: art creates percepts and affects. Percepts are not perceptions, and affects are not affections; they are not what actually takes place, as a general rule, in the organism. A percept is that which *would be perceived,* and an affect is that which *would be felt.* Can the painter create, in materials, the power of color to produce sensations? Can the material be released from what it is for the measuring and adaptive organism, and be allowed to stand alone in its pure potentiality to be sensed?

This returns us to the digital. How is it that 'we' are given a world of formed matters? For Kant this must refer us back to a forming power, a subject's capacity to distinguish and organize. For Deleuze what the work of art intimates is not a subject who must have synthesized matters but matters that enter into relation to produce quantities. In the beginning is neither the hand of man, nor the digit, but a force from which quantities emerge. It is only by splitting the creative hand of the artwork from the enumerating hand of quantifying judgment that thinking will be liberated from its self-enclosing paralysis.

In some ways Deleuze's distinction between the artistic or creative hand that is liberated from function and the hand of calculation emphasizes a Romanticist ethic and aesthetic of anti-subjectivism, in which the force of creativity is no longer determined in advance by the already socialized and organized self – an anti-subjectivism (Hartman 1970). In a similarly destructive manner – using the word '*Destruktion*' in its phenomenological sense – Blake's aesthetics begins with a genealogy of systems (*The Marriage of Heaven and Hell*). Blake speculates that there must have been distinct and incommensurable powers (the pure receptivity of innocence) subsequently organized by the limiting judgment of the understanding. His later epics oscillate between the drive for a unified accord among powers, all operating as aspects of a whole (the single human form), and an undecidable suspension of powers in which difference is irreducible. More often than not, it is sexual difference that provides the figure through which the problem of the unified whole of 'man' is negotiated. Either the feminine is incorporated within divine man in a repose of final order, or man remains distinct and different from a female emanation whom he no longer fears nor whom he reduces to nothing more than his own reflection.[4] Humanity has been 'man' because it has rejected its integrated and original femininity (Jerusalem) and externalized and elevated an independent and dominating female form (Vala). In *The First Book of Urizen* Blake anticipates the emergence of the female form that he will narrate at fuller length in *Milton:*

9. All Eternity shudderd at sight
Of the first female now separate
Pale as a cloud of snow
Waving before the face of Los

10. Wonder, awe, fear, astonishment,
Petrify the eternal myriads;
At the first female form now separate

They call'd her Pity, and fled

(U, 18–19: 9–15 & 1, E: 78; K: 231)

When woman serves merely as an external reflection of male selfhood, solipsism, as well as alienation, occurs. Los does not see an other self in a relationship of mutual recognition but his own divided likeness:

Eternity shudder'd when they saw,
Man begetting his likeness,
On his own divided image.

(U, 19: 14–16, E: 79; K: 232)

This use of sexual figuration by Blake at once reinforces and problematizes the organic figure of man: on the one hand all powers remain distinct but unified within man, drawn back into the enlightening immanence of self-positing humanity; on the other hand man is not the ground of powers but becomes – alongside another female power –a capacity to intuit worlds and infinities not his own. On the one hand there is a figure of the ordered body as unification and reduction of difference to a single system; and on the other hand a sense of the force of life as that which exceeds and extends systematization beyond all closed forms. If the feminine figures as the body's ambivalent and curious outside (never decidable whether femininity is a part of a greater man or a different power in its own form and right) then the hand is also curiously double. At once part of an organized and enumerating body of rigid systems and survey, the hand is also the organ of touch and exteriority. Both femininity and the body have this curious double nature of being both a site of splitting and alienation, and of expansive unification.

The hand is both digital in its capacity to count, reduce, and master, and dis-organizing in its capacity to be released from the body. The hand of the poet, in Blake's work, receives forces from without – printing, marking, and inscribing forces from the outside that are not the body's own. In *Milton* the poet receives inspiration, not through the influx of divine breath, but when Milton 'enters' Blake's left foot; and it is from this intrusion that the poet then goes on to write, becoming populated by a multiplicity of voices:

> But Milton entering my Foot: I saw in the nether
> Regions of the Imagination; also all men on Earth,
> And all in Heaven, saw in the nether regions of the Imagination
> (M 21, 4–6, K: 503; E: 115)

It is not surprising that Blake was concerned with the organization of the body and its discordant faculties or 'zoas'. Blake's art is an art of the hand and the hand's passage from bodily organ to agent of vision, where vision is not the surveying eye of calculating reason but an experience of the haptic. The eye is assaulted by or feels the influx of powers not its own; this eye destroys the selfhood – the organized subject of reason – and then releases what, for Blake, remains ambivalently poised between a cosmos of pure differences on the one hand, and an ultimate or redeeming subject of life on the other. Blake's work is situated between these two possibilties – subject and chaos. This is also to say that Blake's work is a dramaturgy of the analog and digital. He affirms the genesis of quantities that must have emerged from an originally productive life, and seems to veer towards an analog aesthetic in his engraving method that will allow each letter to emerge from the hand, to be directly expressive rather than mediating. And yet Blake, also, through the very same commitment to printing, will constantly rail against indistinction, and will not posit some undifferentiated ultimate or plenitude: 'The Man who asserts that there is no Such Thing as Softness in Art & that every thing in Art is Definite & Determinate has not been told this by Practise but by Inspiration & Vision because Vision is Determinate & Perfect & he Copies That without Fatigue Every thing being Definite & determinate (K: 457; E: 646). Not only does his aesthetic theory and method celebrate the forging of differences, Blake will also present the ultimate foundational life or 'original' body as already plural. It is as though in the beginning there is not a unity that falls into distinction, but a multiplicity of powers – although Blake does occasionally seem to suggest a body that becomes divided by sexual difference:

The globe of life blood trembled
Branching out into roots;
Fib'rous, writhing upon the winds;
Fibres of blood. milk and tears;
In pangs. eternity on eternity,
At length in tears & cries imbodied
A female form trembling and pale
Waves before his deathly face
All Eternity shudderd at sight
Of the first female now separate

(*U* 17 [18] K: 231; E: 338)

The body that seems to suffer from division is originally distinct and multiple (composed of various powers), but then falls into submissive or hierarchical difference (where one power organizes or explains the whole). Two figures of sexual difference occupy Blake's poems: the first is an irreducible difference in which male and female remain distinct, as though life can only be released from paralysis through a recognition of an opening to otherness. The second is a humanizing and organizing difference in which the body of man internalizes a femininity he had mistakenly expelled as other:

Jerusalem! Jerusalem! deluding shadow of Albion!
Daughter of my phantasy! unlawful pleasure! Albions curse!

I came here with intention to annihilate thee! But
My soul is melted away. Inwoven within the Veil
Hast thou again knitted the Veil of Vala, which I for thee
Pitying rent in ancient times, I see it whole and more
Perfect, and shining with beauty!

(J 23, 1–8 K: 645; E: 168)

Blake's final redeemed wholes, insofar as there is any finality or redemption, are at once distinct and unified. Blake's aesthetic project is at once an attempt to seize hold of the forces of repetition, communicability, and digitalism – and so Blake will resist the commodification and mass production of art, restoring the process of printing and writing to the poet's own hand, as though the work of art might once again be analog, emerging seamlessly from the artist's vision. At the same time, the very condition of returning the forces of systems to the individual hand requires a more profound sense of the 'digit,' of the coming-into-distinction and separation of the letter. What Blake's works will rehearse is the inherent impossibility and destructiveness of digitalism, alongside digitalism's persistent necessity. The digit or unit is at once required for the repetition and circulation of any distinct (traced, marked) sense, and yet the digit both mutates and differs in its circulation and breaks with the very sense it supposedly articulates. In order for any quality or sensibility to endure or live on it must take on a body; it must be inscribed or take on a separability that also (in the case of the artwork or linguistic expression) possesses a material support. And yet it is this very digitalization (for the sake of endurance) that will also entwine the work's survival with its distortion and decay. The digit will enable separation and distinction from the gesturing hand, just as the artwork will be possible only through the materialization of sense. A sensation can only endure or be rendered repeatable through the form of sense, and form cannot be actualized without matter, just as matter cannot be materialized – cannot appear *as matter* – without form.

This problem was already present in Kant's aesthetics where the beauty of nature or the artwork occurred in sensation's ready passage to communicability. What is perceived, in the experience of beauty, is not yet conceptualized, but appears as if formed for universal accord: it is as though the world were destined to harmonize with the subject's conceptualizing powers – as though the gap between the world in itself and the world for us could be overcome with the thought of a nature progressing towards universal understanding. Concepts and forms are at once distinct from the world of nature, and yet we approach nature as if it could only arrive at its proper fulfilment through the ordering of conceptual systems. It is in this tradition of the Kantian problem of the concept that Paul de Man will deconstruct the opposition between physis and techne: any nature in itself can be imagined *as nature, as prior to writing* only after the recognition of the separation of writing. It is not surprising, then, that de Man's deconstruction is articulated through the passage from enlightenment to Romanticism. Like Blake, de Man approached the enlightenment of Rousseau with a double attitude (de Man 1976). On the one hand Rousseau's return to nature signals a rejection of constituted laws and systems in favor of a will, language, and law that would emerge from humanity itself; on the other hand, any nature that would be retrieved as prior to social systems can only be known *as nature* in its having been lost. The notion of nature or origin is required to criticize the derivative nature of systems, but any nature that has been retrieved as original must, in turn, be articulated and formed through a system that will, also in turn, appear as secondary. Writing, or the taking on of an external body, is not secondary to the fullness and continuity of an original experience. On the contrary, the seeming self-sameness of an original and lived bodily presence is already digital, already divided into the retention and anticipation of that which could be repeated, beyond the present, into an indefinite and anonymous future. For this reason de Man will use the word 'text' not to describe some organization, differentiation or representation of materiality, but something like materiality 'itself' which *is* or becomes matter only through a punctuation or deferring in which it divides from itself through time. There would be an original digitalism in life, a non-presence, disarticulation or dispersal whereby any supposed continuity that passes into text, any original presence or being, could only be posited ex-post-facto from text.

The literary text or the literary work brings this general writing to the fore precisely in its bracketing or suspension of voice. For what occurs in the convention and framing of a literary text is text *as text* detached explicitly from authorial presence; when one reads a literary text the question of who is speaking can never, unproblematically, be identified with the author. There would be something counter-prophetic in literary texts. Despite first appearances, this is especially so in Blake whose most prophetic voices – those that have broken free from the noise of idle chatter to judge and pronounce – are also exemplary of a fallen and violent self-enclosure. It is difficult, despite first appearances, to establish a simple moral binary between Blake's *Songs of Innocence* and *Songs of Experience,* as though the former expressed an unproblematically good innocence, and the latter a fallen world of moralizing. Blake shifted some poems from one book of *Songs* to the other, suggesting that the relation between the two contrary states was just that – *contrary* – implying each other through dynamic relation. The problem with innocence is its luring self-enclosure, its sense of the world as always harmonious, never radically other. What the state of experience indicates, by contrast, is a world that can only be an object of judgment, given only through experience – as object – never felt: the voice of experience possesses no sense of voice as anything other than law, accusation or command. Both these problematic tendencies come out in Blake's later work in the very possibility of prophecy, for prophecy must at once open to a potentiality for redemption of the present at the same time as breaking with the present. There must be at once the hopefulness of faith, alongside the rupturing distance of a genuinely prophetic future. Even in *Songs of Experience* the voice that 'past, present and future sees' intimates both the opening of messianic hope and the annihilating enclosure of a totalizing vision. There would be tyranny if prophecy were impossible, if voices were only descriptive or affective; but there would also be tyranny in a purely speculative tone, in a leap beyond this world and all its particularity for the sake of a unifying judgment (Derrida 1993). It is not surprising then that the tone of prophecy marks Blake's work at its most decisive and most undecidable points. Voices emerge prophetically to declare a potential redemption, and yet that very break may also be read as a despairing incapacity to live in the world as it is (as already holy, as immanently divine). Consider the following example from *Jerusalem,* where Los battles with his specter, and describes the immobilized and imprisoned Hand:

"Hand sits before his furnace: scorn of others & furious pride
"Freeze around to bars of steel & to iron rocks beneath
"His feet; indignant self-righteousness like whirlwinds of the north
"Rose up againt me thundering, from the Brook of Albion's River,
"From Ranelagh & Strumbolo, from Cromwell's gardens & Chelsea,
"The place of wounded Soldiers; but when he saw my Mace
"Whirl'd round from heaven to earth, trembling he sat: his cold
"Poisons rose up, & his sweet deceits cover'd them all over
'With a tender cloud. As thou art now, such was he O Spectre.
"I know thy deceit & thy revenges, and unless thou desist
"I will certainly create an eternal Hell for thee. Listen!
"Be attentive! be obedient! Lo, the furnaces are ready to receive thee!
"I will break thee into shivers & melt thee in the furnaces of death.
"I will cast thee into forms of abhorrence and torment if thou

> "Desist not from thine own will & obey not my stern command
> "I am clos'd up from my children: my Emanation is dividing,
> "And thou my Spectre art divided against me. But mark,
> "I will compell thee to assist me in my terrible labours: To beat
> "These hypocritic Selfhoods on the Anvils of bitter Death.
> "I am inspired. I act not for myself; for Albion's sake
> "I now am what I am!...' (J: 7–8, 71–17, K: 626–27; E: 151).

On the one hand the voice is positively prophetic, demanding attention, refusing 'deceits', and opposed to 'hypocritic Selfhoods.' And yet there is also a vein of fallenness in Los's punishing and accusing tone: 'I will break thee ... I will compel thee... I will cast thee.' While Los's ire is directed at his Spectre, and can therefore be seen as a redemptive annihilation of his reified or frozen self, there is also a tone of regressive punishment: 'I will certainly create an eternal Hell for thee.' Not only is there an ethical complexity in prophecy insofar as it must at once speak of a future of hope, while allowing a break with the present to be articulated from the present; prophecy also operates with a formal and logical duplicity. The voice of the prophet is necessarily double, at once breaking free from systems and yet productive of a further system and judgment. Once voice gives itself forth in text it is not only quotable, repeatable, and liable to mutation and distortion; it also becomes detached from any authentic presence or guarantee. The prophetic view must emerge from the chaos and difference of dissident voices. And yet despite clear markers of sincerity, and despite the voice's claim to be *the* final authoritative voice, the very intoning or taking on of distinct form and diction renders any voice particular and finite, liable to inauthentic repetition.

Stanley Fish noted this problem in relation to Milton: Milton at once claimed to be the prophetic voice of divine inspiration and yet also to be *Milton,* a poet with his own singular originality (Fish 2001). Fish dealt with this as a conflict between Christian fidelity and literary desires for originality. Blake's similar problem takes the conflict beyond the Christian tradition in its narrow sense to the very possibility of speech and sense. Speech is only possible through system, through submission and fidelity to a communicative structure that has a history and shared set of understood conventions (and so Blake's prophecies take up the Greek, Roman or originally Christian tradition of speaking in common, not falling into the nightmare world of interiority). Yet, Blake's prophecies reject the notion of remaining as hireling or servant of the daughters of memory: 'We do not want either Greek or Roman models if we are but just & true to our Imaginations, those Worlds of Eternity in which we shall live for ever' (M 1, E: 95).

Acknowledgments

I am grateful to the support of the UK's Arts and Humanities Research Council, The University of Edinburgh, The British Academy, The Carnegie Foundation and the Huntington Library Visiting Fellowship scheme for providing valuable research assistance for this project.

Chapter 1

Media, Mediation, and Materiality

We live in an age of digital media. The capacity for artworks to be reproduced, or for artworks to be events of reproduction – photography, film, digital music – is not some event that is added on to the art object (as though art began as pure self-contained original only to be overtaken by techniques of doubling and simulation). The very techniques of art, and even the setting apart of an object *as art* already rely upon systems of recognition, circulation, and repetition. Yet something does occur when the techniques of reproduction take on a greater intensity. Writing and system may be necessary conditions for any event of expression, but some expressions are more formalized than others. A bird or monkey may respond to something like a generally recognizable sound of its own kind – and this because something in each instance is recognized as the same across time. More formalized systems, such as logic or mathematics, have less concrete and material thickness but a greater range of repeatability: we do not hear the timbre and pitch of the voice of Plato (as we would in the immediacy of a cry), but we do read and recognize the highly singular signature of *Plato*: as an individual expressing his own time for all time (Stiegler 1998). Once a system abstracts something like number or sense in general, it can be articulated in a greater number of forms and matters. A mathematical equation has the same sense whether expressed in prose, roman numerals, or Arabic numerals. The purity of its form relies on a logical abstraction that no longer requires an individual voice or signature. Natural languages differ from the sign systems of animals in higher degrees of formalization, and yet they are not the pure forms of logic. One could chart a spectrum between the sonorous qualities of cries and screams, through natural languages (with generalities and concepts), to pure functions (of logic and mathematics). For Deleuze and Guattari these different tendencies – of the sensations of art, concepts of philosophy and functions of science – allow us to discern distinct differences of kind (not just of degree). Philosophical concepts enable a repetition of a sense that carries across infinite instances of sensations, and yet concepts rely both on an articulation in some system of sense, and the creation of some 'plane': we could not have the concept of 'justice' without relations of law, order, judgment and a somewhat impersonal or formalized humanity. Just as concepts rely upon relations among forces (so that the concept of the 'subject' ties thinking to self-awareness, to doubting and to reflection), so the sounds or marks that enable systems of concepts to be formed require some distinction of sonorous or textural matters. Some matter – such as the signs of a language in the form of sounds or marks – is required to release *from matter* that which could be identified, repeated, and expressed beyond material instances. While acts of writing are never fully original – for one can only write and speak via some pre-existing and never individually authored structure – there is also a degree of mutation in every use of a system. Modes of formalization and repeatability differ not only in degree but also in kind. Standard communication may not have the non-ambiguity of logic and mathematics, but it is more regular and formulated than the deviations of poetry.

It is attention to this problem of degrees of formalization that distinguishes Blake's post-enlightenment Romanticism. Unlike, say, Wordsworth for whom nature could be imagined or intimated as a lost plenitude inevitably belied by any system of writing, Blake's inscriptive aesthetics operated with the formalizing process of textual production, both by producing variation in the formalized system of English (engraving letters, creating new words, producing undecidable cases poised between repeatable letter and visual mark) and by narrating the emergence of systems and their destruction. Writing for Blake was part of a more general problem of life: without a destructive imagination life falls into the same dull round of systemic repetition, but without some forming of system there can be no individualized life, only undifferentiated chaos. Blake's productive method explored the genesis of inscription by engraving each letter as both repeatable and singular: the letter was at once part of a system *and* a matter or presence in its own right. His epics also took the emergence of systems as their subject matter, describing the genesis of laws from singular voices, and then the capacity of those created voices to appear as self-present systems.

Rather than read Blake's works through the structuralist model of a signifying system that produces its own oppositions, or a historicist model in which literary forms can be explained as having emerged from the content of an articulated context, Blake's problem of formalization can be best approached through a non-binary understanding of the relation among form of expression, form of content, matter of expression and matter of content. That is, it is not a question of a system imposed on an otherwise inchoate matter, nor of a system that flows directly from a matter that possesses a potential system that merely passes into actuality. Systems are forms of expression, or ways in which life takes on order and relation; but such forms of expression require forms of content (Deleuze and Guattari 2004B, 158). (To use the example Deleuze and Guattari take from Foucault: if there is a legal discourse of reform, guilt, criminality, and deviancy, this supervenes on bodies distributed for surveillance, monitoring, self-observation, and exercises of discipline. A form of expression – such as a language, system of figures, or range of gestures – is one side of a creation of differences, which also includes a form of content. What is expressed has its own relatively distinct relation among differences.)

The form of expression of Blake's work includes the letters of the English language, the visual iconography of his human figures, ornamental and scriptive figures, the genres of epic and prophecy, and his unique mode of illuminated manuscript. His form of expression was a unique interweave of letters and figures, with letters sometimes being poised undecidably between readable mark and visual lure. But such formal systems have a matter or matters: in Blake's case these are the inks, plates, colors, washes, and incisions. The form of expression is a combination of visual figure and linguistic mark; the matter of expression is the engraved plate, including the thickness of the color and the manipulation of materials on the plate. But there is also a form of content, so that Blake's works express a world already formed – a world of bodies, laws, systems, competing discourses and oppositions. In Blake's time bodies were distributed in factories, schools, churches, and cities, in a manner that has been studied by Michel Foucault and his concept of discipline (Stempel 1981). An elevated, centralized or 'deterritorialised' figure – in Foucault's *Discipline and Punish* the prison guard, in Blake's world the priest – subjects bodies to a form of organization whereby bodies fall into a seemingly immanent or self-generating order. The body is imprisoned by the soul: for Foucault this is evidenced in all the forms of analysis and reflection that turn the self in upon itself (Foucault 1979). In Blake, we witness the despair that follows from the self that is closed in upon itself, trapped as a mind looking out from a body. The key point in this critique of transcendence is that what Foucault describes as the discourse of discipline and legal judgment does not exist without a concomitant formation of bodies and spaces. Form of expression – legal discourse – is determined by and determines form of content, or the distribution of bodies and spaces. Similarly, Blake's form of expression (the prophetic book) corresponds both to a matter of expression (ink, plates, sounds, marks), and to a form of content: a world of high systematization that also seems devoid of sense. In addition to form of expression, form of content and matter of expression, there is also the matter of content: the physical bodies and substances of Foucault's prison system, or the factories, laboring bodies and work houses of Blake's world of chimneys, churches, and schools. The matter of the world is formed in a way that is not reducible to the form of expression: forms of expression – judgments, accusations, prayers, poems, natural languages, calculating systems – have as their condition of possibility a world of formed matters. The form of expression and form of content do intersect, but they are not the same. There will always be a problem of analysis in detecting the ways in which the forms of content (the ordering of bodies) intersect with the forms of expression. There will also be a further problem of composition: how might one write or speak, or create new forms of expression, in a world of already formed expressions and bodies? Indeed, we might say that there is a *formal* problem posed by Blake's world: how does one write poetry or create art – how does one formalize – in an era when formalization (or the coming into being of social and natural systems) is itself a problem? What happens when formalization, writing, and the organization of life by systems comes to be recognized both as necessary for sense and yet, also, as that which threatens life's capacity *to sense*?

Deleuze and Guattari have suggested that the domain of art is that of the 'least formalised' elements, somehow finding an element in language or systems that has not yet reached systemic rigor. Blake's works describe the coming into being of formed bodies (where matter is molded and put into relation) and the genesis of forms of expression, where acts of naming or animation fall into rigidity and become reified. Without form the world has no consistency, but without some latitude in degrees and relations of formalization life is condemned to the same dull round.

The contemporary theorist of the history of technics, Bernard Stiegler, argues *both* that something like writing is inherent in the very structure of the human brain – for our neural networks are developed in tandem with a historically embedded system of technical objects – *and* that a new threshold is reached with modern formalized modes of writing. When we read Plato or Blake (at least in a poetry anthology) the voice of the original intention has been given form by a repeatable system that allows it to be re-articulated beyond its original context, and yet also be marked as the voice of a singular intending individual. We might be able to see marks in the sand as the sign of an animal, or even read basic symbols, such as road signs, as signaling a repeatable sense, but 'signed' works that are expressions of a voice and intent require highly sophisticated and particular systems that enable the inscription and maintenance of voice, at the same time as voice itself becomes structured by the system that enables its preservation and extension:

> Recognizing orthographic writing's specificity is not a matter of restoring a phono-logo-centric principle in it: the inscribed orthothesis's meaning is not to be found in some fidelity to the *phone* as self-presence but in the literate/written recording of the past as past, as the passage of the letter, or of speech through the letter – a certain mode of repeatability of a having taken place (if not a having-been) of the play of writing's repeatability (Stiegler 2009, 35).

There is, according to Stiegler, a strange 'pharmakon' quality of writing: it allows the individual voice to be repeated beyond the isolated location of its own context, but can do so only if that individuated voice has taken on the structure of the system that gives its intentionality a repeatable form. (Just as the 'individual' brain becomes more complex and more self-aware because it has a conceptual capacity enabled by the development of symbolic systems and the accompanying neo-cortex or neural 'hardware', so works of art can transcend their context and be repeated anew in later times only because they take up the history of previous forms.) As Walter Benjamin noted, the work of art in an age of mechanical reproduction does not simply make the same corpus of works available to more viewers, it alters the time and body of the work (Benjamin 2008). If a work is *repeatable* then it has already anticipated, in its form of expression, a life beyond its own context.

Perhaps no pre-postmodern writer was more aware of the poisoned chalice of digitalization than William Blake. Art can only have force if it survives, and it can only survive if it takes on a form capable of being copied, repeated, re-articulated, and stored beyond the life of the animating intention. At the same time, however, if the animating intention were nothing more than a fully comprehensible and transparent move in a shared language game, then the work would not *say* anything. An individual is possible *as an individual* only via a system of marking and inscription, even if the individuation of the individual creates some distortion of the system. Something like digitalization therefore marks not only all speaking and communicating but all life: living beings are expressions of potentialities that precede them (not just the codes of genetic material but the possible forms that any viable body might take on), and yet *as living* they are also singular combinations, replications, and mutations of the fragmentary potentials that make up their being:

> What some call properties of human beings – technology and language, tool and symbol, free hand and supple larynx, "gesture and speech" – are in fact properties of [a] new distribution.... the hand must be thought of not simply as an organ but instead as a coding (the digital code), a dynamic structuration, a dynamic formation (the manual form, or manual form traits). The hand as a general form of content is extended in tools, which are themselves active forms implying substances, or formed matters; finally, products are formed matters, or substances, which in turn serve as tools (Deleuze and Guattari 2004B, 67–68).

The problem of digitalism is at the heart of Blake's compositional method: by engraving each word of his corpus he seizes the means of expression from mechanized commodification, and yet the movements of the poet's own hand and the figures that dominate his plates are those of formalized natural language and religious iconography, along with echoes of other already circulating figures. The very return of poetry to the hand of creation and praxis, also renders the hand itself into a component of *techne*, for the hand now follows the traces of script. The same double movement of retrieval and distance (or analog genesis and digital alienation) marks the voices of Blake's poems, and the voices' relations to each other. By writing *prophecies* Blake aims to take a language of judgment, accusation, despair, and moralism back to a declarative moment of openness and inauguration. The prophet or poet – unlike the priest or Urizen figure who operates from an already constituted system of law – is a voice of creative decision and formation. But by granting the act and event of voice a certain force – by setting the prophecy of poetry against the mechanism of empire – prophecy threatens to become one more detached power. In order to rail against system, inertia, the rigidity of moralism, and the closure of religion, a voice must take on a certain form, and be incarnated in a self and body that sustains itself beyond the immediate gesture of negating attack. Blake's prophecies are ostensibly dramas that operate between fallen characters of life-denying and moralistic accusation, and poetic characters of active creation and forgiveness: Los as forging artist-craftsmen versus the judging and enclosed Urizen. Composed of a multiplicity of voices and transformations of single voices from redemptive vision to totalizing despair, Blake's prophecies are at once diagnostic in their capacity to distinguish voices of creation from voices of mechanistic repetition, and yet they also render such distinctions disturbingly undecidable. Individual characters insistently and shrilly assert their absolute self-creation, signaling both a fall into the rigidity of selfhood, but also a possible emergence from mechanistic sameness:

'"I am God alone: / "There is no Other! Let all obey my principles of moral individuality" (M 9, 25–26 K: 490: E 133). Blake's works are at once dramatic explorations of different modes of voice – opposing the fallenness of moralizing judgment to the hope of a viewed and renewed future; at the same time, the composed whole of voices often precludes easy and clear distinctions among characters, or characters and poet. Although the diction of Blake's poetry is decisive, declarative, and marked by vehement pronouncements of distinction and difference, the overall effect is one of a confusing multiplicity. The voice of prophecy that supposedly breaks with the tyranny of law seems to metamorphose into one more negating sound of fallen accusation. The imagination that takes flight from the same dull round of mechanized existence seems to be disturbingly similar to the judgmental and overseeing voice of despair.

If, as Deleuze suggests, art strives to generate an analogical language, or to liberate differences from constituted and formalized systems, it must also always be contaminated by a digitalism against which it labors but without which it cannot survive. That is, the coming into being or intensive genesis of language from the complexity of life must occur by some composition of consistency. Blake's works do not form systems of expression once and for all, but constantly play out the labor of inscription, insistently generating new terms and relations, as though systematization were always oscillating between creation and decreation. What must be warded off in the continual labor of forming, inscribing, writing, and molding is the fall into stagnation – the passage from the active creation of system to the passive submission to system.

That labor of a continual genetic deduction of system in the face of a perpetual relapse into inertia is played out in both the form and content of Blake's epics, and in the relation between form and content. At the level of form Blake's works are curiously fragmented bodies: the order of the plates can be unclear; epic wholeness is suggested by apocalyptic motifs and diction, even though revelation never arrives; and the very mode of inscription that supposedly stems from a drive to clarity and distinction also produces scriptural and figural ambiguity. Blake created his own mythic language and landscape to maximize distinction and individuation, and yet that same gesture also led to a necessary untranslatability such that no Blake dictionary can ever fully realize its task. Blake's epics narrate drawn-out battles between characters who accuse, judge, and negate, and characters who create, see, and forgive. The same character can start as accuser, only to be redeemed by recognizing the expansive power of forgiveness; or a voice may begin as a creative formative prophet only to fall into systematizing and despairing judgment. At the level of form, the epics take up the genre and iconography of grand cultural re-ordering and totalization, only to fragment that genre into multiple voices and narrative lines. Enclosing and telescoping unity occurs alongside chaotic multiplicity. The form of expression – epic poetry, but with multiple endings; the diction of redemption and revelation alongside an inscrutable lexicon of neologisms; a prophetic point of view and framing coupled with multiple voices and dramatis personae – answers to a form of content. Blake's form of expression ties a tendency towards unifying redemption with an emphasis on particularity, just as the world he describes (or the form of content) is a uniform and homogeneous modernity that nevertheless suffers increasing fragmentation. Blake's urban context is characterized by mechanization and technological formalization, the 'single vision' or 'same dull round' that nevertheless lacks any sensed order. This hellish world can be thought of in terms of an extensive multiplicity: what exists is already numerated and rendered equivalent; the addition of one more body or one more voice does not change the nature of the whole. This is a world of maximal and increasing production, but production that merely repeats and extends what is already actualized.

By contrast with the world that has become nothing more than extended substance, Blake imagines an intensive multiplicity, where each event or addition changes the nature of what counts as an individual or event. The reduction of difference to generality yields nothing more than an extensive totality; what is lacking is any intensive wholeness, any sense of the world beyond the sum of its merely assembled parts. Reacting against this dulling generality, Blake's epics are formed as unifying wholes that preside over fragmentation, as though they somehow give poetic consistency to a modernity that is both structurally rigid yet capable of generating proliferating complexity. In this respect, Blake's works are modern in a quite specific sense. They are not only *of their time* – describing a world of immanent order where there is no longer (as there was for Milton) an appeal to a transcendent ordering principle that might yield the world's sense (Colebrook 2008). They also disclose something like 'time in its pure state': not merely the passage from one point in time to another, and not merely a series of events where time is the mapping of a sequence, but time as the creation or genesis of difference as such. Time can be thought of extensively – as clock time or series of 'nows' – or, as Blake describes it – a prophetic or messianic time. The present flow or series is arrested or halted, opening not to a past or future, but to eternity. If there were no single point of view or system, or if the world had not yet been mapped or distributed into a certain space or chronology, then all we would have would be the infinite and eternal order of events. That which is actualized in the concrete world (from the point of view of bodies located in time and space) is only possible because there are eternal potentialities *to differ.* Time in its pure state is not the difference between one event and another, but what Blake describes as the eternity or vortex that opens from the smallest of particulars, but that is indiscernible to the localized observer: 'How do you know but ev'ry Bird that cuts the airy way,/Is an immense world of delight, clos'd by your senses five?' (MHH, (7 K: 150, E: 35). In addition to describing that temporality, Blake's work performs or creates something other than a narrative time: voices and narrative trajectories proliferate and interweave precluding a single order or logic of events. If the genre of the novel was structurally homologous to capitalism – with an individual facing a world of contingency to be overcome (Goldmann 1974) – this was because the novel described a temporal arc or journey that proceeded from a disturbance or incompletion that would then be resolved, but in good narrative time (Brooks 1984). But while we might note that capitalism is entwined with a temporality of forward progression, there is a more profound 'abstract essence' of capitalism: life has no order outside the entering of forces into relation (Deleuze and Guattari 2004A, 330). In modern capitalism those relations are axiomatized as the relation between labor and capital. Accordingly, the responding literary form – or form of expression of this form of content – is the novel with the individual encountering, mastering, and making his own a series of worldly (or already actualized) powers. If the abstract essence of capitalism – differential relations as such – were to be given a form of expression, it might result in the multiple temporalities, voices, and narrative lines of a Blake prophecy.

Blake has been read as a prophet against empire – railing against the commodification and totalizing reification of life – and yet his epics do capture the very mode of capitalism in their form of expression. Powers, forces, and voices enter into exchange without any grounding or transcendent norm; relations are not given in advance by some over-arching order, but occur as various potentials to enter into relation. There is a fractal and combinatory logic whereby encounters generate further encounters and voices generate further voices; there is no ground from which differentiation occurs, for it is from competing and differential forces that the ultimate body of Blake's epic emerges. If Blake is a prophet against empire it is not because he seeks to ground capitalist exchange and relations in some governing form, but because he seeks to release exchange from the single logic of utility, money or production. Capitalism is, after all, not only a single economic system that can take up and commodify any event; it also discloses and brings to the fore the condition for the possibility of all systems (Deleuze and Guattari 2004B, 500). Life takes form through the interaction of potentials: the eye becomes a seeing organ in its encounter with light, the body becomes a speaking and reasoning complex of organs in its relation to other bodies, and bodies become individuated through the organization of their potentials in relation to other potentials. There are not relatively closed forms that then enter into exchange; rather, in the beginning is the dynamically productive relation among powers – the event of exchange that is life:

> ... this becoming-concrete appeared in the differential relation; but it must be borne in mind that the differential relation is not an indirect relation between qualified or coded flows, it is a direct relation between decoded flows; outside this conjunction they would remain purely virtual; this conjunction is also the disjunction of the abstract quantity through which it becomes something concrete (Deleuze and Guattari 2004A, 270).

Blake's epics have a form of expression: a striving towards wholeness and integration of competing powers that is stratified with a form of content. The form of content is both modern capitalism's 'single vision' imposed upon reified fragments (or life's tendency towards the composition of ordered relations) *and* capitalism's destruction of the body politic (or life's tendency towards fragmentation): the two 'contrary states' of integrating order and isolated simplicity. When Blake writes epics he does so both in the manner of *Paradise Lost*, whereby the prophetic voice appeals to some future that would be different from the inertia of the present, but also in a way that breaks with epic notions of a retrieval of transcendent order. As a form of expression, epic tends towards the modes of totalizing vision that Blake constantly undermines. Whereas *Paradise Lost* was a theodicy justifying the ways of God to man, and did so by arguing for a redeemed humanity capable of recognizing man's properly divine potential, Blake's epics generate a divinity beyond humanity, a holiness that emanates from 'everything that lives.' In Blake, the epic's redemptive direction is coupled with a counter-messianic tendency towards the proliferation of minute particulars, with vortices in each moment opening to the infinite.

At a level of content Blake's epics play out the dialectic between enclosing system and opening prophecy, and it is here that the binary of sexual difference comes to act as a crucial figure. The female emanation can appear as a negated and terrifying otherness that drives the prophetic voice to accusation. Sometimes this is symptomatic of an inability to see otherness or sexuality as anything other than horrific, while at other times this is because the feminine has separated itself from creative life to become a tyrannizing power, overtaking the 'man' of humanity of which she should be a part: 'The nature of a Female Space is this: it shrinks the Organs/Of Life till they become Finite & Itself seems Infinite' M 10, 7–8, K: 490; E: 134). At other times it is the distinction of the feminine that is required for redemption, as though the new Jerusalem will occur only with a liberation from the self-sufficiency of man and an openness towards an otherness that is not that of the already actualized world of rationalism. (It is man's internalization of otherness – his reduction of all alterity to nothing more than his own subjectivity – that is nightmarish.) In the following section from *Milton* we are given a complex war among competing modes of sexual difference, whereby a redeeming Jerusalem can be achieved only if the femininity of cruelty and virtue is vanquished by another femininity of weaving (or tying):

> Because Ahania rent apart into a desolate night,
> Laments! & Enion wanders like a weeping inarticulate voice
> And Vala labours for her bread & water among the Furnaces
> Therefore bright Tirzah triumphs! putting on all beauty.
> And all perfection. in her cruel sports among the Victims.
> Come bring with thee Jerusalem with songs on the Grecian Lyre!
> In Natural Religion: in experiments on Men,
> Let her be Offerd up to Holiness: Tirzah numbers her:
> She numbers with her fingers every fibre ere it grow:
> Where is the Lamb of God? where is the promise of his coming?
> Her shadowy Sisters form the bones. even the bones of Horeb:
> Around the marrow! and the orbed scull around the brain:
> His Images are born for War! for Sacrifice to Tirzah:
> To Natural Religion! to Tirzah the Daughter of Rahab the Holy!
> She ties the knot of nervous fibres. into a white brain!
> She ties the knot of bloody veins. into a red hot heart!
> Within her bosom Albion lies embalmd. never to awake
> Hand is become a rock: Sinai & Horeb. is Hyle & Coban.
> Scofield is bound in iron armour before Reubens Gate!
> She ties the knot of milky seed into two lovely Heavens.
>
> (M 19, 42–61, K: 501; E: 113)

Yet even when something like the female emanation *as difference* appears to be necessary for redemption, it is not clear whether the feminine is to be included within 'man' or whether the final resolution requires a recognition of difference and relation, a balanced duality of male and female. Is the 'man' of Blake's epics a sexed subject who relates to an other sex (defined against 'hermaphroditic' forms)? Or is 'man' the unified whole as such who includes the feminine as one of his complementary aspects or 'emanations'?

That such a question remains unanswerable is not an accident of Blake's work. Deleuze and Guattari also present the same problem when they argue that 'becoming-woman' is the key to all becomings (Deleuze and Guattari 204B, 306). In doing so they (like Blake) at once repeat tired notions of woman as pathway to 'man's' redemption, and yet also mark the ways in which the problem of sexual difference is not one problem among others but tends to organize the ways in which we think about difference as such. Should there be a *man* for whom art (or becoming, creativity and difference) is disclosive and self-productive? Or, should one think of becoming as *other than man* – as possible only with the destruction of organicist thinking? Here is perhaps *the* problem of immanent modes of ethics and aesthetics. Immanence, as Deleuze and Guattari argue, is usually regarded as immanent *to* some transcendent ground: if we aim to return all forces and events back to the ground of experience, then the experiencing subject or 'man' becomes one more foundation (Deleuze and Guattari 1994, 46). The critique of alien systems, along with the immanent drive to return all logics to their point of genesis, always risks falling back into one more foundationalism. If Blake is critical of external systems and an imposed priesthood, he nevertheless establishes a point of view of prophecy and creation as a (possible) totalizing viewpoint.

Sexual Difference

Sexual difference can be figured either as the redemption of rational and calculating 'man' via the influx of difference (so that difference is incorporated), or as the abandonment of man for the sake of difference as such. The figure of sexual difference is not one figure among others, for the very notion of man as the being who forms himself from himself, representing the world in order to measure and master an undifferentiated matter, is integral to the very problem of aesthetics, ethics, and the way we figure the relation between the two. If we begin with aesthetics or sensation, then the primary relation is one of perception and an openness towards what is not oneself. However, if ethics or ethos is primary then we begin from the locatedness of the self, with all difference or otherness always being effected from the standpoint of the same. If one assumes that the world is given to be presented, represented, synthesized, and understood, then the man of speech, reason, and self-understanding is its ultimate principle (Irigaray 1985). A certain mode of Blake's epic and aesthetics is in line with this necessarily sexed humanism: all that appears as external, alienated, machinic or technical – and especially a nightmarish feminine to which masculine desire might be enslaved – should be returned and revivified by active and prophetic man. The form of his epics – each letter engraved, the creation of a new lexicon, an emphasis on the act of cutting and marking – all reinforce the man of modernity, the being whose external world is created through his own synthetic and reasoning powers, and whose history will tend towards self-recognition and internalization of all that appeared to be radically other. In accord with this, there is also a horror at female nature. A female nature appears to lie beyond the decision and mastery of the self. Tirzah and Rahab must be overcome through internalizing and softening a femininity that appears terrifyingly other.

Blake rejects any simple denunciation of female sexuality as evil; the very word 'harlot' (used in 'London' and elsewhere) is a symptom of a fallen way of seeing the world as something alien and not something immanent to the one poetically creative life. Even if Blake targets a priestly misogyny that denounces sexuality as a 'dark secret,' he nevertheless demands that a femininity that appears to be terrifyingly other must be reinscribed as the good 'emanation' that will complement the poetic mastery of form. Blake's project of writing draws what appears to be other, alien and inert back to the creative hand; in doing so Blake's poetics at once sexualizes the voice of prophecy by granting the poet/prophet a desiring and particular body. The sexual status of the originating hand is expressive of a profound and essential ambivalence: does Blake's inclusion of dynamic sexuality open prophecy to a principle of embodiment and generation that is not the unfolding of a single will, or does the reinscription of femininity as good emanation perform one more domestication of alterity?

If critics have squabbled about the sense or possible feminism of Blake's project, this is no accident, and cannot be settled by some better and closer reading. Sexuality, *like writing*, has a pharmacological structure. There can be no living body without a border or membrane that closes the self in upon itself, allowing it to be a living *being*; this is what grants a body its ownness, allows it to be a certain individuated kind or genre. But if that body is to live on it must also open out towards a world of desires that are not its own; sexuality is given in this strange double tendency of a body maintaining itself through desires that also expose it to risk, otherness, and a time not its own. If sexuality has been figured in terms of *gender* this has been to manage this existential exposure to otherness in organic and binary terms. What the figural lure of gender discloses is an oscillation in living desire: between an openness to otherness that is requisite for time and becoming, and a self-enclosed sameness that is necessary for the sense of a being that goes through or lives time.

Similarly, sense or meaning can only occur through transcription, or the marking out of sameness through time; but that exposure to the mark or trace also threatens sense with its annihilation. Blake's works have a duration because they take on a body; the force of his hand survives because of his inscriptive labor; and yet that very submission of the sense to an enduring material also exposes the sense of Blake to extinction. (Wordsworth's *Prelude* has a higher degree of formalization, for it relies less on specific materiality – such as the inscribed plates. But *The Prelude,* too, could be annihilated if all copies and memories were erased. By contrast, Newtonian physics or Euclidean geometry could survive textual annihilation, but would still require something like a material basis for formal survival – in the memories and practices of sciences and machines, and so on). It was because Blake wanted to command the memory, cicrculation, and survival of his corpus that the very work he sought to maintain – the work of his hand – will decay, even if printing and digitalism will allow the sense to continue in some other (spectral) form.

The attempt to return the system of text and speech back to the hand of the poet exposes the work to an unmasterable fragility and alterity: it was because Blake brought the conditions of production back to his own control that his works also have an exceptionally high degree of exposure to loss and decay. Elements of his work that are not formalizable or even digitalizable – the textural scratches, the color overlay that has an almost three-dimensional quality, the differences among illuminated prints – preclude the work from operating as a material and surviving unity, even though survival requires just those material supports that expose the work to extinction. The more a work or body wants to maintain itself, or wants to remain close to itself (as did Blake's printing method) the less able that work will be to survive. There is an inverse relation between the singularity of a text and its formalization: the art of writing lies in negotiating the degree to which the artist wants a work to be *his own* (with a unique and singular expression) in relation to some system of repetition and form, or a shared language or repeatable matter that allows the work to circulate beyond his own hand. In this respect textual production is a mode of desiring production: for desire must extend beyond itself towards what is not itself and not yet given, but must also have some minimal degree of self-maintenance.

The play of sexual difference within Blake's epics – suggesting that *man's* redemption requires an openness to life not his own, while that other life must also be incorporated – is played out in the form of the epic and its matter. The continued sense and readability of the work requires incarnation: taking on a form of expression and a matter of expression. Such formed matters will articulate and maintain the interiority of sense, but must do so through a system that is never fully the poet's own. The event of incarnation is central to Blake's work: in the passage from sense to formed expression, in the passage from spirit to body, and in the production of poetic objects that are at once the poet's own and yet possible only because there has been a submission to, and articulation of, materiality that is both extension and alienation.

Chapter 2

Art and Life: Analog Language

Art and life are, therefore, intrinsically digital: a living being or poetic object requires some form of articulation and distinction, and can only maintain itself through time via a repetition of identity. Repetition of identity, or repeated articulation, requires difference and reproduction. An artwork survives through copying, memorization, and preservation, all of which entail that it be submitted to conditions and matters not its own. A living body (or living kind) also maintains itself only through differing from itself. All bodies – living bodies, bodies of artworks, social bodies – are always already digitalized. There is no pure and self-present whole that is not already (*as a unity*) articulated into differentiated and mutually constituting forces. A living system of relations requires some minimal establishment of a unit in order to establish order. Social wholes produce, but also require, the individuation of bodies. Poetic works require and create minimal units of expression (such as phonemes and marks). Living bodies – as organisms – demand the articulation of organs. How can we think about the genesis of the digit, or the emergence of distinction, from a life that is infinitely varied (and anything but undifferentiated)?

In many ways one could read the work of William Blake as achieving what Gilles Deleuze (writing about Francis Bacon) has referred to as the creation of an analog language. This achievement of the analog would not be a return to the flow of *life itself*; there can be no original plenitude that happens to become accidentally corrupted by technical or digital systems. Nor can there be a *proper* digital system that is a full capture or faithful expression or extension of an analog original. What Deleuze refers to as analogical language, and what Blake describes as 'creating a system' rather than being 'enslaved by another man's' would not be the annihilation of a differentiating system to return to a prior unity.

There is a tendency to think of systems as imposing distinction upon chaos, where chaos is thought of as undifferentiated. For Deleuze and Guattari this is the error of Oedipal logic: either submit to the paternal law or fall back into the dark night of the pre-Oedipal plenitude: 'Oedipus informs us: if you don't follow the lines of differentiation daddy-mommy-me, and the exclusive alternatives that delineate them, you will fall into the black night of the undifferentiated' (Deleuze and Guattari 2004A, 87). For Blake, this is the error of Urizen and priestly terror: remain within logic and selfhood or be overcome by the horrors of the void. But the error lies in thinking that outside systems of difference there is indistinction. The contrary is the case: systems of difference are contractions or reductions of difference. There can only be the sound spectrum of phonemes if infinitesimal differences are discounted and one attends to broadly distinguished units of difference; there can only be some general 'humanity' or specified races if one discounts the complex genetic differences that make up individuals. Beyond digitalism and system there is neither chaos nor continuity. Rather, the analogical, genetic or prophetic would operate by creating *more* difference: differences so minute, particular and singular that they would scramble or corrupt repeatable codes, even if this would be to risk the silence of madness. One arrives at the analog not by destroying the distinctions and articulations of the digital, but by creating so many distinctions that any shared or sustained code would no longer be possible.

This drama of forming an analogical language, of *not* working within the already given units or digits of the given system, is for both Deleuze and Blake what defines art against the abstract formalism of logic. On such an account art would essentially be at war with its own survival: at once oriented to the creation of singular and non-formalizable events outside systems of replication and yet also striving to survive beyond the work's own time for all time.

It would be difficult to grant a historical date to the event of art's splitting from itself, or the moment at which the material support that enables art's formation also operates to reduce its unique signature. The invention of the printing press, photography, digitalization, cinema, file formats and new imaging technologies that enable 'perceptions' beyond those of the human eye to enter the world of circulating art objects would all be contenders, but so would the human hand. At once an extension of the body and means of touch and gesture, the hand is also the first tool, weapon and formalized sign. The hand is at once an organ, crucial to the human body as a sensory motor apparatus that enables a functioning organism to approach and work upon a masterable world. At the same time, the hand is always digital: never purely itself but already formalized or 'deterritorialised' into repeatable functions that maintain their identity beyond any single body: 'For with the hand as a formal trait or general form of content a major threshold of deterritorialization is reached and opens, an accelerator that in itself permits a shifting interplay of comparative deterritorializations and reterritorializations – what makes this acceleration possible is, precisely, phenomena of 'retarded development' in the organic substrate. Not only is the hand a deterritorialized front paw; the hand thus freed is itself deterritorialized in relation to the grasping and locomotive hand of the monkey' (Deleuze and Guattari 2004, 68).

Deleuze and Guattari's distinction between the human hand – as deterritorialized, or freed from the mere body to become part of a world of work – and the front paw, was also one of Jacques Derrida's concerns. He, too, realized that one could neither assume that humanity was a self-sufficient natural kind or essence, nor that it could remain within itself in its immediate animality. Criticising Heidegger's assertion that the human hand is radically distinct in its gestural and meaningful capacities, Derrida insisted that the signifying hand and grasping paw would always be in a relation of strange co-determination. Commenting on Heidegger, Derrida writes: 'Man's hand will then be a thing apart not as separable organ but because it is different, dissimilar, (*verschieden*) from all prehensile organs (paws, claws, talons); man's hand is far from these in an infinite way (*unendlich*) through the abyss of its being (*durch einen Abgrund des Wesens*). This abyss is speech and thought ...The essential moment of this meditation opens onto what I shall call the hand's double *vocation*' (Derrida 174). One of the great achievements of the work of Jacques Derrida was the deconstruction of the analog-digital binary. This has implications not only for the voice, but also for the hand. There can be no rigorous or sustainable distinction between the human hand of responsive touch, gesture, and indication and the animal paw or claw of instinctive grasping. In his criticism of Martin Heidegger's attempt to distinguish *Dasein* (or what can no longer simply be referred to as humanity) from animals, Derrida points out that the distinction between the simply instinctive paw/claw of the animal and the reflective, responsive, and gestural hand of the existential subject will always rely on a certain blindness. The human hand of gesture, writing, world-disclosure, and reflective labor must, in order to operate in such a 'human' or self-aware manner, have some *sense* of itself. It must, in order to have this required sense of world and self, pass from simple sensation to a sensation that senses itself – must pass to *sense or meaning*. But this is possible, Derrida argues, only through a temporal inscriptive process whereby the simple self-presence of the pure now is marked as having some sense or quality that could be repeated and maintained through time. The human hand of speech/gesture, meaning, praxis, and self-consciousness is only possible because of a certain machinic technology. The animal claw/paw that operates by an unreflected instinctive immediacy (and that does not anticipate or synthesize a sense of the world) is not outside the rational world of human reflection but *is its condition.* The organized human body— whereby the hand counts and masters a world surveyed by the measuring eye that is, in turn, articulated by the voice of reason (as ratio or common sense) –is only possible through a process of auto-affection, which is always hetero-affection. The self can only be itself, can only realize and recognize itself, through a self-touching that passes through an unmasterable and unreflected mechanism or techne. Put more concretely: those tools that *extend* the hand from being a mere body part to an organ of sense are never the body's own but are always technologies: touching, gesturing, writing, speaking, and looking are never isolated acts of pure and self-inaugurating openness but are always installed in already constituted differential systems.

Rather than regarding tools, technology or writing as *extensive* – as systems that merely allow the body to further its own range – we can regard them as *intensive.* The relations among forces produce new events: when the hand encounters writing systems it ceases to be a body part and becomes part of a technical system not the body's own: 'These movements are movements of deterritorialization. They are what "make" the body an animal or human organism. For example, the prehensile hand implies a relative deterritorialization not only of the front paw but also of the locomotor hand. It has a correlate, the use-object or tool: the club is a deterritorialized branch' (Deleuze and Guattari 2004, 191).

Even though Blake's work would seem to emphasize moments of genesis or inauguration, such as the pre-systematized gaze of the 'enlarged and numerous senses,' his work also operates with an equally important attention to bodies as organized and inter-related systems. Blake is aware of the ways in which body parts are subjected to the central vision of calculating reason, or released into actions of creation and production. The voice, also, is – as Derrida said of Heidegger's hand – *vocative*: it is destined to take on a part that is not fully its own. Blake's voices are contaminated by received discourses.[1] The voice of the priest, the judge, the accuser: all these can invade and overtake the aspects of the self (or the 'zoas') that compose existence. Blake's works are populated less by characters than by powers: the possibility of judgment, of creation, of spirit, or of passivity. And all these powers can become reified in certain fixed discourses: the declarative mode in its rigid manifestation is the blind systemic judgment of Urizen. Blake's bodies are often similarly coded in advance by dominant systems. In the early *Songs of Innocence and of Experience* black skin is lived as a mere covering, concealing a properly white self– 'And I am black, but O! my soul is white' (E: 9; K: 125). In *Visions of the Daughters of Albion* female embodiment is lived as fallen ('But the terrible thunders tore/My virgin mantle in twain' [K: 189; E: 45]), and in the later prophecies the body of rational man is experienced as a cavern with 'chinks' through which the world is viewed. If Blake's entire corpus is motivated by prophecy and a destruction of received systems, he nevertheless acknowledges that the voice with which one begins, and the body which one regards as one's own, are overtaken by systems that are not one's own. Neither the voice nor the body is a force unto itself; both come into being heteronomously.

Voice and Techne

Voice is never pure self-affection, nor is the body ever an organism unto itself. The voice becomes a speaking voice through a system of relations not its own, just as the body is organized in its relation to systems, technologies, and histories of discipline, labor, and sexuality. For all Blake's manifest declarations of an original moment of 'cleansed' perception, he writes also of the imprisonment of bodies in systems of measure, judgment, and calculation. For all his emphasis on the voice of prophecy and the capacity for 'the Daughters of Memory [to] become the Daughters of Inspiration' Blake is also insistent that the voice of the poet is always a voice that opens to an infinity beyond chronological time, beyond the body – despite being always marked by previous systems. This, indeed, is the problem that drives Blake's striving for analogical language: how does one speak and write in a world of necessary systems and technologies? How does one avoid the 'same dull round', the 'one law', or becoming nothing more than the destruction or negation of what one beholds? This is not only to say that there is no private language; it is to recognize that the condition of language – a systemic and decentered distribution – invades the seemingly singular, personal, and private events of touch and self-sameness. This enables us to come to terms with a strangely double quality in Blake's works that was already signaled in his early notion of contrary states. A voice is at once always already part of a repeatable, communicable, and determined system, and so the *Songs of Experience* appear to intone an inescapable structure of iterability – not only the 'marks' that are noted in 'every face' but also the sense of rigid or 'fearful' symmetry. In the later prophecies this sense of the system and structure of any voice is given in the dramatic repetition of received diction, and the ways in which the attempt to break free from determination continually falls back into accusation and despair. It is as though the condition for voice and experience in general is that of an inviolable order and system. At the same time, as in *Songs of Innocence,* a voice, no matter how enclosed nevertheless harbors an utopian singularity. Consider the tragic, 'I am black, but O! my soul is white'; this at once signals internalized oppression at the same time as it testifies to a faith and hope beyond the very system within which it is enslaved. Similarly, the voice of Oothoon, in *Visions of the Daughters of Albion* cries, in a manner that evidences her subjection, '"I call with holy voice! Kings of the sounding air/"Rend away this defiled bosom that I may reflect./The image of Theotormon on my pure transparent breast' (VDA 2, 16–18, K: 190; E: 47). It is the *holy* voice that compels Oothoon to have a sense of herself as defiled, and yet she also discloses an awareness that such a 'pure' feminine would be nothing other than a reflection of Theotormon. There is a double sense in the verb 'reflect': at first appearing as an active verb, so that Oothoon might break away in order to reflect upon her subjection (and this is suggested by the full stop at the end of the line). This is then undercut by the second passive sense of reflection that is in line with the other images of stamping and branding that occur throughout *Visions.* Reflection is at once the capacity for an innocent retreat from the torments of enslaving voices – voices that imprint themselves upon the breast – and reflection is also the means by which bodies appear to be determined in advance (as 'defiled' if the feminine does nothing more than reflect masculine torment back upon itself). Theo*tormon* can be read as the torment of theology, both the ways in which theology torments by accusing, but is also itself tormented in its incapacity to break from its own systems. Such voices disclose a splitting within any accusation, whereby the accuser appears as the damned and blinded figure: how could Theotormon see feminine *defilement* if he were not already fallen and enslaved to a world of guilt?

Experience, or the fallen world of condemning judgment, discloses its own self-punishing limits, intimating a world beyond the totalizing viewpoint that 'past, present and future sees.' In 'The Tyger,' the questions regarding the origins of animated life can only be posed in the most mechanistic and lifeless terms: 'What the hammer? what the chain?/In what furnace was thy brain?/What the anvil?' (SOE K: 214; E 15). Innocence, or the voice of passive submission, also signals its own counter-redemption from within. The voice of 'The Lamb' already admits the lamb's functioning in an economy of human purposes, projecting the lamb's use-value into some divine order: 'Gave thee clothing of delight/Softest clothing, woolly, bright' (SOI K: 115; E: 8). By assuming a necessarily benevolent world, in accord and harmony with the speaker's own being, the poem at once discloses innocence as a paralyzing lure, but also indicates a capacity to think beyond the actual world of reduced and mechanical systems, to imagine a wholeness that is not simply that of an assemblage of completed parts: 'Gave thee such a tender voice/Making all the vales rejoice?' (SOI K: 115: E: 8).

What these two contrary states and their contrary tendencies of voice display is an unavoidable problem of the relation between analog and digital: the analog is always already on its way to digitalization, for it is the coming into distinction of repeatable and identifiable qualities. (The lamb of pure innocence and nature is already anticipated as being part of a commodity culture, while the tiger of the fallen world of experience intimates the limits of a mechanistic and calculating imagination.) Digitalization does not add difference to an analog continuity, but it does code those differences into units: digitalization allows the differential force of the analog to be *extended* – copied, repeated, circulated – even if *intensity* or infinitesimal differences are lost. Deleuze's notion that art strives for *analogical language* captures this problem of an art that must not remain within already formed systems: art must introduce differentials into 'digits' that allow for the release of an expressiveness in matter, at the same time that the force of materiality must take on some repeatable or recognizable form.

Just as the analog harbors intensive differences that require digitalization to be extended into systems of reproduction and repetition, so the supposed fullness of the body's cries and screams already bears a proto-articulation that enables the formation of structured systems of sound and language. Speech, as the sound that remains close to the living body and (seemingly) expresses and extends itself without break or rupture, would appear at first to be opposed to the digital, to the system of discrete, repeatable or 'dead' units that allow for copying, repetition, manipulation, division, and circulation in the absence of the living voice. But how is speech or self-presence possible? How does the artist, the bearer of the living word par excellence, produce a sense that is expressive of his individual being? In order to speak, or even to *be,* the living voice must be itself, sense itself, regard itself *as* the unique being that it is. This can only occur through some distinction or discretion. The *voice* can never be pure analog, can never emerge seamlessly from the living body but must, always already, be articulated and drawn into some repeatable form.

Whereas Derrida regarded the invasion and possibility of the voice by inscriptive systems to be essential – that is, one could not write a *history* of voice because any history would already take part in the articulations of speech – Deleuze and Guattari insist on a speculative or universal history.

From our current position of subjects submitted to signification, we can write a genealogy of the body. We can think of the genesis of man as a speaking animal who represents a world of truth and order. We do this by asking, as Blake did, what distributions of power or despotism would allow a voice to emerge, whose truth is that of a world that is there to be viewed and determined, in advance, from a single point of view with its own inscribed and transcendent logic.

> What changes singularly in the surface organization of representation is the relationship between voice and graphism: it is the despot who establishes the practice of writing (the most ancient authors saw this clearly); it is the imperial formation that makes graphism into a system of writing in the proper sense of the term. Legislation, bureaucracy, accounting, the collection of taxes, the State monopoly, imperial justice, the functionaries' activity, historiography: everything is written in the despot's procession … graphism in one and the same movement begins to depend on the voice, and induces a mute voice from on high or beyond, a voice that begins to depend on graphism (Deleuze and Guattari 2004A, 220).

The hand is never pure sign or digit – never fully released from the pathos and singularity of the body; nor is the hand ever simply *of* the body, for the body is always – as body – organized, assembled, synthesized, maintained as itself through time by means of a whole series of technologies, including speech and vision: 'these are the three sides of a savage triangle forming a territory of resonance and retention, a *theater of cruelty* that implies the triple independence of the articulated voice, the graphic hand, and the appreciative eye. Such is the manner in which territorial representation organizes itself at the surface, still quite close to a desiring machine of eye–hand–voice' (Deleuze and Guattari 2004A, 207).

Blake's prophecies describe the drama of the organized body: the limbs forming around the stabilizing center of the brain, the brain becoming a technology of measurement by viewing the world through eyes that are 'chinks' in a cavern: 'In chains of the mind locked up/Like fetters of ice shrinking together/Disorganiz'd, rent from Eternity' (U 10, 25–7, K: 228; E: 336). And yet the process of Blake's works destroys the organized body. His mode of production is led by the hand that is guided not so much by the eye-brain but by forces from elsewhere – the spirit of Milton entering his foot, the vortices opening from the pulsations of every artery, or the poem being dictated from Eternity: 'Eternals I hear your call gladly, Dictate swift winged words, & fear not/To unfold your dark visions of torment' (U 2, 5–7, K: 222; E: 70). One cannot, then, mark either a simple opposition, or a straightforward transition from analog to digital. There is no seamless emergence of systems from the flux of life; nor is there a direct transition from the lived body in its supposed immediacy to the organism structured by technology and functionalism.

No artist brought this more to the fore than William Blake, whose images of prophecy, vision, singular imagination, and expression were set alongside figures of digitalization, systematization and inscription – with no clear moral binary organizing either series into an opposition between origin and supplement. Consider the above-quoted lines from *The First Book of Urizen*: on the one hand these describe the world as fallen and indicate a prophetic call to eternity, and yet the voice that makes this diagnosis is despairing and can only view an abominable void:

> 1. Lo, a shadow of horror is risen
> In Eternity! Unknown, unprolific!
> Self-closd, all-repelling: what Demon
> Hath form'd this abominable void
> This soul-shudd'ring vacuum?–Some said
> "It is Urizen", But unknown, abstracted
> Brooding secret, the dark power hid (U 3, 1–7, K: 222; E: 70).

The fluidity and expressiveness of vision and life (the enlarged and numerous senses) must take on the form of a counting or marking hand. Without processes of forming, marking, and inscribing, life 'itself' would remain in a condition of unreflected stagnation (the infantile enclosure of innocence or Beulah: 'There is a place where Contrarieties are equally True/This place is called Beulah, It is a pleasant lovely Shadow/Where no dispute can come' [M 30, 1–7, K: 518; E: 129]). In *The First Book of Urizen* Los, the prophet figure, tries desperately to give Urizen some semblance of bounded form, 'affrighted/At the formless unmeasurable Death.' But the act of marking and discrimination that synthesizes and forms, allowing life to take on body, also leads to distinction, separation and a necessary alienation from the sensation it would express. The marking out of form is at once matter's extension or expression and its enslavement to system, order and form. Blake diagnoses the fixing of laws, through inscription, as a retreat from eternity into single vision:

> 6. Here alone I in books formd of metals
> Have written the secrets of wisdom
> The secrets of dark contemplation
> By fightings and conflicts dire,

With terrible monsters Sin-bred:
Which the bosoms of all inhabit;
Seven deadly Sins of the soul.
7. Lo! I unfold my darkness: and on
This rock, place with strong hand the Book
Of eternal brass, written in my solitude.
8. Laws of peace, of love, of unity:
Of pity, compassion, forgiveness.
Let each chuse one habitation:
His ancient infinite mansion:
One command, one joy, one desire,
One curse, one weight, one measure
One King, one God, one Law (U 4, 36–40, K: 224; E: 72).

Matter cannot be identified with either the analog or the digital. The analog and digital – before they appear explicitly in modernity as different modes of synthesis – operate as figures, or ways in which we think about the transition from the immediacy of flux to systems and order. It might seem commonsensical to think of matter as simply continuous stuff – requiring form for distinction. Alternatively, one might think of matter atomistically, as disarticulated units that require form and system for organization into distinct substances. Such a basic distinction between matter as undifferentiated continuity *or* as disarticulated units yields two notions of the emergence of language and systems: either language as structure is imposed on matter to produce differences, or language generalizes differences that are already present. Matter is, however, neither undifferentiated stuff requiring form, nor already formed substance: 'Unformed matter, the phylum, is not dead, brute, homogeneous matter, but a matter-movement bearing singularities or haecceities, qualities and operations…' (Deleuze and Guattari 1987, 512).

Form emerges from matter's own tendencies to difference. It would be wrong to say that matter is continuous and undifferentiated before its organization into systems, but it would be no less erroneous to regard matter as already fully formed, with systems of measure being nothing more than maps of what already exists. Analog and digital are different modes in which life becomes formed as matter. In the digital understanding of the body's relation to matter, the hand imposes itself upon 'hyle' or matter. The hand is a set of digits and is coupled with a calculating mode of vision. Matter is pressed into the service of the hand, while the hand becomes a part of the world and system beyond the body. The relation between the two terms – hand and hyle—is one in which each term becomes what it is through an encounter, transforming matter into substance, and hand into functioning organ. The eye views the world as so much quantifiable material available for manipulation, while the hand that allows for mastery of this nature is a hand of digits. Digitalism would seem to imply a matter that has no order in itself, and that is nothing more than a medium for synthesis.

Not surprisingly, in contrast with the hand–eye–brain coordination of traditional perspective and aesthetics, Blake's *Milton* will depict Milton's spirit as entering the poet's *foot* as he walks through eternity; Blake will describe 'doors,' not windows of perception that the body as a whole must walk through rather than view from a distance, and he will align poetic writing less with thought than with a tactile perception. Blake's work is neither manual (with the hand remaining as body part) nor digital (reducing the body to system), but *haptic*: the engraving method enables the inscriptive process itself to be seen, as though the eye can *feel* the incision of text, or sense the layers of color and wash.

In the first plate of *Milton* we note two features that cannot be marked by digitalization: the depth that is discernible by the eye – the discernible incision of the line into ink that in digitalization is marked as a difference between light and dark – and a luminosity or difference in visual intensity between the black/colored inks and the gold letters that frame the page and that are themselves cut into by the hand of the poet/prophet. 'To Justify the Ways of God to Men' is written in luminous gold at the bottom of the page, but the upward curve of the 'n' in 'Men' indiscernibly becomes part of the swirling borders around the page, and – in moving from signifying letter to figural border – also passes from being the overlay of gold ink to the incision of a line into black ink. Elsewhere, as the 'P' of 'Poem' curls up and also passes from gold ink into incision, the fine incised lines are overlaid with white ink – so there are two modes of the absence of color, a whiteness that occurs as the black ink is scored, and a whiteness that is achieved by the overlay of ink. Whiteness is both digital and analogue, both extensive and intensive. In the digitalized version there is no gold luminosity, no distinction between intensities of whiteness, and no discernible hatching that stipples the prophet–poet's body. The hand that cuts into 'Milton' on the digitalized version appears as a colored-in inked outline, while in copy B (held at the Huntington library) the outline appears as scored into the ink.

Before digital media in its narrow sense there is already a process and problem of digitalism. The condition for any voice or vision taking on a form that will survive and be readable (both for the artist and beyond the artist) is the passage from the hand to the digit. A *manual* art would

maintain a proximity between hand and work: in its extreme or pure form manual aesthetics would yield either works of art that *are* the body, such as mime, dance, a music of body sounds, or even canvases that pass directly from the hand and paint to the final work. The eye can see the ways in which paint is almost 'thrown' on the canvas when one looks at the work of Jackson Pollock. More recently than Pollock many artists work directly with the materials of their own body, using blood and saliva, or impressions of body parts, to stand alone. Such manual modes of production create a direct passage from tactile hand to surface. The closer the distance of the artist's touch, the more difficult becomes the task of reproduction. (We can easily read Blake's poetry in its formal dimension in print form, but it is less easy to get a sense of the illuminated books' surfaces from even the most sophisticated copies.) Digital media, by contrast, allows for replication without diminution and also, at least ideally, does not distinguish between an original that is then submitted for replication but is 'in itself' already a replication. Blake's illuminated books were all copies, but Blake introduced essential variants in each print through the addition of inks and colors to the print surface. It is as though Blake seized the means of poetic production, returned the making of text to his own hand, and then allowed the works of the hand to take on variations that were poised between difference and repetition. He allowed the copying process itself to introduce singular variants. Rather than copying being a mutation that introduces variation beyond the artist's hand, Blake rendered each copy – at least at first – as his own, by coloring plates individually. Again, though, it was precisely the attempt to draw the process of copying back to the artist's intentional touch that led to a greater exposure of the work to death. If the *sense* of Jerusalem occurs not in a single circulating text, but a series of varying copies, all concretely marked as different, then this reduces the work's survivability (because the variants and not just the idealized form must be maintained). There has been interpretive work on variations across different versions of a plate, but such critical attention must labor against the tendency of the anthologized, circulating and widely consumed Blake.

Blake's poetry occupies a curious position in relation to the problem of the digital. On the one hand he is the poet par excellence of an analogical language: this is captured within his poetry in the many narrations of the transition from the inner spirit (inspired and prophetic) to formed systems. In the later works this transition will be a struggle, with the figure of Los battling against specters. The more joyous description of the passage from sense to expressed sensation occurs in *The Marriage of Heaven and Hell.* In the beginning is the poetic act of animation that becomes systematized by 'priests:'

> 'The ancient Poets animated all sensible objects with Gods or Geniuses, calling them by the names and adorning them with the properties of woods, rivers, mountains, lakes, cities, nations, and whatever their enlarged & numerous senses could percieve.

> And particularly they studied the genius of each city & country, placing it under its mental deity; Till a system was formed, which some took advantage of & enslav'd the vulgar by attempting to realize or abstract the mental deities from their objects: thus began Priesthood; …' (MHH 11, K: 153; E: 38).

Inspiration passes from 'enlarged senses' that view the world, to the printing and writing hand, and then to the written and incarnated word. Blake is critical of any calculative, mathematical, systematized or quantifying reduction of the world to so much neutral matter. When one looks beyond formed systems it is mistaken to think of the void or chaos, for what is encountered are infinitesimal distinctions, eternities, and infinities. How might one have an 'infinitesimal eternity'? If, as Blake insists, every aspect of the actual world opens to reveal more and more difference and distinction, then the eternal is not some abstract 'beyond' but occurs when vision departs from the point of view of the self-interested and enclosed organism and intuits forces beyond its narrow range: 'What is Above is Within, for every-thing in Eternity is translucent' (J 71, 6, E: 225; K: 709). In *The First Book of Urizen* Blake describes the 'abominable void' as a consequence of the retreat of vision to an imprisoning interior: 'Self-clos'd, all-repelling: what Demon hath form'd this abominable void/This soul-shudd'ring vacuum?' (U 3, 3–4, K: 222; E: 70). Blake's visionary materialism will always be critical of closed systems, and will do so not by imagining some God or spirit beyond all matter but by regarding matter itself as vital. Yet, at the same time, and in tension with a prophetic poetics of visionary transition and the emergence of text from spirit, Blake did not see print, text or line as vehicles for a voice that could exist independently of its concrete support. He did not see matter as the medium through which forms would be actualized. Matter itself bears its own tendencies towards distinction and, even more significantly, possesses singular and individuated points from which the infinite or eternal unfolds.

In a manner that is curiously proto-digital Blake will allow for the infinite repeatability and recurrence of a world of singular events. All events possess an incorporeal sense that opens chronological and linear time to what Blake will refer to as a time of vortices:

> As the eye of man views both the east & west encompassing
> Its vortex; and the north & south, with all their starry host:
> Also the rising sun & setting moon he views surrounding
> His corn-fields and his valleys of five hundred acres square,
> Thus is the earth one infinite plane, and not as apparent

To the weak traveller confin'd beneath the moony shade.
Thus is the heaven a vortex passd already, and the earth
A vortex not yet pass'd by the traveller thro' Eternity.
(M 15, 21–35, K: 497; E: 109).

In the vortex each point of the present has at one and the same time its actual temporal location and a sense that is infinite and eternal. Blake's statements on line, articulation, delineation, lineaments, distinction, and difference – against the horrors of indifference, vagueness and 'hermaphroditism' – are tied to a broader aesthetics and ethics that one might want to call radically digital or proto-digital. The horrors of chaos and the void are only partially ameliorated by the female figures of weaving, binding, veiling and singing to the 'sounds of the loom's treddles.' Genuine redemption for Blake comes with a mode of digital aesthetics that occurs beyond, or redeems, the analog-digital divide:

...with bounds to the Infinite putting off the Indefinite
Into most holy forms of Thought...
Antamon takes them into his beautiful hands:
As the Sower takes the seed or as the Artist his clay
Or fine wax, to mould artful a model for golden ornaments.
The soft hands of Antamon draw the indelible line,
Form immortal ... (M 28, 4–17, K: 515; E: 126)

There is at once a requirement for distinction, system, incarnation, and circulation of repeatable forms alongside an attention to the genesis of the digits or units that enable art's extension and survival.

Blake's figures of cutting, stamping, hammering, forging, writing, and engraving do not give a body to a spirit that in itself is disembodied:

The Clouds of Ololon folded as a Garment dipped in blood
Written within & without in woven letters: & the Writing
Is the Divine Revelation in the Litteral expression:
A Garment of War (M 42, 12–14, K: 534; E: 143).

Despite first appearances, Blake will never begin with a pure spirit that either falls into, or is lamentably mediated by, a body. On the contrary, spirit is properly actualized in body: 'Man has no Body distinct from his Soul for that call'd Body is a portion of Soul discern'd by the five Senses, the chief inlets of Soul in this age.' When the body appears to be nothing more than a container this is because of a diremption; it is not the body that is fallen. Rather, the illusion that the body is fallen – that the body is a part of an alien world of matter – is a symptom of our 'contracted' perception: 'All Bibles or sacred codes have been the causes of the following Errors/That Man has two real existing principles Viz: a Body & a Soul' (MHH 4, K: 149; E: 34).

The experience of the body as fallen is symptomatic of an inability to see the infinite, divinity, eternity or spirit in the created world. The fall for Blake occurs *both* when the world appears to be nothing more than matter and when some separate spectral world is posited above and beyond matter. Both a naïve realism – the world as mere matter to be encountered through a detached perception – *and* idealism (or the notion that there is no reality beyond the self's images or ideas) are fragmentations and distortions of a world that is properly viewed as a spiritual matter that realizes itself in forms. Incarnation is not a passage to death – or it is so *only* when the expressive passage from spirit to body is forgotten and the body appears as nothing more than a limit. Properly conceived the body is an expansive and enabling actualization of a potential that requires expression.

Similarly, language for Blake is neither some pure sense that only accidentally requires writing, nor some reduced material system that exhausts meaning. Writing is neither a dead letter that simply mediates or contains spirit, nor a material system that can account for the totality of sense. Blake, like Deleuze, would need to be contrasted with a certain reductive pragmatism whereby writing would be nothing more than a system of conventions or moves in a language game: writing cannot be reduced to communicative functions or practical force. This is both because writing is the expression of sense, or a body given to a potentiality that exceeds formal textual systems, *and* because writing itself bears a force that goes beyond natural man. Writing is at once matter that expresses spirit, and yet possesses a spirit or life of its own. Blake will celebrate arts, such as sculpture or engraving, where the matter worked upon has its own vitality and force. Form is not imposed from without but is drawn from, or actualizes, matter's potentiality. This haptic aesthetics (an aesthetics that has a feel for matter) is at once opposed to hylomorphism (or the notion of form imposed on chaotic matter) and abstraction, where form exists in itself, requiring matter for presentation (Deleuze and Guattari 2004B, 407).

At the level of sound Blake's poetry expresses a variation of matters: the proper name Urizen is like a mutation of Reason, Horizon, 'Your Reason', 'Ur-reason.' 'Theotormon' is a mutation of theological torment, while other names seem to twist and turn in various directions: 'Los' being perhaps both an inversion of central light ('sol') or spirit ('soul'), or perhaps a stopping short of 'loss.' Urthona may be 'earth-owner' or 'Ur-thona.' There is a suggestive and yet non-etymological playing with the sounds of language and its contingent connections with multiple senses (including the two characters Hand and Hyle). It is as though the very system through which 'man' comes into being – speech and text – has a power of variation beyond human intentionality. The lines of the engraved letters can merge with marginal ornaments and figures, just as human figures can seem to metamorphose into leaves, borders, trees or ornamental lines: here, it is as though we can see again the emergence of script, hear again the distinctions of phonemes, and the event of naming. The poet arrives neither at a blank page nor a silent milieu but must hammer, bind, weave, sculpt, and forge figures and sounds from already formed matters. Blake's work is at once about distinction – about overcoming a world of vague and generalized forms to arrive at clarity and distinctness of each singular and minute particular – at the same time as each distinguished and determined figure bears a power of genesis and variation that allows it to mutate into new and distinct forms: 'Distinct General Form Cannot Exist. Distinctness is Particular, Not General' (K: 461; E:649).

Blake's aesthetics is also an ontology, for if matter possesses its own tendencies to form, then this means that artistic creation is a question of intuiting (and being guided by) matter's spirit, rather than imposing difference and distinction on an otherwise neutral or undifferentiated mass. This is most apparent both when Milton moulds a body for Urizen in *Milton* – suggesting that one gives bodily form to what is already at least partly a body – and when Blake creates a method of printing whereby the letters are not stamped in upon the page but emerge from the page, in relief.

> Thus Milton stood forming bright Urizen. while his Mortal part
> Sat frozen in the rock of Horeb: and his Redeemed portion,
> Thus form'd the Clay of Urizen; but within that portion
> His real Human walkd above in power and majesty
>
> (M 20, 11–14, K: 502; E: 114.)

What makes this figuration of the aesthetic *proto-digital* is that Blake will not see the work of art as a seamless extension of the world; there is no direct and continuous emergence from voice and spirit to word and object. Rather, the passage towards incarnation occurs as a break with pure spirit: writing and figuring is never simply an expression or double of an already distinct and formed world. The incarnation of spirit into/through matter depends upon the artist attaining the proper mode of the hand. When the hand is guided by matter, feeling its way towards proper form, then the body or text that emerges possesses the correct distinction:

> Come into my hand,
> By your mild power descending down the Nerves of my right arm
> From out the Portals of my brain, where by your ministry
> The Eternal Great Humanity Divine Planted his Paradise,
> And in it caus'd the Spectres of the Dead to take sweet forms
> In likeness of himself … (M 2, 5–10, K: 481; E 96)

A good digitalism occurs when the distinction and articulation that allow sense to be expressed in system proceed from a feeling and responsive hand. If, by contrast, the hand is digital in a fallen sense – a hand that is a series of digits that merely counts and quantifies – then the text or body that emerges has no life of its own and is a pale, spectral or lifeless copy. A few plates after the above-quoted passage it is the 'cold hand' of Urizen that pours icy water on Milton's *brain.* Throughout Blake's work it is the body that is centered on the brain, the body of cognition and central organizing command, that is both fallen and stulifyingly self-enclosed ('the orbed skull around the brain' [M 19, 52 K: 501; E: 113]). By contrast, the body that is grounded on the active limbs – a body that begins with movement – is the body that opens to the world. After Urizen freezes Milton's brain with 'icy fluid from his broad cold palm' Milton responds by sculpting a clay body for Urizen, feeling the clay with his body as he rebuilds Urizen from the ground up:

> But Milton took the red clay of Succoth, moulding it with care
> Between his palms and filling up the furrows of many years,
> Beginning at the feet of Urizen, and on the bones
> Creating new flesh on the Demon cold and building him
> As with new clay (M 19, 10–14, K: 500; E: 112)

There is a certain mode of incarnation or digitalization – a passage from spirit to distinct and circulating work – that is neutralizing, deadening, and produces an indifferent difference: a differentiation of the world into so many equivalent and comparable units. Here, the hand that writes is a hand of digits – a counting hand subordinated to the surveying eye. It is a hand of the organism: a body coordinated around a central point of view, dominated by 'single vision.' The analog, the world of continuous, vague, and non-quantifiable differences, is effaced, repressed, or expelled to some external chaoic and threatening void. (This is Blake's Beulah – a 'space' that offers some promising outside to the world reduced to so much system. It remains at once alluring, yet also partial because it has been detached from the incarnate world, the world of matters.) Blake's redeemed digital aesthetic is quite *literal.* There is a commitment to the hand's relation to the formation of the letter. The hand (properly) follows the world's own tendencies to distinction; it is not a hand of equivalent digits, but a hand tied to a body of 'enlarged and numerous senses.' This expansive body of writing – a body that comes forth through writing – is presented, figurally, within the text in references to the body's distinct powers, and the properly productive distinction of forces.

Blake's text itself is also a body of distinction, with marks of script, lines of visual figuration, and forces of color that rarely converge or reduce to the mimetic double of a prior and self-sufficient sense. Sometimes the writing has an almost machinic quality. The drama of voices is populated with names (usually Biblical) that have no clear force or reference. In plate 24 of *Milton* Los's declarative mode slows down with a series of names that appear here but do not make up any part of the sense or drama: '"Of Palamabron's Harrow & of Rintrah's wrath and fury:/"Reuben & Manazzoth & Gad & Simeon & Levi/"And Ephraim & Judah were generated ..."' (M 24, 1–4, K: 508; E: 119). It is as though the writing itself is going through the generative process it describes. In addition to the intruding lists of names or places, there is also a repetition of seemingly key Blake terms, such as 'terror', 'fires', 'flames', 'pity', 'cruelness' or 'mildness', and yet such terms have no clear reference or axiology. Sometimes, for example, it seems as though pity is part of a redeeming complex of mercy and forgiveness, sometimes as though pity is a paternalizing and weakening gesture ('pity divides the soul/And, man, unmans'):

> Jerusalem. Reply'd, like a voice heard from a sepulcher:
> Father! once piteous! Is Pity. a Sin? Embalm'd in Vala's bosom
> In an Eternal Death for. Albions sake, our best beloved.
> Thou art my Father & my Brother: Why hast thou hidden me,
> Remote from the divine Vision: my Lord and Saviour.
> Trembling stood Albion at her words in jealous dark despair He felt that
> Love and Pity are the
> same; a soft repose!
> Inward complacency of Soul: a Self-annihilation!
>
> (J 23, 9–15, K: 646; E: 168)

Visually, the same doubleness of sense also invades Blake's corpus: it seems as though flames can be at once those of fiery imagination and creative furnaces, while at other times they are terrifying (though 'terror' too is not clearly a negative in Blake, for it is sometimes an apocalyptic and awakening terror). Added to this is the disjunction among the semantic, the visual, and auditory: 'Tyger, Tyger burning bright,' seems to be utterly simple, almost childlike. It speaks of terror, and yet – as Harold Bloom (1963) noted – the tiger depicted appears as harmless as a stuffed animal (and Blake certainly knew how to depict terror). For all its formal simplicity and clarity of diction, the poem's ultimate sense is enigmatic. Just what 'And when the stars threw down their spears' *means* (or refers to) is far from straightforward. And for all the childlike simplicity of the verse, the poem ostensibly refers to terror and dread: *fearful* symmetry (or the horror of an ordered world that seems to suggest an inscrutable hidden law). Blake's works are at once multi-media works, but they take on this form not through processes of integration whereby the visual, literal, and tactile reinforce each other, but through a dis-organization of the sensory-motor apparatus.

Blake's own work does much to destroy the reading eye, the eye that – today – is also facing different modes of destruction. Many media and cultural theorists have lamented the degree to which the new era of visual culture threatens to destroy the connective and organizing eye of reading and grammar (deep attention), to give way to a simple and fragmented eye as stimulus response mechanism (what N. Katherine Hayles refers to as 'hyper attention') (Hayles 2007). The eye that reads, according to Deleuze and Guattari in *Anti-Oedipus,* emerges from a history of deterritorialization, and this process, in turn, is possible only because sensations or formed matters bear their own force. The eye of the organism follows from territorialization whereby brain, eye, hand and body coordinate to view and act upon the world. In the beginning the eye (like all body parts) is synthesized as a collective organ. The eye sees/feels the public event of scarring or ritual circumcision, and this affect then organizes the body as a part of a network or web of bodies:

> ... what enables the eye to grasp a terrible equivalence between the voice of alliance that inflicts and constrains, and the body afflicted by the sign that a hand is carving in it? Isn't it necessary to add a third element of the eye: eye-pain, in addition to voice-audition and hand-graphics? In rituals of affliction the patient does not speak, but receives the spoken word. He does not act but is passive under the graphic action; he receives the stamp of the sign. And what is his pain if not a pleasure for the eye that regards it, the collective or divine eye that is not motivated by any idea of revenge, but is alone capable of grasping the subtle relationship between the sign engraved in the body and the voice issuing from a face – between the mark and the mask. ...

> The signifier is the sign that has become a sign of the sign, the despotic sign having replaced the territorial sign, having crossed the threshold of deterritorialization; *the signifier is merely the deterritorialized sign itself.* The sign made *letter.* Desire no longer dares to desire, having bcome a desire of desire, a desire of the despot's desire. The mouth no longer speaks, it drinks the letter. The eye no longer sees, it reads (Deleuze and Guattari 2004A, 206, 225).

In the beginning is not an isolated eye/brain that looks out from a single body; rather, there are events of seeing and feeling, and it is the relation among these events that enables bodies to be formed and organized. (Blake also describes how the self-enclosed body is *contracted* from life: as though in the beginning there is an expansive openness to the world, and from there something like the enclosed body is formed – belatedly, and through the rigidity of the generalizing intellect: 'Opacity was named Satan, Contraction was named Adam' [M 13, 22 K: 494; E: 107].) Further, this contraction occurs with the formation of *man,* the man for whom the feminine is some exterior space or beyond: 'The nature of a Female Space is this: it shrinks the Organs/Of Life till they become Finite & Itself seems Infinite' (M 10, 6–7, K: 490; E: 104). After the territorialization that forms bodies in relation to each other, the body can become privatized; turning in upon itself. The eye no longer relates directly to an outside but views the world *as* something to be deciphered. This is *de*territorialization because the eye–world relation is mediated by another transcendent point or system: what *is* this world that I am viewing; what does it *mean*? Reading (or an eye that de-codes rather than feels) and the privatization of the organs occur as two sides of the same synthesis, and for Deleuze and Guattari this synthesis is a theatre of cruelty and then despotism: the eye *reads* the knife that enters the flesh – not feeling the wound collectively – by interpreting the cut in flesh as punishment from some over-seeing despot. When the eye becomes a reading eye the organ is no longer part of a larger affective 'socius' but becomes an organ that turns the body inward. If the outer world is to be read – as the sign of a world of laws and punishments that come from 'on high'—then the body is lived as subjected to an order not its own. When the eye becomes a reading eye, the world beyond the body is viewed and calculated at a distance, neither felt nor touched.

Blake, too, notes the ways in which a world of laws and commandments encloses the organs within a body that is subjected to an alien outside world that appears to lack any order or distinction of its own: 'Urizen lay in darkness & solitude, in chains of the mind lock'd up … Rolling around into two little Orbs, & closed in two little Caves, The Eyes beheld the Abyss'

(M 3.6–15 K: 482; E: 76). It is not the case that there are seeing–hearing–speaking organisms that come to represent and order a world that would otherwise have no sense. On the contrary, man – as an animal whose eyes read a world that is so much manipulable matter – results from a history in which the very mode of the humanized body is possible because of a prior organization of sensations.

Blake's epics were concerned both with the genesis of the organized body and the divergent relations among the body's powers; these divergent relations did, eventually, converge on the unified man of reason – on the body dominated by a calculative mind for whom the senses present so much data. But prior to this organized body of the man of reason, there had been perceptions as such, intuitions that were forceful and disturbing, not yet sensations as the sign or double of an external world.

It is possible to locate both Blake and Deleuze in a counter-enlightenment tradition, which also includes Friedrich Nietzsche. Nietzsche, too, narrated a fall from an originally expansive and active perception – in a Greek tragic mode capable of confronting the intensity of existence – to a reactive and intellectual judgment of the world in terms of transcendent value. Nietzsche's counter-enlightenment, like that of Blake before him and Deleuze after him, is therefore a dramaturgy of man as organism – a critical genealogy of the transition from an open and forceful encounter with the world to a *reading* of the world in terms of a posited 'higher' world (Deleuze 2006, 186). Counter-enlightenment, in this sense, is not so much a reaction *against* enlightenment as it is a *counter*-enlightenment. Blake, as many have noted, objected to mystification, subjection to unexamined external authorities and any general notion of transcendence – the notion of a higher authority that lies outside and gives law to the world. The key enlightenment gesture was one of internalization and deduction: any authority that seemed to order the world from without should not be passively accepted but recognized as emerging from the powers of human reason (internalization) and justifiable according to how human reason may know the world (deduction). Key to this enlightenment strategy was a certain relation between mind and body. There can be no rigorous or reliable mode of thought that is immediate (for feelings and passions are *pathological,* and require concepts in order to be known or communicated). Nor can there be *knowledge* of what is not given to the self in a mediated (conceptualized) manner: one cannot *experience* God, the infinite, or the good. These cannot be *objects* of knowledge. Rigorous thinking must pertain to what is communicable, and one can only speak reliably and responsibly about that which can be shared, legitimated, and known by an other as it would be for oneself.

Kant therefore insisted that while we may be able to *think* of ideas beyond possible experience (such as God, freedom or the infinite) we can have knowledge only about that which appears within the temporal and spatial world of concepts that we ourselves have synthesized. Of that which we cannot speak we must remain silent.

As a consequence, art becomes important: it is in art that we *feel*, once again, the synthesizing power that has formed the world as a conceptually ordered and therefore reasonable world. Writers from Kant to Habermas have insisted that the beauty and worth of a work of art, or nature, lies in its expression of the faculties' harmony. We feel the world, not as already formed and known, but in its process of formation:

> ... under the *sensus communis* we must include the Idea of a communal sense, i.e. of a faculty of judgment, which in its reflection takes account (*a priori*) of the mode of representation of all other men in thought; in order *as it were* to compare its judgment with the Collective Reason of humanity, and thus to escape the illusion arising from the private conditions that could be so easily taken for objective, which would injuriously affect the judgment. This is done by comparing our judgment with the possible rather than the actual judgment of others, and by putting ourselves in the place of any other man, by abstracting from the limitations which contingently attach to our own judgment. This, again, is brought about by leaving aside as much as possible the matter of our representative state, i.e. sensation, and simply having respect to the formal peculiarities of our representation or representative state (Kant 136 [40]).

For Kant, nature is beautiful when its perceived order is intuited with a feeling of harmony, *as if* it were in accord with our capacity to form concepts. Rather than perceive the world as conceptualized, art gives us sensations that appear conducive to conceptualization. It is as though the world were not just data for me, but given in a manner that tends towards a communicable and shared order. I feel what is given not as bodily sensation but as an intuition in accord with subjective powers of synthesis. For Habermas this Kantian indication of a *sensus communis* – a posited community of like-minded speakers oriented towards common feeling and judgment – allows us to arrive at modernity, and an enlightened attitude towards writing (Habermas 1973, 75). From this perspective there is no final and proper form of the world. Even if such finality does not actually arrive we nevertheless communicate according to the *ideal* of a shared and rationally agreed upon world. We speak and act *as if* there would be one ideal common realm of truth, with all speech and action being oriented towards this ideal of consensus.

Politics, on such an account, is a transcendental horizon: it is not the case that we have our humanity and then enter into relation with each other. Speaking, acting, perceiving, desiring – and the world we perceive – emerge from a common and intersubjective tradition of world-formation achieved through working and speaking collectively. Modernity occurs when this ideal, but not actuality, of legitimation is reflected upon. A counter-tradition, running at least from Blake's own time, and possibly emerging from a mystical tradition that affirms the positivity of forces beyond cognition, function, the organism, consensus, and formed polities, seeks to destroy the convergence of intuition, perception and life on a single logic. Such a tradition is both digital and multi-media in the broadest sense. It is multi-media because it stresses the distinct lines of formation and technology that possess their own tendencies (multiple modes in which matters are formed). There is a technology of the eye that overlaps with, but is not reducible to, the systems of voice, concept, touch or ear. This counter-enlightenment is digital in its insistence on the capacity of systems of code to bear their own tendencies: systems begin as formalizations or idealizations of continuous and complex matters, but take on their own autonomy. Blake's position in this tradition is given both in his printing method – uniting and dividing text, color, figure, and mark – and in his epic allegories that will chart the passage from relations among divergent powers to the reduction and deadening generalization of all faculties in the calculating body of the man of reason. Such epics are *counter*-political insofar as they begin with territories of divergent powers that become (for Blake, lamentably) domesticated to a single voice; the mildness and conciliatory tones of reason are a symptom of a disastrous waning of affect.

Deleuze and Guattari, similarly, will argue for a counter-political model in which the polity – the body of social consensus – can only occur at the expense of a multiple and individuated (but not individual) perception, which is why they argue that desire is directly revolutionary. Deleuze and Guattari, like Blake, regard perceptions or organs as initially broader and more expansive than the individual's sense organs. It is from perceptions that the social body is formed, and from those collective perceptions that individual bodies are eventually contracted. Organs are originally collective – there is just seeing, hearing, feeling, touching – but once those movements are 'territorialised' or take on a certain rhythm, pattern or refrain, then it is possible *first* for a social body to be formed and *then* for individual bodies to experience sensations as their own, as private: 'For it is a founding act – that the organs be hewn into the socius, and that the flows run over its surface – through which man ceases to be a biological organism and becomes a full body, an earth, to which his organs become attached, where they are attracted, repelled, miraculated, following the requirements of a socius' (Deleuze and Guattari 2004A, 159). The eye is originally a collective organ, all the bodies in the tribe 'feeling' the incision of the tattooing knife upon flesh. Privatization of the organs occurs when sensations are not lived intensively – felt as such – but become extensive: sensations as signs (for me) of a world (out there). The eye is privatized when it reads marks as signs of some general meaning (or signification) available for all to see. Prior to the privatization of the organs, the senses or capacities of each power were not organized into a coherent and self-bounded whole, but created divergent lines of sense.

Blake wrote of 'enlarged and numerous sense' and wrote epics about the properly divided labor of each of the living being's 'zoas'. Blake's hand is, in its redemptive mode, composed of receptive powers that receive and transform the distinctions of a world of singular and unfolding powers. So critical is Blake of the digital hand that is nothing more than the calculating instrument of a world of rational matter that he has Milton's descending spirit enter his foot. Even the standard figure of the descent of the muse is given in a manner that is visceral and nervous:

> Come into my hand
> By your mild power; descending down the Nerves of my right arm
> From out the Portals of my Brain, where by your ministry
> The Eternal Great Humanity Divine, planted his Paradise
> And in it caus'd the Spectres of the Dead to take sweet forms
> In likeness of himself. (M 2, 11, K: 481; E: 96)

Blake narrates a relation between hand and hyle that occurs within a whole series of other distinctions, divisions, relations, and negotiations. His epics both demonstrate and thematize the distinctions that occur in the incarnation of sense, or the passage from spirit to the distinctions of script and figure. This always involves some form of break or rupture. But Blake's many narrations of scriptural or figural incarnation – the formation of digits from continuity – occur alongside the equally frequent intimation that there is always some force or remainder that the body of the work never fully exhausts. Although Blake will argue against the idea that man is an isolated body shut off from the infinite, he will also insist that the body is a fragment of an eternity of sense: 'Names anciently remember'd but now contemn'd as fictions/Although in every bosom they control our Vegetative powers' (J 5, 37–38, K: 624; E: 148).

By the same token, just as the human body is an incarnation of a world of spirit of which it has only a partial sense, so language is at once the expression of some greater whole while also being a distinctive force and body in its own right. This is why the bard in *Milton* will demand, 'Mark well my words! They are of your eternal salvation.' The mark of the word possesses a distinct force. Signs are neither passive doubles of the 'vegetative world' nor generalizing systems. The passage from spirit to body occurs neither by the straightforward flowing forth of sound from the body (as though language emerged as some cry or scream of the body); nor is language a system of differences imposed on an otherwise indifferent matter. Rather, matter itself has its own tendencies towards distinction. But the distinctions of matter are always exceeded by other possible distinctions – such as the force of the mark or word.

For Blake, as for Deleuze and Guattari, there is a strange confluence between an affirmation of the externality of relations, alongside a primary expressivism. To say that relations are external is to refuse organicism: there are powers or potentials that have produced the relations and systems of this world, but those same powers could have been actualized differently. It is not the case that every part has its proper place in a whole, for even though bodies – social and biological – are assembled from various powers, those powers could have produced other relations. Even so, just because the systems and relations of this world of ours are not necessary – or could have been actualized differently – does not mean that they are absolutely contingent. Life is expressive insofar as all signs, bodies, distinctions, forms, and texts emerge from and indicate the nature of a life of which they are genuine signs (and not simply arbitrary signifiers). The world that is formed and expressed in this manner, with life issuing in these bodies and these systems of signs, bears a potentiality to have been expressed otherwise. If we view the world *sub specie aeternitatis* then we see it not only as it is now but also as it would be for other times and other perceivers. For Blake this is why every power opens inward to eternity, for nothing is fully exhausted in its present actuality. Blake expresses this thought as an infinitive, so that the form of expression enables the thought of an unactualized potentiality: 'To open the Eternal Worlds, to open the immortal Eyes/Of Man inwards into the Worlds of Thought, into Eternity/Ever expanding in the Bosom of God, the Human Imagination' (J, 5, 18–20, K: 623; E: 402). This is a double structure: if the body opens inwards to the 'Bosom of God,' it is also the case that God is 'not a God afar off, I am a brother and friend;/Within Your bosoms I reside, and you reside in me' (J, 4, 18–20, K: 622: E: 401). The infinite is not, as it is in the critical Kantian–Hegelian tradition, that which prompts thought to go beyond its conceptual limits in order to think the *negation* of what it can know; the infinite resides in the smallest of things, in each 'fibre,' 'molecule' or perception. Minute particulars bear their own singular relation to an infinite of which they are but one expression. This ability to think the infinitely small is part of a counter-enlightenment tradition that is also given in Deleuze's reading of Leibniz's monadology: the world we perceive is one way of expressing an infinite, but there would be other worlds – other openings to the infinite. We perceive the world the way it is because of the organization of our bodies, and the history of our senses, but there is nothing in the forces themselves that entailed this particular structure of relations:

> ... insofar as the same world is included in all existing monads, the latter offer the same infinity of minute perceptions, and the same differential relations that yield in them strangely similar conscious perceptions. All monads thus perceive the same green color, the same note, the same river, and in every case a single and same eternal object is actualized in them. Yet, on the other hand, actualization is different for each monad. Never do two monads perceive the same green in the same degree of chiaroscuro. It could be said that every monad favors certain differential relations. At the limit, then, all monads possess an infinity of compossible minute perceptions, but have differential relations that will select certain ones in order to yield clear perceptions proper to each. In this way every monad expresses the same world as the others, but nonetheless owns an exclusive zone of clear expression that is distinguished from every other monad (Deleuze 2006B, 103).

This counter-enlightenment (or the thought of powers beneath our thresholds of perception) is also a counter-organicism: 'Man's perceptions are not bounded by the organs of perception' (NNR [b], E: 2; K: 97). From the point of view of an organicist aesthetics, which dominates ways of thinking about the incarnation of sense from Kant to the present, individuals only have the sense or identity that they do because of their relation to a whole. *Relations* are dominant and determine what something is; it makes no sense to speak of a force or power outside its relation to a whole. For Kant, it is illegitimate to consider things as they are in themselves, for we know the world only as it is given to us, and through our powers of reason that organize the intuited world into a whole. By contrast, one might consider powers, potentials or sensations *from which* relations (such as languages, bodies, texts or social systems) emerge, but such powers might also have yielded quite different relations. Powers or forces do not have intrinsic relations. Light might be perceived by us (humans) as color, just as vibrations might be perceived by us (humans) as sounds. A bat, by contrast, 'sees' by hearing. Blake will write of the worlds or infinities that open up for fleas, pebbles, clods, and every other singular power: 'The nature of infinity is this: That every thing has its/Own Vortex' (M 15, 21–22, K: 497; E: 109). For Blake the consequence of affirming distinctions themselves, *not* reduced to a single world that is the same for reason, art, politics, and sensation, is two-fold. If everything is One this is only because there is a One in which each particular is so defined as to be incapable of subsuming any other – a One of univocity: 'Seest thou the little winged fly, smaller than a grain of sand?/It has a heart like thee, a brain open to heaven & hell,/Withinside wondrous and expansive' (M, 20, 27–29, K: 502; E: 114). Such a commitment to the externality of relations or univocity (or the same world articulated in infinite modes) requires a different notion of aesthetic production. The forces of matter take on a certain autonomy, freeing sensations from the 'single vision' of calculation. Further, univocity *as a pluralism* is destructive of the notion of *the political* – whether that be a social world or horizon of sense from which individuals emerge, or a collective ideal of consensus towards which all speech and action would converge.

Chapter 3

Incarnation

The passage to incarnation in Blake's work is never straightforward: bodies emerge from bodies, dividing sometimes to create fruitful and productive difference, but sometimes to create deadening negations rather than contraries. Just as there are two modes of digit – a uniform system of equivalences versus a hand that can feel the distinctions of matter – so there are two modes of incarnation. There can be the emergence of a body that creates illuminating distinction, giving the potentials of matter an actual and richer difference. Here, the body or incarnated work yields greater articulation and has more reality than the site from which it emerges. As an example we can think of Milton's molding of a body for Urizen in *Milton,* an act which takes the rational ideality and spirit of Milton's poetic vision and gives it a richer distinction, also allowing for the sexual difference and multiplicity that Milton had subordinated by situating the female as different in degree, not kind, from the male. By contrast there can be false, 'covering' or spectral bodies: not bodies that give distinction and enrich the potential differences of matter, but bodies that cover over the fluxes of force. Blake refers to 'hermaphroditic forms' or political bodies, such as the institution of the church, that create indifference. When Blake refers to 'one man' or Albion it might appear that he invokes a unified and unifying body, a body that covers over difference to yield something like 'mankind.' But Blake's founding body is articulated, composed of distinct powers that are not different in degree but in kind, each power bearing its own body, time, signature, and world:

> Loud sounds the hammer of Los, loud turn the wheels of Enitharmon
> Her Looms vibrate with soft affections, weaving the Web of Life
> Out from Ashes of the Dead; Los lifts his iron Ladles
> With molten ore: he heaves the iron cliffs in his rattling chains
> From Hyde Park to the Alms-houses of Mile-end & old Bow
> Here the Three Classes of Mortal Men take their fixd destinations
> And hence they overspread the Nations of the whole Earth & hence

The Web of Life is woven: & the tender sinews of life created
And the Three Classes of Men regulated by Los's hammer, and woven
By Enitharmon's Looms (M, 6, 27–35, K: 486; E: 100)

Incarnation in its neo-Platonic, Christian (and possibly contemporary genetic[1]) sense marks a distinction between the actual body in this world and the essence, idea or form of which it is an expression. In neo-Platonism the world of actual incarnate bodies is an expression of Ideas that require the passage to embodiment to realize their full potentiality. In Christianity, the incarnation is the contraction of God into the body of Christ, so that embodied humanity might once more return to its original intimacy with spirit. It is by passing into human form that divinity can take on the sins *of man* and then (through sacrifice) allow humanity to express, once again, God's image. Such a theological and neo-Platonic sense of incarnation both expresses a need for the passage towards body, at the same time as the actualized body never fully exhausts the spirit of which it is an expression. Incarnation is traditionally the giving of body to spirit, *and* the passage from sense to expressed body (of writing or figures). This first sense is theological and is expressed thematically in Blake's work as the relation between this life that we live here and now, and the spirit or divinity that is life's properly animating truth. Such a sense is also specifically Christian, and yields a particular (proto-secular and proto-digital) aesthetic. In the Christian tradition spirit takes on a body, in the case of Christ, so that incarnated divinity can sacrifice its bodily being: humanity is then redeemed from its original overvaluing of itself in the fall.[2] From Christ's sacrifice on, every human body is an incarnation that must also make the journey towards spiritual fulfillment, the body being the necessary vehicle but also the very medium of redemption. Embodied life in this world is an art of the soul; the body would be properly guided towards spirit, not by mortification or negation, but by acting as an expression of divine life.

The status of incarnation in this Christian-theological sense is ambivalent in Blake, for he both asserts (visually and poetically) the integration of spirit and body, while also often reducing one side of the dualism to the other. We appear to have a natural body that would be a portion of a material and external world; this can, and will, give way to a unity of spirit where sexual difference, personal individuation and the natural man appear to be what they are – limits to a vision that is properly infinite: 'The Mundane Shell is a vast Concave Earth, an immense/Harden'd shadow of all things upon our Vegetated Earth,/Enlarg'd into dimension & deform'd into indefinite space' (M 17, 21–23, K: 498; E: 110). This aspect of Blake's work would be closest to philosophical idealism, mysticism or cabbalism were it not for the contrary claim that this seemingly spiritual unity is composed of minute particulars, and that even the seemingly most trivial entities – such as fleas – possess a spirit and infinite holiness. To this end, Blake was highly critical of the denigration of the body, the 'hermaphroditism' of sexual indifference and the illusion of disembodied mind.

> The Twofold form Hermaphroditic: and the Double-sexed:
> The Female-male & the Male-female, self-dividing stood
> Before him in their beauty, & in cruelties of holiness!
> Shining in darkness, glorious upon the deeps of Entuthon.
>
> (M, 19, 32–35, K: 501; E: 113)

The narrative trajectories of his epics proceed both as journeys from bodily fragmentation and sexual division to spiritual unification, *and* as progressive attainments of distinction and autonomy for the world's smallest points of difference:

> Terrified Los stood in the Abyss & his immortal limbs
> Grew deadly pale; he became what he beheld: for a red
> Round Globe sunk down from his Bosom into the Deep in pangs
> He hoverd over it trembling & weeping. suspended it shook
> The nether Abyss in tremblings. he wept over it. he cherish'd it
> In deadly sickening pain: till separated into a Female pale
> As the cloud that brings the snow: all the while from his Back
> A blue fluid exuded in Sinews hardening in the Abyss
> Till it separated into a Male Form howling in Jealousy
>
> (M, 3, 28–36, K: 483; E: 97)

This ambivalence regarding the status of the body and its matter is the very motor of Blake's poetry and visual work, and relates to the other two senses of incarnation, not only inflecting a relation between form and content but anticipating a productive undecidabilty whereby *form is content*. For it is precisely because Blake will neither affirm the primacy of the body, nor the purity of spirit, nor assert the full union between the two that his epics play out the disjunctions between spirit and body, and that his printing method affirms the distinction of text, and yet does so in order to assert the expressive force of sense.

Although Blake will occasionally assert the unreal nature of the body, with body being but a distortion of a properly spiritual world, he will also proclaim the thorough reality and immanence of this life, refusing any notion of soul or mind that is not the form of the body. Alongside this, Blake will also often place the relation beween mind and body as two substances at war. The dynamic conflict of mind and body in Blake is frequently figured as a moral narrative in which an initially embodied and active humanity becomes seduced or enclosed by images of a pure, detached, 'spectral', and judging mind. The figure of the specter captures the accusing, life-denying, moralizing fragment of the self that is no longer recognized as having emerged from desiring life:

> The Separation was terrible; the Dead was repos'd on his Couch
> Beneath the Couch of Albion. on the seven moutains of Rome
> In the whole place of the Covering Cherub. Rome Babylon & Tyre.
> His Spectre raging furious descended into its Space
>
> (M, 9, 49–52, K: 490).

The disembodied mind that appears to be set over against, and above, embodied life, can only be redeemed via a process of incarnation that destroys the appearance of mind as a distinct or separate substance. Blake dramatizes this renewal of incarnation through the battle against Urizen, both in *The First Book of Urizen,* which describes the detachment of mind into its own inner space, and in *Milton,* where the figure of Satan is also described as a retreat from perception to an 'opake' interiority:

> Thus Satan rag'd amidst the Assembly! and his bosom grew
> Opake against the Divine Vision; the paved terraces of
> His bosom inwards shone with fires. but the stones becoming opake:
> Hid him from sight. in an extreme blackness and darkness,
> And there a World of deeper Ulro was open'd, in the midst
> Of the Assembly
>
> (M, 9, 30–35, K: 490: E: 103)

Blake creates his character of Urizen as a hybrid of Cartesian rationalism and Old Testament legalism; these are the two modes of transcendence against which Blake's poetic project labors. The shift from a tyrannical external and punishing God to a subjective moral law still subjects life to an authority that is not its own. Against such despotisms Blake sets the project of poetry. And here we can take *poeisis* in its sense of a creation that, unlike *praxis,* creates an end beyond itself. Against the idea of a law that is set over and against the world, and against the idea of life's subjection to a transcendent God or Reason, Blake strives for a genesis of form from life. This would be a reversed Platonism, whereby there are still eternal forms but they are those that arise from life's striving towards its own proper potentiality:

> The task of modern philosophy has been defined: to overturn Platonism. That this overturning should conserve many Platonic characteristics is not only inevitable but desirable. It is true that Platonism already represents the subordination of difference to the powers of the One, the Analogous, the Similar and even the Negative. It is like an animal in the process of being tamed, whose final resistant movements bear witness better than they would in a state of freedom to a nature soon to be lost: the Heraclitan world still growls in Platonism. With Plato the issue is still in doubt: mediation has not yet found its ready-made movement. The Idea is not yet the concept of an object which submits the world to the requirements of representation, but rather a brute presence which can be invoked in the world only in function of that which is not 'representable' in things (Deleuze 1994, 59).

Incarnation is not a fall from pure law or reason into embodiment, and so must be set against a notion of the body as a corruption or mediation of spirit:

> It is sufficient to understand that the genesis takes place in time not between one actual term, however small, and another actual term, but between the virtual and its actualization – in other words, it goes from the structure to its incarnation, from the conditions of the problem to the statement of its solution, from the differential elements and their ideal connections to actual terms and diverse real relations which constitute at each moment the actuality of time (Deleuze 1994, 183).

For Deleuze, although Platonism still bears some sense of the genesis of actuality from a virtual power that cannot be reduced to human calculation and representation, this is soon lost with the subordination of the categories of judgment to the human subject. Blake, too, also marks a distinction between a truly dynamic eternity that opens the world beyond its concrete actuality to its animating spirit, and a rigid reason that reduces the actual world to a single law. Urizen is both a punishing form of law and judgment set over and against life, and a calculating reason that enables an individual to be subjected to a law that he forms and finds within himself. For Blake, the legalistic judgment of Old Testament theology and modern rationalism perpetuate the subjection of divine life to some putative and ghostly (or spectral) 'higher' world.

4. Dark revolving in silent activity:
Unseen in tormenting passions;
An activity unknown and horrible;
A self-contemplating shadow,

(U 3, 19–23, K: 223; E: 71)

Both aspects of Urizen (as *Ur-reason* – theological or rationalist) can only be overcome through a redemptive process of re-embodiment and an embrace of sexual difference. Both the body and sexual difference are sites in which reified, detached and seemingly ideal or disembodied spirits need to be regrounded in this world of passionate and desiring life.

If Blake's corpus seems to be oriented towards an integrated or embodied vision of mind, or mind as properly emergent from bodies, there is another strand that is just as critical of any simple affirmation of body. Although Blake clearly sets his poetics and visual production against the Cartesian image of mind and the notion of divinity as some detached and overpowering deity, he will be no less critical of a new scientism in which time and space are accounted in terms of extended substance, and in which the matter of the world might be reduced to quantity, calculation, and actuality. Blake will therefore intertwine the notions of incarnation as the taking on of body by spirit – the Christian sense of incarnation – with the modern and secular (immanent) notion of incarnation as the relation between the two substances of mind and body.

This combination of figural and conceptual traditions opens a complex ambivalence. For the tension between the Christian sense of incarnation as passage from divinity to flesh, and the philosophical problem of mind's relation to body, are played out in Blake's own artwork in a manner that is *problematic*. That is to say, rather than decide or assert the primacy of matter or spirit Blake's works perform and demonstrate the emergence of inscriptive form from the sense and sensation of the artistic imagination. In so doing, sense is at once grounded on sensation, while sensation in turn can no longer be reduced to a reductive conception of matter. This yields two intertwining temporalities: a cosmic sense of a divine life that embodies itself in the historical world, and a human time of the struggle between a detached reason and a lived body. These are played out in Blake's work through a figuration of the various modes of incarnation.

Christian/neo-Platonic incarnation is progressive and linear: the taking on of body is necessary for the soul's journey and allows the body to live a life of futural redemption and spiritualization. The modern or philosophical sense of incarnation as the relation between two substances is binary and conflictual; incarnation is not a journey towards matter's redemption but a process of violent splitting. These first two thematic strands of incarnation in Blake – the passage of essences into some actual instantiation, and the necessity for mind or soul to be housed in some spatio-temporal body – allow for two interpretive approaches. Let us say that the first is to read Blake as providing a traditionally Romantic or ideological resolution to political problems: after the early revolutionary affirmations Blake will assert a spiritual integration that will be set against actual, worldly, and material disorder. Alternatively, we can set Blake against Romantic Ideology and regard his labor as material, as disturbing a naïve or reactionary spiritualism by affirming the text as a social act. Blake's texts are either redemptive, in their narration of eventual spiritualization through integration, *or* in their giving body and force to his radically distinct political vision. Blake can be housed within a spiritualizing and depoliticizing Romanticism of final unities – stressing the figures and formal devices of integration – or he can be deployed to argue for a radical textual materialism that would give the lie to any spirit or sense beyond the letter. Late twentieth-century reading practices tended to favor the second, political-materialist mode (Mee 1992), although there are still highly philosophical approaches to Blake that would, if political at all, locate his transformative potential at the level of ideas (Otto 1991).

How is it that the spiritualized Blake is deemed to be de-politicizing, while politics is aligned with materialism? If spirit is assumed to be a specter, a dominating ghost that is divorced from political actuality, then it follows that a return to matter would be a form of politicizing demystification (Colebrook 2011). Why the apolitical and political would line up with mystical/spiritualist versus materialist/immanent approaches might seem to be self-evident in an age when the return to materiality, praxis, and the body is taken as synonymous with demystification (opposed to spirit and ideality). However, it is just such a chart of mapped binaries that the readability of Blake's work ought to question. Blake's work is poised between two conceptions of politics: politics as the demystifying return to matter, alongside politics as the radical affirmation of spirit beyond matter. It is the strange doubleness of Blake's form and content that disturbs the very possibility of 'the' political. If, as many appeals to 'the political' today seem to indicate, politics is lost when language becomes nothing more than circulating and reified noise, and when vision becomes nothing more than captivating spectacle, then Blake would appear to be the political poet of the future. His entire aesthetic mode of production was oriented towards returning language to animating and inscriptive origins, and to opening vision beyond the confines of 'man.' And yet this very project was essentially pharmacological in Derrida's sense: the very process that would be used to return language to the regenerating polity would grant Blake's poetry a strange and inhuman autonomy (Derrida 2004, 131). If poetry is restored to the hand, once more allowing poetics to emerge from the individual rather than being organized by systems of literary commodification, then this also reduces the degree of formalization and subjects the sense of the poem to a fragile materiality. This is the transcendental or essential problem of the politics of writing: a sense can only be sustained through time if it takes on a body, but that body – continuing and repeating itself through time – is necessarily distinct from any living voice. A text or inscription is required to give body and continuity to a voice, but that voice will therefore be subject to repetitions and mutations not its own. A voice, insofar as it speaks, is always already systematized and alienated. By the same token, there can only be politics or the formation of a common body through some shared system of conventions, norms, and discourses, and this too means that politics will always already partake of an apolitical, alienating, reified or spectral otherness.

At first glance Blake's work may seem to support *both* the self-evidently radical materialist nature of politics – where a return to the polity of active physical bodies is necessarily the creation of a proper future from our proper potential – *and* the opposite claim: that politics is possible only through the influx of a transcendent truth. Indeed the structure of the *political* divide – the problem of whether the body politic would be generated from within or oriented by a transcendent form – seems at once to be central to the very form of Blake's work, at the same time as the execution or incarnation of his project short-circuits this type of political thinking. Blake does seem to reject the idea of a transcendent deity in his critique of the emergence of accusing specters, in his negative figuration of Urizen and Nobodaddy, and in the very form of his work: each letter, mark, shade, and figure emerges from a relation between the engraving hand and expressive spirit. And yet Blake's redemptive trajectories are also dominated by the image of imposing form: Milton's molding of a body for Urizen in *Milton*, the acts of stamping, forging, marking, pressing, weaving, and inscribing, and – most importantly – the resolution that occurs with the form of the final body of Christ/Jerusalem. Each of these aesthetic formations would, if allegorized, suggest a different political metaphysic. One would be hylomorphic, whereby matter in itself is chaotic and unruly, almost in a state of non-being, requiring the infusion of form to bring beings into existence (and this would be in accord with figures of molding or stamping – acts that are frequently but not always valorized in Blake's work). Another aesthetic–political paradigm would be haptic, the eye being guided by matter's own potentialities, the hand being led by matter's own tendencies – arts that are more akin to weaving, or even unveiling. Engraving – Blake's own art – holds both possibilities: it is both an incision on tabula rasa (imposing order and distinction on the undifferentiated), and a reception or inspiration from what is taken in by the senses (disclosing an order from the depths 'to reveal the universal which was hid' [MHH 14, K: 154]).

Blake's prophecies rehearse this ambivalent aesthetic–politics between active and vital inscription (or hylomorphism) and a mode of 'self-annihilation' that abandons itself to the influx of sensations. There is a profound emphasis on act, inscription, forging, determining, and proclaiming – an apocalyptic tone of overcoming mystery – as well as a mystical abandonment to rhythms and perceptions that are not the poet's own and that lie in an eternity beyond natural vegetative man (and the 'mundane shell'). For this reason Blake inverts the classic Christian corporeal and global imaginary, a maneuver that is most evident in his refiguring of Milton's spiritual geography.

At the level of the body, Milton had depicted inwardness, or the turn of the self towards its own interiority as definitive of Satanic fallenness, and this because – like Blake – Milton was aware that the turn inward would be limitless. The clearest expression of this problem was *Paradise Lost* and the alignment of Satan with a regressive interiority: 'Which way I fly is hell; myself am hell;/And in the lowest deep a lower deep,/Still threat'ning to devour me opens wide' (PL 4. 73). There is an infinite divisibility or unboundedness in centrifugal or vortical movements: for Milton, true virtue ascends and moves upward and outward towards transcendence. Satan can only find a hell within because when he reflects he sees only himself; genuine spiritual inwardness finds not itself but God's inner light. Milton's self is, therefore, properly given form not by itself but by the divine life of which it is a sign. The human body is evidence of a divinity that is always and everywhere formed. For Milton the universe is *bounded*, a balanced orb, a pendant world, with a clear circumference: '... hanging in a golden chain/ This pendant world' (PL 2.1051–52); 'And the earth self-balanced on her center hung' (PL 7.242). Correct direction for contemplation and ethical attention is outwards and centrifugal.

For Blake, by contrast, the bounded earth is the 'mundane shell'; the eternal is approached via increasing movement inwards, opening up the infinite from the smallest of things: 'Every thing in Eternity shines by its own Internal light' (M 10, 17, K: 491; E: 104). This interiority occurs both beyond the body, with vortices that open from the smallest of creatures, and within the body. But this inwardness is not a mode of subjectivity, for the self does not find its own person or self-sameness, but an infinite that is also beyond natural man. In terms of the self and the body, Milton advocated the self finding its proper form by focusing on the divinity towards which it tends: as though humanity begins as a fragment of the divine and must regain paradise by journeying towards higher and higher forms, becoming more and more sublime. By contrast, for Blake the infinite is not the boundedness of some great and totalizing whole, subject to a transcendent God towards whom contemplation ought to tend. The infinite opens from each creature, atom, and pulsation, while an eternity unfolds from each moment: 'Eternity is in love with the productions of time' (MHH 7, 10, K: 151; E: 36).

One might consider here a distinction drawn by Deleuze in *Difference and Repetition* between humor and irony, or between a movement towards the infinitely small and an orientation to the infinitely large: 'the art of the aesthetic is humour, a physical art of signals and signs ... an implicated art of intensive quantities' (Deleuze 1994, 245). Deleuze explains Leibniz's monadology in this manner: each moment or point in the universe has its own perception of the infinite, but always according to its own degree of clarity and distinction. And each perceptive point is itself composed of openings to the infinite, monads within monads, all seeing and singing (in their own way) an expression of the infinite. The truth of the world is perspectival – which is not to say there is no truth because everything is relative, but that there is a truth of the relative. There is a truth of the harmonious monads, all opening to the whole of life from their own perceptive singularity. Deleuze identifies this Leibnizian monadology with humor and a passage to the depths, precisely because it is an abandonment of mastery and transcendence; it celebrates the crowds or swarms of being, a certain not-knowing or exposure to that which befalls:

> There is a crucial experience of difference and a corresponding experiment: every time we find ourselves confronted or bound by a limitation or an opposition, we should ask what such a situation presupposes. It presupposes a swarm of differences, a pluralism of free, wild or untamed differences; a properly differential and original space and time; all of which persist alongside the simplifications of limitation and opposition (Deleuze 1994, 50).

By contrast with humor, Deleuze describes the movement of the infinitely large as Hegelian and ironic. For Hegel the notion of the infinite as ever-expanding would be a bad or false infinity: such an infinite would always be capable of being extended and would therefore not be truly infinite. The infinite in Hegel occurs with full and adequate self-realization, when the Idea completes itself, finding itself given in and through self-limitation.

Such a notion is ironic. From Socrates onwards, irony has been defined and achieved via a recognition that concepts are self-surpassing. Justice is not this or that just thing or event. Justice is an Idea; one can think of what justice *would be* beyond concrete instances. Hegel's philosophy is ironic in its identification of the self-exceeding nature of events and concepts. The *Phenomenology* demonstrates that any finitude will always, as finite, imply or pass over into the infinite of which it is a negation. Even the most concrete reference to 'this' is the most general of indicatives, while specified concepts – such as justice – will always push thought beyond any of its determinate instances (Hegel 2009, 169). Whereas Leibniz's monadology, like Blake's aesthetics, accepts the multiple series of infinities or eternities that open from each singularity, creating a dizzying world of multiple expressions and 'worlds', Hegel's irony surpasses all that fragmentation to define the Idea as that which negates itself to recognize itself as self-negation. This creates a politics of self-recognition, whereby man properly arrives at a law that is not so much imposed from without but recognized as that which man gives to himself to arrive at his own self-expression. Such a notion is figured in Milton's God, who creates from himself, freely and without necessity, in order that his own being may be reflected back through the expression of divine creation. Accordingly, each being of creation is properly oriented to the divine whole or order of which it is a limited part.

Humor returns to the 'depths' while irony views from 'on high.' Not surprisingly, Milton's *Paradise Lost* is framed with tropes of poetic elevation, with the poet's blindness enabling a spiritual vision that transcends the distracting light of day. In terms of form and aesthetics, Milton foregrounds an ethics of reading whereby the task of the human soul is to see each creature, body and event as a sign of God's divinity. By contrast, Blake's eye is not a reading and interpreting eye, oriented to *the* sense and order of all things, but a destructive and self-annihilating eye, in which the influx of the outside multiplies rather than unifies, expanding perceptions to open series of worlds beyond man and any single order. The return to the smallest things, and the destruction of a single law or single vision, is not an abandonment of sense for the sake of sensations. Rather, the self-annihilation that occurs with the openness to the eternities disclosed in all the world's creations and pulsations reveals a spirit beyond the natural vegetative man – beyond the self-enclosed body – even if this is not a sense of some whole or divinity beyond humanity as such. The final unity is, for Blake, insistently human and revealed by opening the infinite from the depths or heart of the world's minute particulars. At the same time this eternity is an annihilation of bounded selfhood:

> There is a Negation, & there is a Contrary
> The Negation must be destroyd to redeem the Contraries
> The Negation is the Spectre; the Reasoning Power in Man
> This is a false Body: an Incrustation over my Immortal
> Spirit: a Selfhood. which must be put off & annihilated alway
> To cleanse the Face of my Spirit by Self-examination.
> (M 40, 32–37, K: 533; E: 142).

This doubleness of an opening of the infinite beyond 'man' but from the human form is also what marks Blake's work as ambivalently digital in its negotiation of incarnation. There is at once a privileging of articulation and distinction such that we might say, with Deleuze, that the problem with modernity is not the fragmentation of the world (or even systematization) but simply that the fragments or units are too large, too blunt to yield any real distinction. A genuinely redemptive aesthetic would not be a simple continuity of the analog but a finer and finer digitalism, an ever more nuanced and distinct system. On the one hand, Blake's act of engraving each word and of refusing the general commodity system of mass-produced printed texts was a counter-digital gesture that resisted the submission of the (analog) sense of the work to a pre-formed and formalized system of units. There is no law or ratio of the whole; indeed, for Blake the 'Vegetable ratio' is directly tied to the self-enclosed organism:

> Can such closed Nostrils feel a joy? or tell of autumn fruits
> When grapes & figs burst their covering to the joyful air
> Can such a Tongue boast of the living waters? or take in
> Ought but the Vegetable Ratio & loathe the faint delight
> Can such gross Lips percieve? alas folded within themselves
> They touch not ought but pallid turn & tremble at every wind
> (M 5, 28–37, K: 485; E: 99)

On the other hand, Blake's printing processes were also hyper-digital, seeking to grant each word and sense its own delineation, creating a sign for each unique sensation, drawing the text closer to the hand of digits, where the latter are not equivalent units but articulating powers.

Blake will present the imposition of form upon matter as both necessarily redemptive and impossibly partial. The imposition of form enables the articulation of what otherwise would be a nightmarish chaos, but an overly rigid or abstract form leads to self-enclosure and blindness to anything beyond the constructed system. The act of forming is therefore ambivalent, poised as it is between two modes of the hand: either a hand that feels matter's proper forms that lie in wait to be revealed (a haptic digitalism), or a hand that encloses or stifles sensations through the reduction of complexity to unity (a quantifying digitalism). Passive receptivity can be both a radical and vital opening to the influx of spirit (circumventing cognition and mind, by a direct passage to the engraving hand) while also being a paralyzing position of reductive stasis (where the hand blindly copies or traces, and which Blake will oppose to the active body of walking, forging, sculpting or dancing).

Chapter 4

Force and Form

One of the most copied and circulated of Blake's images is that of Newton the pantocrator. The scientist is bent over, eyes focused on the ground, hand and eye co-ordinated and guided by the mapping compass that merely traces the world's order but is able to do so only because the hand is twinned to the technology of the measuring compass. Blake will elsewhere depict a bent-over Urizen, transcribing 'the' law onto stone tablets, again twinning a seeming passivity (the hand as transcriber) with a violent annihilation of matter's own force. Both the formalization of science and the universal laws of religion and reason are *reactive,* for they present the formation of systems as nothing more than the ordering of a lawful world. Creations of force are presented as simple copies or transcriptions, presenting action as innocent reaction. By contrast Blake depicts bodies on their way to redemption as dynamic, athletic, coupling, dancing, all limbs engaged.

There are forms in Blake's aesthetics, and in a thoroughly Platonic or neo-Platonic manner, these forms are eternal. But Blake (in a manner akin to Deleuze's 'reversed Platonism') stresses the *forming of form,* especially through bodies that sculpt, mould or touch the matter upon which they work. The artist is more like an engraver or sculptor who works with the resistance and depths of matter, than a painter whose blank canvas offers no tendencies of its own or a draftsman who can form a model, in advance, in abstraction.

If such creating bodies are active it is not in any simple sense, for Blake's active bodies are also receptive. The acts of accusing, imposing law, judging, and condemning are reactive actions (or negations of what is contrary). Accusations, rapes, enslavements, judgments, and the imposition of rigid or reifying systems that diminish complexity are typical of what Nietzsche referred to as *ressentiment*: rather than act from itself, a body feels a pain or sensation and responds by attributing guilt or menace to a punishing other.

This then yields the reactive logic of: 'I suffer therefore someone else is guilty:'

> Meanwhile wept Satan before Los. accusing Palamabron;
> Himself exculpating with mildest speech. for himself believ'd
> That he had not opress'd nor injur'd the refractory servants.
> (M 8, 1–3, K: 487; E: 101)

By contrast, active forces are those that allow the body to be affected or to receive what is distinct from itself, and thereby become other than itself.

Blake's work in this respect is, again, counter-political: there is no polity or system through which actions and judgments take place. In a world dominated by *the polity* there is no action, only reaction; what occurs takes place only in terms of defined relations of an already constituted or imagined whole. In Blake's imagined prophetic future, action occurs when bodies do not have a common space or public sphere, when there is no count, measure, unit or 'digit' of political grammar. Rather than see political models as either activist (the demos producing itself through democracy) or pacifying (the loss of the political that occurs in totalitarianism or media culture), Blake describes different modes of the active–passive relation. Rather than parse these out with the notion that politics occurs actively when individuals form the world and law for themselves, and that politics is lost when individuals are subjected to external forms, Blake makes the relation between action and reaction an ongoing dramatic problem. The problem of this active/passive relation that cannot simply be mapped onto any politics bears two features.

First, it renders the conceptualization of 'the political' difficult, if not impossible: if there is no clear relation or distinction among bodies, or bodies and world, then the very formation of a polity as a bringing together of parts into some cohering whole becomes problematic. Blake's prophecies never arrive at a distinct body politic where parts compose a whole, precisely because the relation between part and whole remains undecidable. Sometimes the voices of the poetry are aspects of a single body, at others they are between a body to be redeemed and its other, and sometimes the voices operate at confused registers, appearing now as aspects of a whole, later as wholes that require reunification. It is never clear in these epic journeys towards redemption who or what is being redeemed: are the prophecies allegories of a humanity that has fragmented into 'four zoas,' *or* morality tales of a war between a naturalized fallen humanity and its properly spiritual end, *or* a theological drama in which man must find his redeemed soul, *or* are we reading a political call to revolution that would urge humanity to overthrow illusions of transcendence? It is not only *not* clear at what level the allegory is operating – whether Blake is referring to a humanity that requires redemption through spirit, or a humanity that suffers from the illusion of a spiritual other – it is also impossible to decide whether redemption should occur by way of unification and assertion or by self-annihilation and submission. In the following passage from *Milton* 'self-annihilation' is coupled with humanization:

> To bathe in the Waters of Life; to wash off the Not Human
> I come in Self-annihilation & the grandeur of Inspiration
> To cast off Rational Demonstration by Faith in the Saviour
> To cast off the rotten rags of Memory by Inspiration
> To cast off Bacon. Locke & Newton from Albions covering
> To take off his filthy garments, & clothe him with Imagination
> To cast aside from Poetry. all that is not Inspiration
> (M 41, 1–7, K: 533; E: 142)

This is further complicated by the fact that the active–passive relation is sexualized, with an active mode of femininity being tyrannical, while the passive mode of femininity is either a seductive and dangerous lure or a redeeming medium through which the enclosed male subject can expand his being:

> and those in immortality gave forth their Emanations
> Like Females of sweet beauty. to guard round him & to feed
> His lips with food of Eden in his cold and dim repose
> (M 15, 14–16, K: 496; E: 109)

Here, again, something like a sexual *politics* is precluded precisely because of the lack of a proper body: it is sometimes the case that the body politic includes male and female components, but also that it is a male body redeemed through the feminine, or even a balanced duality with no sex or gender overall (generically 'man'). In *Milton* redemption occurs when Leutha takes on the burden of fault (in a manner of Christ-like sacrifice):

> All is my fault: We are the Spectre of Luvah the murderer
> Of Albion: O Vala! O Luvah: O Albion! O lovely Jerusalem
> The Sin was begun in Eternity, and will not rest to Eternity
> Till two Eternitys meet together,
> (M 13, 9–12, K: 494; E: 107).

But this redemption, via female sacrifice, seems to be required because of a prior demonization or mystification of female sexuality: 'For then the Body of Death was perfected in hypocritic holiness./Around the Lamb. a Female Tabernacle woven in Cathedrons Looms' (M 13, 25–26, K: 494).

Both of these problems of politics – of sexuality and activity/passivity – are problems of incarnation and are figured through Blake's own presentation of engraving where the line is both a decisive act of prophetic marking and something that emerges from the depths when appearances are burned away. The line is both creation and revelation, both the hand's own, and discovered through touch. The body politic and the body of the work are poised undecidably between definitive unities where each part contributes actively to the whole, and mystic, fragmented and open processes or networks without any possibility of comprehension. One could describe the unities towards which Blake's prophecies tend as 'open wholes': there is a sense of connectedness among parts, and a sense of over-arching unity, and yet both the relations and the totality are also open to variation. One might also describe this as 'transcendence in immanence': the sense of the whole that is greater than the parts is always given from some specific and distinct singular point, for there is no unity in general. Consider two competing senses of the end: the final visual image of *Milton* accompanies an infinitive: 'To go forth to the Great Harvest & Vintage/of the Nations.' And although Milton's *Paradise Lost* also concludes with a futural direction ('They hand in hand with wand'ring steps and slow/Through Eden took their solitary way'), Blake's use of the infinitive is without subject and expresses the potentiality of an event as such. The visual image has at its center a female figure with arms held high (almost another variant of what has come to be known as 'glad day' or a joyous celebration of the liberated body, this time feminine), but she is surrounded by two bodies as pillars, with androgynous heads looking towards her, with torsos that could either be organic (as though emerging from leaf-life pillars) or architectural (bodies that are like columns). Even though the epic has figured Jerusalem as the ideal counterpart or unifying emanation, the visual conclusion is tripartite, with a centered female figure surrounded by desexualized almost non-human forms. Similarly, the final plate of *Jerusalem* depicts three bodies: this time a central male figure, holding compass and hammer (as a figure of redeemed labor), but again the two bodies on either side are (at least in one case) androgynous. The bodies appear to have the musculature of a male but the head on the right, turned towards the center, is feminine with arms opened that present the moon, with the figure to the left appearing as masculine and holding the sun. The unity is, again, closer to being a trinity, and one in which each figure seems (more so than in *Milton*) to bear equal force and weight. The textual conclusion is more definitive than *Milton,* ending not with an infinitive but with an act of definitive naming. Here, though, the conclusion that brings all forms together is still one in which each power is granted its singularity (and Jerusalem is plural):

> All Human Forms identified even Tree Metal Earth & Stone, all
> Human Forms identified. living going forth & returning wearied
> Into the Planetary lives of Years Months Days & Hours reposing
> And then Awaking into his Bosom in the Life of Immortality.
> And I heard the name of their Emanations they are named Jersualem
> (J 99, 2–6, K: 747; E: 259)

What counts, then, as an epic and narrative unity? Is it the inclusion of all elements within a final whole (visually three bodies appearing as a trinity, or each element bearing the one name of 'Jerusalem' – although this is the name of the emanation not the elements themselves). Or, is resolution achieved through distinction – every body granted its own force, and every form 'identified'?

Reading what remains of Blake's engravings usually also brings its own politics: either looking beyond the scars of the text to an ideal, circulating, repeatable sense, or focusing on the minute particulars and singularities that would preclude any general meaning beyond the work. Politically, one would extrapolate these two modes of aesthetics – where aesthesis begins from the eye's receptivity – into two modes of synthesis: either an imposition of political order from without (that assumes unified sense), or the generation of the body politic from life itself and its intrinsic tendencies (the text's materiality). If Blake is claimed to be a political visionary – a figure of the left with a definitive system of revolution – then the parts can cohere into expressions of a whole. The text would be an expression of ideas that one could read through the text and that could then enable a determination of less clear passages. This mode of reading via a hermeneutic circle has been the dominant in Blake criticism, whereby Blake's vision finds its actualization and incarnation in the plates and the decisions that went into the formation of those plates. From David Erdman and E. P. Thompson to Saree Makdisi and Jon Mee, everything in Blake's work can at least begin to be understood through reference to a context of ideas. In contrast Jerome McGann has argued for the text's specific materiality, both against a general Romantic 'irony' that would supposedly allow literature of the time to gesture to some reconciliation beyond fragments and disunity, and against an effacement of the text's specific difference. Politics, for McGann, would not lie in the unity of vision or historical context, but in the pragmatic forces of *speech acts*; each text is an act and cannot be understood by referring distinctions back to some originating sense. Instead one looks at the text itself as a force in its own right: 'Blake's work is important in this context because it consistently foregrounds the material, social and institutional bases of its productive modes. … His illuminated poems are especially clear examples of his understanding that if art is to be an agent of change, its agencies will be operating at the earliest stages of conception and through all later productive, distributive and reproductive phases. None of this may be allowed to escape poetry's concrete transformative deliberations' (McGann 232). Even if one does not adopt McGann's theory of texts as acts, and politics as a pragmatic and contested arena rather than an unfolding of ideological visions, the Blake of revolutionary ideas and vision has always been contrasted with a craftsman Blake. From the latter point of view one ought to focus on Blake's own hand, on the text itself, and its productive genesis (Viscomi 1993). Against a history-of-ideas approach in which Blake would be understood as an expression of his time, there would be a positivist historicism that would fracture any notion of a general polity, granting the text as material object its own generating force. But perhaps Blake is best approached through what Paul de Man referred to as 'unreadability': what we have is not a text as an access or mediation of vision, nor an object that can be tied back to a series of actions. Blake has left us a text. We have nothing other than a dispersed series of fragments, all of which indicate a whole of which they would be parts; and yet any such intimated whole is only a projection *from* the remainder or fragment. To read a text politically, either as caused by, or expressive of, some network of meaningful intention, is to subdue the text's force as a detached remnant. Any sense of the text as an outpouring, expression or extension of spirit is always an effect of the text itself.

It has become a commonplace of the literary critical establishment 'after theory,' that all readings are political readings. It is accepted that all reading occurs in some context, is embedded in a series of institutional, community, and historical practices and operates, however, minimally, as a move in an ongoing language game. Such a commitment to 'the political' would seem to demand a theoretical approach: as Terry Eagleton argued in his introduction to theory: 'the claim to be without theory is really a disavowal of one's enabling theory' (and therefore a denial of one's implicit and, inevitably, depoliticizing or conservative position): 'all criticism is in some sense political, and since people tend to give the word 'political' to criticism whose politics disagrees with their own, this cannot be so' (Eagleton 2008, 184). Alternatively, if politics were to be associated with a true materialism, such as McGann's reference to concrete and textual acts, then reading would draw more upon specific material and distinct forces: these would include Blake's hand, the means of production, local power relations and networks, and the text itself. Politics as such would be the final horizon, either because one assumes that texts emerge as expressions of some ideology, or because one assumes that texts are social acts, always readable in terms of their context of production and reproduction.

Anyone working on Blake would have a sense of the warring nature of Blake's work. There is at once a high state of concretion achieved through individual and laborious printing practices, alongside an expansive mystical abstraction. There is the creation of a singular mythography and lexicon, which renders the corpus *sui generis,* but this is coupled with place names, Biblical proper names, local historical incidents, and other fragments of literary history that draw the text away from the unity of intention. Blake is at once the most systematic of poets in his formation of an elaborate lexicon, cartography, and alternative universe, as well as being the most chaotic. But this war is not accidental: Blake's work brings to the fore, and intensifies, an essential tension at the heart of literary and cultural production. Forces of production – despite Marxist dreams of returning all creativity to the hand or praxis of a generating humanity – necessarily break with the animating origin and become separate. This is the very nature of *techne,* and the inextricable imbrication of *techne* with life: something lives on or has an identity only by attaining some systemic repeatability that maintains itself through time. Physis and *techne* do not negate each other, but are contraries. One can only posit a proper nature or life *as such* through some ongoing establishment of identity, and that ongoing identification will take the technical form of perceptual recognition, speech or writing. A produced work – as work (as detached and formed product) – leaves its origin, and does so by taking on a form that can never be fully *political*, for it becomes distinct from any assemblage of bodies gathering in common. The work as such, whatever its political origin, operates beyond the polity, which means that it will always require a labor of reading that can never be completed:

> In the manner of a proper name, the work is singular; it does not function like an ordinary element of natural language in its everyday usage. That is why it lets itself be assimilated less easily by culture to whose institution it nevertheless contributes. Although more fragile, having an absolute vulnerability, as a singular proper name it appears less biodegradable than all the rest of culture that it resists, in which it "rests"and remains, installing there a tradition, its tradition, and inscribing itself there as inassimilable, indeed unreadable, at bottom insignificant (Derrida 1989, 825).

Something mystical, unreadable or materially resistant will always remain. Thus it is Blake's manifestly political gestures – to break from the dull round of dead language by forming a new vital system requiring an active new readership – that will render any full politics impossible.

The gestures that contemporary thinkers have associated with true politics – such as Alain Badiou's insistence that politics occurs with a break from the already enumerated and a vision of a new universality – are ultimately destructive of anything like *the* polity (Badiou 2011). Insofar as such gestures are successful, in forming some new act that takes on a form that remains through time, they are also distinct from any context from which they emerge. Similarly, the warring forces of system and chaos in Blake's work are essentially intertwined and impossible to reconcile. Rather than accept a vague generality, Blake seeks to re-name and distinguish every nuance of his envisioned word; each aspect is given both a proper name (thereby resisting the generality of concepts) and has its own cartography and genealogy. But this results in a frenzied proliferation of terms. The desire to name each event or moment in its utter singularity is both a reaction against the tyranny of generality and a 'will to system' that would answer to each specificity's own force (Lacoue-Labarthe and Nancy 1988, 32). What results is a mass of lists, neologisms, place names, proper names, distinctions, and fractal genealogies.

The problems of incarnation in Blake – the problem of expression or sense being inscribed as text, the problem of spirit taking on body, the problem of the mind-matter unity of worldly bodies, both political and individual – open out a space that takes us beyond today's current concept of the political. For although Blake will retreat with horror from the formless chaos of an unbounded, disarticulated, and undelineated void, he will not assert a single transcendent form. Instead, what we are given is an ongoing war between incarnation (or the taking on of distinction and boundedness) and spiritualization where the body's potentiality exceeds any of its actual incarnations. It might seem as though this war leads to a permanent irony: there must be some posited whole, order or system, and yet the particulars made visible by the system always indicate other orders. And there is, of course, a sense in which Blake's work is part of a broad tradition of Romantic irony in its capacity, as willfully fragmented, to intimate a whole that is only given from the fragment and that can never become operative. However, there is another respect in which Blake retreats from the height of irony to the depths of humor. As already noted, Deleuze marks a contrast between Hegelian ironic modes of speculation, in which the range of a concept can always be exceeded or surpassed to indicate a higher ideality – when any instance of justice would always be inadequate to 'the' just – and Leibnizian modes of humor, where any generality can always be seen as composed of smaller and smaller potentials, going to the infinitely divisable: 'The first way of overturning the law is ironic, where irony appears as an art of principles, of ascent towards the principles and overturning principles. The second is humour, which is an art of consequences and descents, of suspensions and falls' (Deleuze 1994, 5).

The idea of the polity is essentially ironic: there is always an idea of humanity, democracy, consensus, the state or justice that guides political action but retreats from any actuality. *The* political is an expansion to some higher or intimated beyond. It is no wonder that Romanticism, in general, has borne some relation to this irony of the heights – a striving to an Idea that will always offer itself in an ever-receding future. Such an ideal is maintained today in the post-Kantian tradition of theory: in Jurgen Habermas's ideal that consensus as an ideal of ongoing political conversation, not something that ever arrives, in Jacques Derrida's insistence on a justice or democracy 'to come' such that the Idea of justice will always disturb any present actuality, while never itself being actualized, and even in more general theories of liberal justice as 'fairness' whereby I decide what counts as justice according to what any individual *would* choose if he or she could not determine their position in the polity (Rawls 1972). Such ironic orientations of the Idea proceed from the conditions of political conversation: insofar as I speak in common I must presuppose a sense of – say – justice, democracy, consensus or the good; to speak without some ideal horizon of agreement would be a performative contradiction. Deleuze has argued that this structure of political thought is inherently bourgeois: on the one hand I desire justice and democracy, while on the other accepting its necessary non-arrival. It is a 'thermodynamic' ideology of more or less, of striving to achieve ideals, while tempering the distance and purity of ideals with the actuality of compromise and conversation. It is a negotiation between the Idea of what must be true or imagined as true for all time, and the compromised complexity of time and space:

> Good sense is by nature eschataological, the prophet of a final compensation and homogenization. If it comes second, this is because it presupposes mad distribution – instanaeous, nomadic distribution, crowned anarchy or difference. However, this sedentary, patient figure which has time on its side corrects difference, introduces it into a milieu which leads to the cancellation of differences or the compensation of portions. It is itself this 'milieu.' Thinking itself to be in between the extremes, it holds them off and fills in the interval. It does not negate differences – on the contrary: it arranges things in the order of time and under the conditions of extensity such that they negate themselves. It multiplies the intermediates and, like Plato's demiurge, ceaselessly and patiently transforms the unequal into the divisible. Good sense is the ideology of the middle classes who recognize themselves in equality as an abstract product. It dreams less of acting than of constituting a natural mileu, the element of an action which passes from more to less differenciated: for example, the good sense of eighteenth-century political economy which saw in the commercial classes the natural compensation for the extremes, and in the prosperity of commerce the mechanical process of the equalization of portions. It therefore dreams less of acting than foreseeing, and of allowing free rein to action which goes from the unpredictable to the predictable (from the production of differences to their reduction). Neither contemplative nor active, it is prescient. In short, it goes from the side of things to the side of fire: from differences produced to differences reduced. It is thermodynamic. In this sense it attaches the feeling of the absolute to the partial truth (Deleuze 1994, 283).

Blake and Deleuze also refer to Ideas but Ideas for these two writers are worked through a structure of humor rather than irony. Blake will insist on the reality of Ideas or forms, with such eternal forms not being apprehended (as they were for Kant) by thinking beyond what can be given. Blake stresses an expanded perception, such that Ideas and forms (to use Deleuze's terminology) arise 'from the depths.' Blake describes the infinite arising from the depths, as having been present all along, if perception could only be cleansed. Deleuze also insists on Ideas – not as higher level abstractions attained by increasing generality to arrive at universality glimpsed beyond this world – but as thoroughly real, ideal, and absolutely distinct.

Similarly, though Blake celebrates a world of minute particulars he will also insist that each tiny fragment of a body, every thread and fibre, opens to infinity. This is so much so that 'self-annihilation' proceeds only with an inspiration that passes directly to the hand:

> To open the Eternal Worlds, to open the immortal Eyes
> Of Man inwards into the Worlds of Thought: into Eternity
> Ever expanding in the Bosom of God, the Human Imagination
> O Saviour pour upon me thy Spirit of meekness & love:
> Annihilate the Selfhood in me, be thou all my life!
> Guide thou my hand which trembles exceedingly upon the rock of ages,
> While I write of the building of Golgonooza. & of the terrors of Entuthon:
> Of Hand & Hyle….
>
> (J 5, 19–26, K: 623; E: 147)

Against the deadening circulation of accepted opinion and democratic negotiation, against a popular taste for the easily consumed, Blake will explicitly affirm an aesthetics of distinction, individuation, and rupture with the present, often by way of violent intrusion. What ensues from this rupture is not 'the' political and does not result in a constituted formal system of consensus. Blake's Jerusalem is not in any way a polity. It is not a gathering of subjects with a view to some created common. However ambivalent Blake's final or redemptive unities may be, they do not map onto current notions of the properly political. They are neither, as the Erdman revolutionary Blake tradition would have it, a reduction of all seemingly transcendent and spiritual forms to the common body of the populace (for there is always the affirmation of Jerusalem as a unity beyond the material collection of bodies); nor are Blake's higher unities governed by some proper form in the Platonic sense whereby human reason is led beyond interests to some ideal procedure that would be free from localized and particular points of view. Blake's final forms are not, in contemporary terms, what Hardt and Negri have referred to as 'the common,' even though Hardt and Negri's manifesto for one self-constituting political dynamic body without an imposed center or mind might appear (at first) to be Blakean:

> The multitude today, however, resides on the imperial surfaces where there is no God the Father and no transcendence. Instead there is our immanent labor. The teleology of the multitude is theurgical; it consists

> in the possibility of directing technologies and production towards its own joy and its own increase of power. The multitude has no reason to look outside its own history and its own present productive power for the means necessary to lead towards its constitution as a political subject.
>
> A material mythology of reason thus begins to be formed, and it is constructed in the languages, technologies, and all the means that constitute the world of life. It is a material religion of the senses that separates the multitude from every residue of sovereign power and from every "long arm" of Empire. The mythology of reason is the symbolic and imaginative articulation that allows the ontology of the multitude to express itself as activity and consciousness. The mythology of languages of the multitude interprets the telos of an earthly city, torn away by the power of its own destiny from any belonging or subjection to a city of God, which has lost all honor and legitimacy. (Hardt and Negri 2000, 396).

Nor are Blake's open wholes what liberal or post-Kantian theory would affirm as purely procedural systems capable of detaching the conversation of politics from the pathology of local interests. Blake's problematic unities lack the self-organizing, immanent or autopoetic qualities that define the contemporary political bodies that have been affirmed against supposedly traditional 'transcendent' political forms. Blake might at first appear to be akin to various contemporary movements of immanent politics, oriented towards destruction of an imposed state form, generating the body politic from its own energy. But even though Blake will constantly turn to the genesis and vital emergence of the body politic, he will also always affirm transcendence or the intrusion of an inassimilable element that cannot be incorporated (with all the senses of the body and its limits that incorporation brings in train). Blake's work remains committed to a radical transcendence that will intrude violently to disrupt the apparent closure of political wholes. But this is a 'transcendence in immanence', or a radical outside that opens from the immediate and the given.

While Blake's poetry works to destroy any imposed state form or any notion of a proper body that would be other than the dynamic life of the present, he is also insistent that this present life is inspired by a life that is not immediately apparent. In this respect, his work exposes the problem of any art of the political. There cannot be a polity that fashions itself from itself as a work of art directly expressive of spirit; and there cannot be a work of art that remains close to the hand of praxis, as though art might be nothing more than the active growth of the polis taking on external form. This is because art, as a work, is incarnate: it possesses a body. The bodies of artworks cannot be organic; they emerge as art only in being detachable from their animating ground, and they live on only if they are released from the immediacy of their originating expression.

The mode of incarnation of Blake's body of work also troubles any consideration of the body as an organism. The three senses of incarnation as they are played out in Blake's work all appear at first to intend some organic fulfillment at the same time as they expose the impossibility of any mode of organic boundedness. The body of the artwork is at once readable, or occurs *as art,* only if it refers back to the hand from which it has emerged. At the same time, the artwork's constitutive separation severs its relation to that hand. The passage from expression to material letter at once requires the incarnation of the artwork's matter, even if that matter takes on life only by being divided from itself. We may imagine the body of the artwork as being tied to the inscribing hand of its author, and we may also imagine it as giving form to the political imaginary, but to do so is to *reduce* the body of the work either to its (supposed) originating sense or to its present actualization. The state of incarnation – the work of art's material body – entails that it cannot be self-present but carries unread (and unreadable) marks and scars of the past, and multiple series of unactualized potentials.

Insofar as Blake's poetry and visual corpus take on the form of a body of *work,* it can be neither political nor common. It cannot be reduced to discursive, repeatable, and rational circulation. In addition to the understood and received sense there will always remain the spatio–temporal and incarnated figure and body of the work. This remainder is both the material letter, or the engraved and detached work as object, and the repeated and digitalized circulating copy of the work (as well as the vaguely understood cultural memory of Blake – all the half-remembered and borrowed phrases that dominate popular music and iconography). The work exists both as common sense – as the work of Blake that is known, read, and repeated – and as a resistant figure that remains unread and unassimilated. Such figures cannot be political for even though Blake's works seem to play an exemplary role in (say) the constitution of the British polity – from the hymn 'Jerusalem' to the widely circulated images of Newton the pantocrator – such events occur alongside an unread or unreadable – inassimilable – element. There is at once the political, circulated, read, and consumed Blake alongside a demonically repeated and destructive element that tears the body politic apart from itself.

What happens when a work is fragmented, or when a fragment of a work becomes detached and circulates, divorced (as it must be) from the sense of its genesis? Consider the hymn 'Jerusalem.' For all Blake's railing against religion, church law and a complacent submission to the notions of 'natural man,' 'Jerusalem' has become one of the motifs of not only the Church of England and an intrinsically royalist state; it also celebrates one of England's least Blakean institutions (the BBC Proms in which the 'high' art of popular classics from Vivaldi to Elgar is distributed and televised to the populace). Taken out of context the use of this part of *Milton* as a hymn and anthem shifts the force of Blake's text away from revolutionary destruction towards nationalist sentiment. But this fall of Blake into a jingoistic nationalism cannot be viewed as a corruption that befalls the work from outside. Blake's corpus faces in two directions at once: a release of the figures and images from their origin in British political history, alongside a regressive retrieval of nationalism and personal humanism against which Blake labored.

One way of reading the politics of this fragment of *Milton* and other circulating fragments of Blake's work is through a theory of irony that would be essentially political. Blake was a radical poet at least in this respect: the very mode of putting the sense of the text into a material body aimed to free art from easy commodification and generic consumption. Each engraved plate would bear the mark of the originating hand, and if some text or part were to be freed from the hand – as in the hymn 'Jerusalem' – then a political reading could always return the text to its originating context. Because the hymn 'Jerusalem' signifies an essentially English and easy nationalism it might then be contrasted with the original force of the text, which aimed to rupture the present in order to open time onto an England that, though green and pleasant, would not coincide with any happy sense of self-affirming and contemporaneous community. There would be an ironic disjunction between the lived (current) sense of the fragments of Blake that circulate to reinforce Englishness, and the original Blake that emanated from a disenchanted, disaffected, and disdainful poet prophet. But this dislocation and ironic split does not affect the work from without, as though a proper sense could be distinguished from a circulating distortion. The condition for Blake's authentic and original rupture – for creating some body of work that would be distinct from the same dull round of already given content – is that there be the creation of a distinct object, a body of work or corpus in the sense of *poiesis*. That is, in order to resist commodification and the dulling of sense as digitalization, or the reduction of complexity to a single technical system, Blake could only resort to a hyper-digitalization, a greater distinction, and separation. He could, and did, draw the sense of the text back to his own hand, but this would then mean that the hand would split from itself: the very scars, marks, inscriptions, and traces of the poet's own hand would remain and circulate after his own life, and would take on a life of their own, appearing to enrich and occlude the animating intent of the inscribing intention.

A work can only live on and be distinct – can only express an artist's individual sense that is distinct from the artist's own time – if it takes on a body; but precisely because the very body that will guarantee the distinction of sense must separate itself from the originating hand, it will always tend towards dislocation. Digitalization is at once necessary, for there can be no readable repetition without the submission to a system of units other than that of the hand itself. At the same time, pure digitalization is impossible: the inscription or marking out of the digit always bears some trace of the distinguishing and singular body. There is something *a*political in any incarnated work. It can only emerge as a bounded, marked, signed, and individuated work if it is not merely one more stock phrase or convention amongst the polity's standard exchanges. And yet the work's ongoing life can only occur – can only be repeated and renewed at other times – if it incarnates itself in a form of expression that is recognizable, repeatable and therefore essentially detached from its originating moment of genesis.

This gives the incarnation of the work a curious and apolitical double status: it emerges as a signed and distinct work in its separation from the ready-made figures of the polity, and therefore possesses a counter-political opening. A text is a recognizable work or act only if it is *not* the already-said and already-formed. Even the use of existing objects *as art* (such as the extreme case of the ready-made) can occur only in an event of detachment or setting apart. (This is why Deleuze and Guattari argue that all art begins with the ready-made: not a faithful repetition of the real, but a displacement that splits what is already given from its present and functioning locus). A text must be counter-political in its creation of a relation that is not already caught up in system and structure. At the same time, a text's readability, circulation, continuity, and sustained life demand that it take on a body that can be essentially torn from the animating intent, and that can then become grafted to the polity that it originally ruptured. In order for a sense to be expressed a work must leave the hand of its author and become a detached object. This necessary detachment not only allows for copying, splitting, scarring, excision, and distortion, it also includes the capacity for the text to become a dead letter. 'Jerusalem' can have the force that it does as a national and enlivening hymn not only because its full context has not been read but also because something of its origin remains unreadable, remains inassimilable to the polity from which it emerged and which continues to invoke its terms. If a text were not at least in part unreadable – if it did not have some non-semantic or non-actualized remainder – then it would no longer require reading. Nothing more would be left to say.

In Blake's own mode of giving sense a body, it was his very act of keeping the work close at hand – of individuating each letter, plate, and figure distinctly so that it would remain inspired and singular – that also led to the body of work's greater death. The body of the work of art must take on a material form to secure a time of living on, and yet it is just that necessity for incarnation that will eat away at the work's very life. By giving sense to a body that will sustain itself through time, the incarnated work becomes open to decay, splitting, distortion, and dead repetition. The very condition of the political – that there be some common context across which difference and discourse can take place – is ruptured by the work's distinct emergence as an event of the not already said. The very condition of the work's continuity is that it in some way becomes political, becomes a text in common: Blake's phrases, aphorisms, images, and figures contribute, at least in part, to the creation of an illusion of a polity, even if the body of that polity is anything but an organic unity in which each part is in dynamic and living relation to the whole.

This dislocation of the body from itself is disclosed both as a problem of incarnation within Blake's work, and as a problem of incarnation in the circulation and 'consumption' of Blake's corpus. Within Blake's work, despite its affirmation of an infinite, a Jerusalem, an eternal man or a redemption from fragmentation, the passage to the infinite is always figured as the passage to 'an' infinite from a singular point. To use the terminology of Leibniz: every point of existence opens to the whole of being in its own highly individuated way. But to add Deleuze's inflection to Leibniz: rather than each point in the whole singing the same tune of one harmonious world, the series diverge into multiple infinities:

> ... insofar as the same world is included in all existing monads, the latter offer the same infinity of minute perceptions, and the same differential relations that yield in them strangely similar conscious perceptions. All monads thus perceive the same green color, the same note, the same river, and in every case a single and same eternal object is actualized in them. Yet on the other hand, actualization is different for each monad. Never do two monads perceive the same green color in the same degree of chiaroscuro. It could be said that every monad favors certain differential relations that hereafter confer on it exclusive perceptions; that the monad leaves other relations below the necessary degree; or, further, that it lets an infinity of minute perceptions subsist

> in it without at all assuming relations. At the limit, then, all monads possess an infinity of compossible minute perceptions, but have differential relations that will select certain ones in order to yield clear perceptions proper to each. In this way every monad, as we have seen, expresses the same world as the others, but nonetheless owns an exclusive zone of clear expression that is distinguished from every other monad: its *subdivision* (Deleuze 2006, 102–03).

If, as Blake affirms, one can perceive the infinite in a grain of sand, this not only proclaims the significance of the grain (the importance of the smallest of things); it also proclaims the insistence of the infinite – its intrusion into all aspects of existence, and its vortical opening from every aspect of the world. That is, one can both assert that the infinite is not some grand foundation or transcendence lying beyond worldly finitude *and* that every singularity perceives and unfolds the infinite in its own way. Even the grain of sand, the flea or a singular pulsation of blood opens out beyond itself to an infinite:

> Timbrels & violins sport round the Wine-presses; the little Seed;
> The sportive Root. the Earth-worm. the gold Beetle: the wise Emmet;
> Dance round the Wine-presses of Luvah: the Centipede is there:
> The ground Spider with many eyes: the Mole clothed in velvet
> The ambitious Spider in his sullen web; the lucky golden Spinner;
> The Earwig armd: the tender Maggot emblem of immortality:
> The Flea: Louse: Bug: the Tape-Worm: all the Armies of Disease:
> Visible or invisible to the slothful vegetating Man.
> The slow Slug: the Grasshopper that sings & laughs & drinks:
> Winter comes, he folds his slender bones without a murmur.
> The cruel Scorpion is there: the Gnat: Wasp: Hornet & the Honey Bee:
> The Toad & venomous Newt; the Serpent clothd in gems & gold:
> They throw off their gorgeous raiment: they rejoice with loud jubilee
> Around the Wine-presses of Luvah. naked & drunk with wine
> (M 27, 12–25, K: 513; E: 124).

Every singularity or minute particular is fully articulated, capable of repetition beyond itself eternally; nothing simply is what it is without also being a repetition of eternity: 'And every Generated Body in its Inward form/Is a garden of delight & a building of magnificence.' Everything is always already other than itself, iterable in advance. And yet the infinite is never given as such, in its plenitude, but is always this finite opening from this singular now.

This provides a way of thinking about Blake's corpus (and art's corporeality in general). Blake's bodies circulate in contemporary culture, and play a formative and yet non-transparent role in the contemporary polity. Britain's body politic is composed, at least in part, of fragments and unreadable remnants: the hymn 'Jerusalem,' the figure of Newton the pantocrator (that emblazons science textbooks and provides the forecourt sculpture for the British Library), the circulating phrases used as book titles, song lyrics, and epigrams (from *Fearful Symmetry* and *Songs of Experience* to 'mind forg'd manacles,' 'doors of perception' and 'dark satanic mills') (Goode 2006). These are not so much quotations or propositions that make up the sense and value of a collective identity, as fragments that indicate gaps and fissures rather than a whole to which they might be returned. What we are left with in Blake is *neither* a proper polity of some final unifying and transcendent form *nor* a gathering of individuals to form a single, immanent, and foundationless plane of conversation. Politics is not the constitution of some universal that might be seized upon from within the present – so politics cannot be the intrusion of truth into the given. Politics cannot be envisioned as some point of final arrival at decision-making following a world that has fallen into and then been redeemed from banality. Blake's 'ends' are undecidable, poised between this world and the next, between a distinct body and a greater unity, between minute particulars and grand wholes. What is evident is that politics cannot be a return to praxis, bodies, matter, and immanence.

Despite a privileging of the hand, the poetic act, the touch of the artist upon matter, and the life of bodies in this sexually creative and fruitful world, Blake will criticize generation and will always write in a counter-narrative mode that resists any resolution of organicist comprehension and any notion of a historically transparent genesis. What needs to be questioned, following Blake's difficult relation to both theological and human modes of incarnation, is the very concept of the political as *polity*. For Blake will affirm neither the political subject who acts and speaks in such a way as to constitute the political body from himself, nor the political body as some common and human collective. The body politic for Blake is neither a purely procedural form (as it will become for liberalism) nor a common whole as it would be for communitarianism or Romantic organicisms. Blake's poetry negotiates relations between individual particulars and final unities while also refusing a *political* body. This is both because the body for Blake, when viewed positively, opens beyond its locus to exceed any form of sociality or lived time, and because the body when negated (as the natural vegetative aspect of the world that must be transcended) opens to a new

Jerusalem that maintains a warring relation among its components; the 'giant Albion' of the Blakean end is radically *impolitic.* Incarnation, or the dynamic relation between animating spirit and actual body, whether that spirit be mystical or human, precludes all the redemptive images of unification and dialectic that have characterized celebrations of the proper political body. To say, then, that Blake is a non-dialectical artist whose work is primarily impolitic is to draw attention to two features in his corpus that may lead us to rethink what it is to read a body of work. The constitution of an artist's corpus, as a circulating cultural commodity, destroys as much as it reinforces the sense of a political whole. Further, even though the condition of reading a work – or of attributing sense to a work – requires that one posit some original animating intent, that intent can only survive if it becomes detached and alienated from its origin.

One notion that characterizes what has come to be known as 'theory' today would suggest that all reading must be political and this because reading is always an activity of the world, embedded in contexts of interest and – even more importantly – always the reading undertaken by this or that subject whose world is always given in terms of their own potentialities. There could be no apolitical reading, no reading outside the polity or outside the relations that enable us to have a world as such. But in many respects Blake's work is destructive of just these seemingly unavoidable conditions. One of the current claims made for the unavoidability of meaning, readability, and an inescapable embodiment relies on the postulation of the organic nature of life: there is, supposedly, no world as such, only a world *for* this or that bounded organism with its possible actions and perceptions (Thompson 2007). If this were so then relations would be primary, and any terms would be effected from relations. There would be no intrinsic qualities. Or, at least, qualities would be given only in their dynamic relations; and this would be in accord with a general organicism that privileges both the primacy and the individuating power of wholes and interconnectedness. One might note that such an organicism continues today not only in theories of bodily life and meaning but also in all the figures of ecological networks, the Gaia hypothesis and various theories of a global brain or living systems (Lovelock 1979; Capra 1996; Bloom 2000).

In contrast Blake's work is counter organicist, especially in its mobilation of the dynamics of incarnation, and in its ambivalent relation to digitalization. While Blake resists a simple digitalism or atomism – a world of so many equivalent units, or a general system of quantification – he nevertheless writes of, and with, intrusive and singular powers or recalcitrant elements that open their own eternities. Not only does the text assert a world beyond the bounded body of 'natural man' and a realm of sense beyond communicative and translatable language; the very form of Blake's work tends to unbind rather than organize its elements.

The text's presentation of itself *as text* – as a surface to be intuited or read through as the sign of a sense – nevertheless perverts the very passage to spirit that it would seem to demand. At the level of sense, Blake's work operates as a performative contradiction, demanding to be read and yet remaining unreadable. The Blakean corpus is a body presenting itself as the sign of a spirit that is at once more present than the mere surface of the text and yet radically distanced by the text's surface operation. Blake's aphoristic style, his epic trajectories that continually end in seeming unifications only to split apart and re-start, and his disturbance of character coherence (with aspects of the self taking on spectral form, only then to become characters with their own fragmentations): all these have an effect that goes beyond standard hermeneutic complexity precisely because Blake will work with the dynamic of incarnation while precluding the formation of a unifying body. From the first two senses of incarnation – the theological relation between divinity and worldly revelation, and the human relation between mind and body – it is not surprising that Blake's work would open another, third, sense of incarnation that would redistribute and problematize form and content.

This third sense of incarnation is textual and has to do with the relation between imagined sense and inscribing hand. The passage from inspiration to inscription is often played out as a scene within Blake's work, where various prophet figures or aspects of life ('zoas') are depicted hammering, engraving, molding sculpting, weaving, forming, imprinting, binding, marking or stamping. The problem of textual incarnation is also foregrounded in every act of reading Blake's work where one *either* attends to the ideal sense that one must assume is posited above and beyond material inscription (so that the singular variations of the engraved words have a significance that is maintained across variation and difference) *or* one focuses on the actual and embodied illuminated books (in which case the singular variant has the highest degree of significance). Blake critics usually, and for good reason, do both: a poem in its general, circulating, and anthologized form is inflected with attention to its singular variants (that cannot be dismissed as simply external or accidental). The local and archival reading of any illuminated book regards some marks of the poet's hand as significant (as attributable back to the intentionality of the engraving body); other traces are regarded as less intentional or not fully historical and have to do with the matter through which the hand expresses itself. We might refer to this as the problem of the relation between hand and hyle: between a living body that animates its world and the matter or medium through which that animation occurs.

This complexity of hand and hyle, or technical expression and material support, is the problem of incarnation in general: on the one 'hand,' a body is never simply itself, for the hand is a hand only as part of a broader organic function expressed and actualized through time and given meaning by the work it performs. There is no aspect of life, in this sense, that is purely matter – simply being what it is without sense or relation. One can, as Bergson does in *Matter and Memory*, regard matter and memory as degrees of contraction and dilation: matter simply is, in actuality, without any reference to anything other that its actualized presence, while memory 'dilates' and allows the present to be flooded with other perceptions from the past which always remains present, though virtual. Bergson defines matter as actuality without anything other than the pure point of the present, while memory is an expanding 'cone' opening further and further to include more and more of the past. Pure matter (or actuality without any virtuality) and pure memory, or the flood of the entire past, are imagined limits. What we always experience are mixtures; matter is always lived with some degree of past recollection, and memories are always to some extent lived with some reference to the present:

> No doubt there is an ideal present – a pure conception, the indivisible limit which separates past from future. But the real concrete live present – that of which I speak when I speak of my present perception – that present necessarily occupies a duration. Where then is this duration placed? Is it on the hither or on the further side of the mathematical point which I determine ideally when I think of the present instant? Quite evidently it is both on this side and on that; and what I call 'my present' has one foot in my past and another in my future (Bergson 2004, 176–77).
>
> Memory actualized in an image differs, then, profoundly from pure memory. The image is a present state, and its sole share in the past is the memory when it arose. Memory, on the contrary, powerless as long as it remains without utility, is pure from all admixture of sensation, is without attachment to the present, and is consequently unextended (Bergson, 2004, 181).

On the one hand, then, the present material object can only be experienced with some inflection of a past and some context. On the other hand, any sense, tradition, ideal object, performance, meaning, intention, or spirit cannot be released from the body or matter that it forms. Nowhere is this more apparent than in the textual and spiritual tradition that might seem to affirm the opposite. The very idea of God as it came to be defined and refined in Christian monotheism would seem to assert the purity of an essence without any requirement for a determined actualization. God creates a world other than Himself, not out of necessity but from a pure expansive gift that is all the more glorious for its not having to be. God is existence as such, not bounded by any form or essence, for He is the forming power that brings all essences or forms into existence. His essence is to exist; He is not an essence brought into existence (Gilson 1983, 164).

Before looking at the dramas of hand and hyle, the eternal and its fragmentation, and the infinite and the particular in Blake's work, we can see how this problem of incarnation is played out in Blake criticism in terms of the relation between the singularity of the mark and the ideality of the poem's sense. For any event to be meaningful, to be experienced *as* this or that specifiable phenomenon, it must be experienced as repeatable. If some of Blake's marks have sense then this is because we read the specific token as a sign of, or repetition of, an ideality. We refer the hyle or matter back to a hand: the mark or trace expresses an intentionality to make a difference. When Jerome McGann refers to texts as *social acts* he captures this sense of the mark as the trace of intentionality. The poem is social, for a mark can only have sense through a convention or context where we assume that, say, this specific token will be recognized and responded to as an event in a presupposed grammar. But the poem is also an *act*, for it is not the case that meaning is some mental content which is contingently submitted to a linguistic sign in order to circulate. To speak or write is not only to make a move in a game, at once invoking expectations and conventions but also creating a specific speaking position, social relation, and potential for a certain range of responses. It is this notion of language as *performative* that explicitly underwrites McGann's defence of a certain way of reading Blake: if we want to read a text we do not assume some pure ideality detached from the context of interacting, convention-enabled bodies. We ask what a text does in a context of conventions and actions. There is only sense (and poetry) if there is some common system through which individuals can be speaking subjects: not conveying some internal meaning or mental content *through* signs, but being created as subjects of speech through each discursive relation, with the world – as meaningful – being also determined through an ongoing system of exchange and interaction. To read a poem as a social act is to assume that a poem's sense is what it wants to do, with any intentionality being only discernible through a consideration of context, convention, and conditions of social recognition. For a work to be *read* it must already be non-identical to itself: the concrete marks on the page that make up 'Oh Rose, thou art sick,' are not simply the material object but function as tokens of recognizable, repeatable, and immaterial sense. This insistence upon reading signs as signs *of intentionality* is what led Walter Benn Michaels and Steven Knapp to write 'Against Theory': texts cannot be considered simply as isolated marks but are always read as signs of some intent (Benn Michaels and Knapp 1982). Their argument against theory was, however, ultimately a confirmation of the problem of 'theory'. They argued that one did not require theory because there was no gap between meaning and intent, and so one did not need to discover or find one's way to meaning by way of intentionality. But Blake's work proves quite the opposite (as would any work): one can only assume intent, or that the text *wants to say* something, because one posits or reads what is not fully present in the text itself. It is because texts continue to be read as signs of what is *not* present that there will always and inevitably be a speculation regarding a sense that is intimated but never presented as such.

For the most part Blake's poetry is readable in this manner – as a sign of prior intent – and this allows his work to circulate in an anthologized, standardized and digitalized format (the latter allowing not only the linguistic material but also the designs, colors, washes, borders, typeface, and minor inflections to be available as a common resource liberated from its initial material support). But digitalization in its literal sense (where the original material object is re-coded into a language of ones and zeros, then given a repeatability beyond its original locus) opens up the question of the analog/digital relation in a much broader sense. Digitilization is possible only through a certain comportment of body and world, particularly a relation between eye–hand–brain and touch. The digit occurs with the use of the hand as an instrument of counting, with the matter to be counted being surveyed by a measuring eye. It is when the hand is formed as a set of 'digits' that a finger or body part relates to its world not through the immediacy of touch but *as* a certain amount or quantity. The matter that is digitalized has to be viewed as a quantifiable field capable of being rendered into relatively equivalent units. Digitalization is the passage from the immediacy and senseless presence of mere matter, not yet formed as this or that identifiable entity, to a world experienced as readable: what is perceived is *seen as* this or that repeatable phenomenon. In this regard all thought is digital in its reduction of the complexity and difference of experience to recognizable and articulable concepts. If there is no such thing as a private language this is because in order to experience, live or think of a phenomenon, event or quality one must have already marked in the absolutely singular that which could be repeated, recognized, and communicated to an other. To *read* a poem one does not attend to the specific materiality but to that which has been digitalized, or has passed from the inchoate to the systematized. This raises the question of the border between that which is textual (readable as a social act with a capacity to be circulated and liberated from its material support) and that which cannot be digitalized. Here we can return to McGann, who argues for the poem both as social act (as circulating, ideal, repeatable and readable as independent of its material support) and as text. The latter dimension, though, is not simply distinct for McGann, and it is the decision – for McGann, editorial – in passing from material text to poem that is itself an act of reading. To include some variants, rather than others, often cuts the poem off not only from those material aspects that are inert, unintended, and senseless, but also to the very act that gives the poem its proper force.

McGann is explicitly attentive to the body of the poetic work, both literally and figuratively. It is this body, as material object with specific conditions of production, emergence, circulation, and preservation which is *dismembered* by any act of criticism (which uses the work for its own located ends) and which demands to be re-membered in a future of open criticism:

> ... the full and dynamic reality of the works is dismembered by the uses to which they are put by later readers. ... we have to see that all literary works, including the texts of those works, are inhabited by lost and invisibilized agencies, and that one of the chief functions of criticism is to re-member the works which have been torn and distorted by those losses (McGann 1988, 6).

McGann is not the first to liken the book to a living body susceptible to violent dismemberment. When Milton used the image in *Areopagitica* he did so with the insistence that destroying a book was a greater violence than killing an actual human body precisely because the literary work harbors a spirit or potentiality for re-reading and 'living on' that is greater than a physical body: to murder a book is to murder a spirit that goes well beyond the matter of either the human organism or the text as physical object:

> And yet, on the other hand, unless wariness be used, as good almost kill a man as kill a good book. Who kills a man kills a reasonable creature, God's image; but he who destroys a good book, kills reason itself, kills the image of God, as it were in the eye. Many a man lives a burden to the earth; but

> a good book is the precious life-blood of a master spirit, embalmed and treasured up on purpose to a life beyond life (Milton 2008, 12).

The work is a body that has *more* life and potentiality – active life as *agency* – than any of the readings or uses that actualize certain of its aspects.

McGann's defence of the book (as opposed to its circulating ideality) is a properly organicist aesthetic; the poem as living body is neither the isolated urn of new criticism's self-referring formalism, nor a simple copy of the world of naïve literalism. By poising the work – as living body – between the self-sufficient and unworldly idealism of pure form (a world unto itself) and the simple snapshot or picture of reality that would deny the work any life of its own, McGann's argument plays out the standard balancing act of all doctrines of incarnation. The problem of a living body is this: in order to *live*, a body must not be closed in upon itself but must possess some relation to the world, and yet in order to be a living *body* it must also have a form or relative stability of its own that would mark it out or set it off against the world. McGann refuses both the closed formalism of a work as mere thing (ideal or material) and a positivism that would see works as copies or doubles of some objective outside. That crime – of isolating the text from the world, truth, and reference (because one takes reference to be a simple copying or doubling) – is laid by McGann at the foot of Paul de Man, Yale criticism and 'academic' postmodernism (all symptomatic of an aestheticism that, since Kant, isolates the work from social networks and vectors) (McGann 1988, 5). If the work is a body and not some ideal entity, then it makes sense to understand it both as having emerged from a world of relations and as itself creating one more possible network of relations in all the readings and exchanges it undergoes. Like a living body that has its dynamic potentiality only insofar as it maintains itself as a responsive network in relation to a world that is also highly relational, the poem is *whole* only by virtue of having a permeable border. McGann insists that while de Man was right in acknowledging that the poem is not some simple representation or copy of the world, and that it refers only by creating its own relations, the poem nevertheless creates its outside or referent by taking up discourses and conventions: not the world as brute thing in itself, but the world as already social, relational, meaningful, and discursive:

> To bring about the accommodation which de Man was seeking, however, we will have to reconstruct a theory of the text, and a practical criticism, that follows sociohistorical and materialist lines which are not, at the same time, positivistic. This entails an opening of the field of 'reading' beyond

> what is now called 'the text' to include that whole range of materials comprehended by the disciplines of history, sociology, and anthropology, as well as traditional philology. Thus, to study, say, *The Marriage of Heaven and Hell* would involve a 'reading' of that work in terms of its entire productive and reproductive histories along the vertical axis of their temporalities as well as the horizontal axis of their socioinstitutional structures (McGann 1988, 6).

That is, a poem has sense and is readable only because it occurs in some context, and is already marked by social, political, and cultural relations: the poem is essentially open. At the same time, *as a poem*, it is also creates a point of relative discursive closure or autonomy. It can only be open to a world of relations if its marks itself off or creates itself as a body in relation to the discourses and conventions upon which it acts. For there could be no act, agency or force of a poem if it were not other than the world of relations of which it is (only in part) a vector: the poem has its integrity only in being at once relatively closed, while maintaining that closure in relation to a dynamism in which it may always intervene. It is this openness that also allows us to approach the work not just as a literal body but also as a living unity:

> … poetry is a discourse deploying a form of total coherence – and thereby a hope of coherence – within the quotidian world, which is dominated by various forms of relative incoherence … Texts governed by memory and imagination – poetic texts – display networks of human interests which are massively heterodox. They are not merely open to various 'readings,' they are inhabited by long histories of complex and often conflicted self-understandings. In this respect they hold a mirror up to the human world (McGann 1988, 9).

Chapter 5

The Body of Work Beyond Good and Evil

The body and ethics of the archive are nowhere given a more complex expression than in Blake's corpus. In addition to refiguring the relation between sense and the passage to the sensible, Blake made a direct theme of the genesis of the literary object, and of meaning in general. This theme is articulated at least as early as *The Marriage of Heaven and Hell*, with the manifesto statement that the poets animate a world with spirits that is subsequently systematized by priests. Already this early work of Blake's is poised curiously between a vitalist and 'continuist' thesis (where all sense, meaning and work can and should be traced back to animating senses, including the very hand that touches the body of the work) and a 'discontinuist' and *poetic* thesis in which the created object has a being of its own that cannot be traced back to, reduced to, or mastered by its origin. That curious ambivalence that at one and the same time privileges the unity of a single ground *and* the production of multiple, dispersed, unknown, and irrecoverable distinctions remains to the very end of Blake's works.

While Blake's works repeatedly narrate a fall, lapse or forgetting of an animating force that becomes enslaved to systems, thereby suggesting that all poetry and reading (and indeed living) should be directed towards regaining an original energy and spirit, he also *diagnoses* that same narrative of fallenness suggesting that the true art of poetry – and revolutionary politics – lies in an abandonment of mourning, an acceptance of the positivity of loss, and a privileging of eternity. Unlike chronological time, which would measure value through either progress towards an end or distance from an origin, the eternal point of view no longer grants priority to any single event or body. It is from the point of view of eternity that we can see that all our narratives of despair, progress, corruption, and purity actually stand in the way of redemption. Frequently in Blake it is the figure of fallenness or evil that is itself life-denying and imprisoning. It is the accusation of evil, or the attribution of sin – rather than any evil itself – that is depicted negatively in Blake. By presenting ambiguous figures of hell, despair, fallenness and evil Blake transformed theoretical questions about origin, time and space, form and matter, hand and hyle, interior and exterior, active and passive, and analog and digital into a drama. Rather than provide an axiology of good and evil Blake's epics play out the relation among voices that variously assert purity, defilement, origin, terror, despair, and judgment. What needed to be thought was not the purity of the origin but the figures and relations through which a sense of the origin is given.

By producing his works in dramatic and multi-voiced form, Blake was able to compose a symptomatology of the modes of life and reading though which evil is figured. Key to that dramatization and staging was the figure of sexual difference. It was this figure that seemingly allowed Blake to moralize a series of oppositions, with the poetic figure of Los being associated with time, active formation, the force of the hand and the creation of distinctions, while femininity would be aligned with a loss of distinction, the passivity of receptive matter, a space that would be variously nightmarish or ameliorative depending on its relation to time, and an alienation of the living and human into a tyrannical transcendence. But while sexual difference seemed to provide Blake with a means of organizing and subordinating terms it was also the figure that disrupted Blake's vitalist ethic. Blake's two great epics, *Jerusalem* and *Milton* present a bifurcated and fallen world that can initially only imagine nature, the body, and what is other than the self as a tyrannical, terrifying, and punishing female (or worse a 'hermaphroditic' form that stands for institutionalized religion, nationalism, and other corruptions). Fallenness occurs through the division of humanity into a self-referring intellect and external feminine matter:

> While the Females prepare the Victims, the Males at Furnaces
> . . .
> The Eye of Man a little narrow orb closd up & dark
> Scarcely beholding the great light conversing with the Void
> The Ear. a little shell in small volutions shutting out
> All melodies & comprehending only Discord and Harmony
> The Tongue a little moisture fills. a little food it cloys
> A little sound it utters & its cries are faintly heard
> Then brings forth Moral Virtue the cruel Virgin Babylon
> Can such an Eye judge of the stars?
>
> (M 5, 15–28, K: 484–85; E: 98)

Redemption is achieved through incorporation and recognition of the female emanation as an essential aspect of the self, a self that is not merely intellect, cognition, and judgment, but a feeling, moving, and coupled body. Blake is thereby able to take relations among the self's potentialities and give it a dramatic, historical, political, religious, and national narration, describing the violence the self inflicts upon itself as variously attributable to modern science's positing of the world as mere matter, the Church's domination of its members' bodies through the doctrine of the corruption of the flesh, a nation's loss of its true myths through being seduced by classicism, druidism or other systems, and even a single body's capacity to isolate itself from the world by taking itself as the origin or locus of experience.

Blake's account of the genesis of the self's emasculation of its powers not only has multiple origins (with the fall occurring through division of labor, sexual difference, priesthood, mathematization, narrowed nationalism, or the forgetting of the value of poetry), it also has various sexual figurations. Sometimes it appears that Blake sees sexual difference as a *symptom* – as long as the feminine is regarded as tyrannically other, we will be locked in the nightmarish world of the pure mind and its solipsism – while at other times sexual difference is the *cause*: it is only through a return to unity, to one eternal man and the incorporation of the female as aspect or emanation, that experience, humanity, history or the imagination (whatever it is that 'we' are) will be redeemed. Sexual difference is therefore a curiously ambivalent opposition, at once a way of figuring relations, of explaining relations, of ordering relations, and of diagnosing relations. The chaotic, ambivalent, difficult and occasionally *mad* production of Blake's sexual dramas should alert us to a deeper problem that is captured by his work, and that is not reducible to the Blake corpus. The problems that Blake uses the figure of sexual difference to explore are, as I have already suggested, problems that concern the very origin of meaning, or the very origin of difference; they concern the relation between self and other, body and milieu, interior and exterior. The ambivalence, chaos, and confusion that surround Blake's figuring of sexual difference could be consigned to this poet's particular madness, or to the particularly accidental nature of the Blake corpus. A more interesting possibility is that there is nothing accidental about the predominance of accidents and madness in Blake's poetry: questions regarding the very borders of the self, of the relation between sense and time, of the origins of meaning and the *value* of distance from that origin will always – if thought through – destroy any organizing opposition or hierarchy.

To make this more concrete we can consider the relation between hand and hyle as it confronts us today with the Blake archive. The highly singular nature of Blake's work lies in its mode of production. In tune with the expressed content of his poetry, Blake did not want his vision to be systematized, generalized, commodified or rendered equivalent through the usual modes of literary production. In order to ensure the continuity between his own vision and the created product Blake took publishing and writing into his own hands. His poems not only narrate the specific hand, touch, inscription, and imprinting of form and difference; his illuminated books are individuated with each letter, page, figure, and color being marked and differentiated by singular differences. In Blake's epics the male figures of Los, Milton or the poet himself are involved in hammering, sculpting, pressing, and imprinting. Blake also described inspiration as flowing directly not from an abstract muse into mind or spirit, but from body to body, from hand to foot.

But it was the very means that Blake employed to ensure the direct continuity from vision to hand to work that also preclude the maintenance or 'living on' of Blake's forms: by marking his works so directly onto material objects that have been touched by his living hand, the works depend upon an archive which is subject to the ravages of time *and* exposed to the errancy of accidents. That is to say, whereas *in principle* one might want to correct a typographical error in a poet whose work was ideally distinct from its printed form, no such distinction in Blake is possible. The illuminated books are not copies of prior models; they are the act of poetry *as object.* When the illuminated book appears to have an accidental or corrupting mark that one might want to 'correct', then one can only do so by assuming that there is an intent or spirit separated from the letter (granting the singular no significance), but this would have to occur against the very spirit of Blake's poetry which is to grant significance to the smallest of differences, presenting the body of the work not as a representation but as an expression of the poet's own hand.

We confront in this curious relation between body proper and its accidents, deviations or corruptions, the necessary myth of techne: does the body have a *proper extension* (such as its own hand, and the works closest to the hand), which can then fall into corruption when disengaged (when the work is subjected to a system, body or difference not one's own)? Or, can a body, spirit or imagination only be what it is through techne? This would suggest that the works of the hand already open a gap or distance within the self's own expression. Replayed in terms of sexual difference, which is precisely how Blake figures this problem of the imagination's distance from itself: should we see that which becomes detached from 'man' as a positive sign of distinction, emanation, and a liberation – an openness to what is not oneself – or should one see all that is seemingly other as ideally and originally man's own? In terms of the textual accident: how do we read that which appears to have liberated itself from the poet's own hand? Must we see the singularity of the text – its material and textual incarnation – as an alienation of the spirit, a spirit that we ought to be able to read *through* the letter?

Life, Economy, Evil

In *A Finite Thinking* Jean-Luc Nancy discusses two ways of thinking about evil: evil as that which befalls a being, and evil as corruption. We could think of that first sense of evil as predominantly pagan, pre-modern, and tragic. An individual or state is struck by an affliction that appears from without, allowing the tragic chorus to express despair in the face of an implacable fate:

> The question of evil has always been posed – and 'resolved' – against a horizon of sense that ended up (without ever really ending) by converting or transforming its negativity. There were two possible models for this conversion (crudely, we could call them the ancient and the modern, even though their actual manifestations were far more complex than this). First, there is the model of *misfortune,* of unhappy fate or tragic *dystychia.* Evil in this sense is given or destined [*envoyé*] to existence and to freedom as such. It comes from the gods or from destiny and it *confirms* existence in its opening to or as sense, regardless of whether this entails the destruction of life. This is why evil is borne, recognized, lamented, and overcome by the community. Terror and pity are responses to the curse or malediction.
>
> Then, second, there is the model of *sickness.* It confirms the normativity of the norm in the very act of rupturing it. Evil in this sense is an accident (and, in principle, can always be mended) and belongs to a lesser order of existence, if one that is not actually null and void (Nancy 2003, 16).

Evil has no real being, no time, and no place. It does not strike life as a force in its own right; nor will evil ever be able to deflect life from its trajectory of fulfillment.

Taking Blake's argument for contraries seriously requires seeing evil not as an accident, negation or corruption of life, but as immanent to life and progression. In terms of meaning and reading, this not only requires that the condition for the progression of time and continuity is a loss, absence and death that can never be recuperated and brought to presence; it also entails that *ethical* reading is only possible with the inclusion of all that has usually fallen under the name of evil:

> Without contraries is no progression. Attraction
> and Repulsion, Reason and Energy, Love and
> Hate, are necessary to Human existence
> From these contraries spring what the religious call
> Good & Evil. Good is the passive that obeys Reason
> Evil is the active springing from Energy.
> Good is Heaven. Evil is Hell,
>
> (MHH 3, K: 149; E: 34)

The voice that strives to free the world from all corruption, the voice that strives to master time, the voice that insists on dominating synthesis, relation, comprehension and understanding is, for a great deal of Blake's poetry, the voice of 'evil' or the Satanic accuser.

> For Satan flaming with Rintrahs fury hidden beneath his own mildness
> Accus'd Palamabron before the Assembly of ingratitude! of malice;
> He created Seven deadly Sins drawing out his infernal scroll.
> Of Moral laws and cruel punishments upon the clouds of Jehovah
> To pervert the Divine voice in its entrance to the earth
> With thunder of war & trumpets sound, with armies of disease
> Punishments & deaths musterd & number'd; Saying I am God alone
> There is no other! let all obey my principles of moral individuality
> I have brought them from the uppermost innermost recesses
> Of my Eternal Mind, transgressors I will rend off for ever,
> As now I rend this accursed Family from my covering.
>
> (M 9, 19–29, K: 489–90; E: 103).

Blake's poetry could therefore be read as taking the general form of a performative contradiction, where the 'I' who speaks does not coincide with the 'I' of the speech act. In his earliest poetry the proverbs for which Blake is most famous – the voice of the devil in *The Marriage of Heaven and Hell* – are neither clearly delimited and distinguished from the implied authority of the poet, nor coherent as a body of thought. Not only are there murderous intentions that are elsewhere tempered by forgiveness and passivity – such as 'Sooner murder an infant in its cradle than nurse unacted desires' – there are other engaging proclamations ('Truth can never be told so as to be understood, and/not be believ'd') that are elsewhere tempered by Blake's acknowledgment of the difficulties of truth's perception and demonstration: 'That which can be made explicit to the Idiot is not worth my care' (K: 793; E: 702). In *The Songs of Innocence and of Experience* the innocent commitment to a benevolent, enclosed, ordered, and blessed world is neither fully endorsed nor depicted as simply deluded. The voice of 'The Little Black Boy' is at once charmingly open to a world of light and joy and yet suffers from seeing this world as necessarily other than his own skin:

> And we are put on earth a little space...
> That we may learn to bear the beams of love,
> And these black bodies and this sun-burnt face
> Is but a cloud, and like a shady grove... (K; 125; E: 9)

Similarly, the condemning statements of the *Songs of Experience* are both true – for London *is* a site of suffering and injustice – and false: for it is the very lament and despair directed to that supposedly fallen world that precludes the vision of a redeemed life. Blake's poetry is at one and the same time a judgment, accusation, and threnody *and* an affirmation of the blessedness of life. It is at once the prophetic voice of a poet *and* a call to abandon the isolation of voice, annihilate the self, and live at one with life. Blake's declaration that 'everything that lives is holy' implies a divinity and blessedness that suffuses life beyond the mind of man. Indeed, it is the image of 'mind' as the point from which the world is represented that has diminished life, and it is this mind-centeredness that leads to the figure of Urizen as an enclosed self who must somehow see outside the cavern of his head and find a world that is always in doubt. At the same time as Blake is critical of the image of Cartesian man he also affirms the true reality of the 'mental' and the ultimate residence of divinity in the human breast. Such seeming contradictions in *what* Blake's poetry says are intensified with the very form of the poetry.

If one is to speak meaningfully then one must, in principle if not in fact, avoid contradiction. For Aristotle this is the unavoidable premise of all reasoning: to say that something *is* is to commit oneself to the identity of the thing, an identity that could be verified and grasped by others. As Husserl argued, any attempt to contest the principle of non-contradiction – to say that it does not apply – already invokes the principle, for we are relying on something being or not being the case (Mohanty 1976, 123). But it is just that torsion or knot of self-contradiction, of not-saying what one is saying, that dominates Blake's poetry.

Blake's poetry is constantly poised between a prophetic declaration that the fallen world we live in has another future *and* a counter-prophecy that calls for the self-annihilation of judgment. It is the structure or relation of voices in Blake's poetry that yields the impossible claim that the very use of the word 'evil' *is* evil: it is the pious, accusing, purifying, and all-inclusive desire for a moral world that corrupts a life which is intrinsically joyful. It is the judgment *that* the world is fallen that constitutes our fall. Saying this, however, places the poet himself in a position of judgment. If accusation itself is our only evil, then how do we avoid accusing the accuser, killing the tyrant only to become what we behold, a 'tyrant in his stead?' If there is an 'answer' to this problem it is not the overcoming of the contradiction but the shift away from poetry as a speech act – a poetry in which the voice, insofar as it speaks, must seek recognition and agreement – to poetry as a monument, in which the voices that cannot be brought to coherence or presence are allowed to remain.

Jerome McGann, as already noted, has argued – against the image of Romanticism as a literary movement that somehow intimates an ultimate unity beyond the fragmentation of speech – for poetry as a social act. If we want to read a text we need to understand what it seeks to do, the linguistic forces and conventions it draws upon, and the new language games that it makes available. Although such an approach to poetry liberates us from the idea of the poem as a sign that harbors an ineffable sense which it would then be the task of the interpreting critic to reveal or disclose, and although such an approach allows us to consider the poem as having emerged in time and being conditioned by forces beyond the words on the page, the emphasis on the poem as *act* maintains a normative image of life and meaning. McGann is explicit about the pragmatic background to his arguments for meaning as act: no word or text exists in isolation but makes sense only in relation to other texts, and only in a context where agents strive to achieve certain effects. What is left out of consideration is the text as a self-enclosed object, detached from conditions of production. But it is just such a detached, enigmatic, self-enclosed, and *inactive* object that exemplifies both the texts that Blake created and some of the ways in which he depicted redemption. Life, seen as always directed towards action, effect, force, and relation, was countered by Blake's poetry and art of resistance and non-relation.

The most powerful image Blake gives of this non-relational potential is the vortex, which appears at first as a point within time and as bound up with our own order of comprehension and purpose. If, however, one passes through that point, detaching the singular from the relations of the world as lived and ordered, then we are given an eternity that is no longer reducible to the 'same dull round' of life as we know it. The singular point of the vortex, far from disclosing sense or giving order, and far from overcoming time to yield a pure present, opens a future that is *not* a fulfillment of the present, but an absent presence: a sense *that* there is a time beyond the sense we make of time, but not *what* that time might be. For Blake, poetry is not the act of a subject who makes a claim in the world, situating himself within a certain discourse or social and artistic system that would include all other speakers. Rather, each speaker, each body, each 'pulse of the artery' opens up its own eternity, its own time.

The performative contradiction is not a special or corrupt case of language but the very condition of poetry, which is also the condition of life. Blake's poetry presents as law that there is no law ('One law for the lion & ox is oppression'), and creates a system that affirms the destruction of systems: 'I must create a system or be enslaved by another man's.' The speech act that *cannot* mean what it says – the performative contradiction of 'don't listen to me'; 'obey only yourself' – is not a special case. To speak is at once to make a move in a game, to demand recognition and to want to take one's place in meaningful time (a time in which each moment carries over the past and works towards a future); at the same time speech is also a resistance to time and life. A text or poem demands to be read not because its sense and order are present or presentable, but because it creates a temporal knot. It is given as what cannot be synthesized or comprehended within our current context. Blake's poetic commitment to vortices, minute particulars, eternities that reside in grains of sand or pulsations of an artery yields a production of voices, each expressing a distinct comportment towards time and space.

Poetry and Evil

The poetics of evil has been dominated by a double symbolism, whereby active and proliferating life is opposed *both* to the chaos of mere elements without unity or bound, *and* to the body detached from all relation and temporal progression. This is perhaps a contradictory imperative in the image of proper life and one that was brought to the fore by both Henri Bergson and Sigmund Freud: life must both maintain itself (and therefore establish a border or boundary) but it must not be so self-enclosed or detached as to cease living. Good life must (ideally) be both self-sufficient and complete, a demand that no organism can fulfill. A body can only make its way in the world by being open to what is not itself, while maintaining some sameness or relative self-permanence through time. The positive symbol of this perfectly poised life is (prior to modernity) God: a complete and perfect being who also creates what is other than Himself. Today that image is given in the homeostatic organism that balances its own state of equilibrium by monitoring its internal states, and by going out into the world only as required for ongoing life. The negative symbol is evil: given both in the completely enclosed, self-absorbed, and self-consuming body and in the unbordered, meaningless, and fragmentary night of chaos.

In Blake the poetics of evil is linked directly to aesthetics, so that he will oppose the bounding line of engraved art to the formless void, and the open and receptive body of the prophetic poet to the inward and isolated 'natural man' of modernity. Los's call for redemption is one of opening humanity towards an expansive brotherhood, but also suggestive of inclusiveness and reduction of difference (in relation to his female emanation):

> I care not! The swing of my Hammer shall measure the starry round.
> When in Eternity Man converses with Man, they enter
> Into each other's Bosom (which are Universes of delight)
> In mutual interchange, and first their Emanations meet
> Surrounded by their Children; if they embrace and comingle
> The Human Four-fold Forms mingle also in thunders of Intellect;
> But if the Emanations mingle not, with storms & agitations
> Of earthquakes & consuming fires they roll apart in fear;
> For Man cannot unite with Man but by their Emanations
> Which stand both Male and Female at the gates of each Humanity.
> How then can I ever again be united as Man with Man
> While thou, my Emanation, refusest my Fibres of dominion?
> When Souls mingle & join thro' all the Fibres of Brotherhood
> Can there be any secret joy on Earth greater than this?
>
> (J 88, 2–15, K: 733; E: 246)

It is not clear at this point of the epic whether Los's voice here is still suffering from fallen diremption (in his demand for inclusion of otherness) or whether it expresses a prophetic opening towards what is not the self. Is divinity achieved through self-annihilation and distinction of what is not oneself, or through recognition and 'Fibres of dominion'?

If we think through the two motifs of evil (as both lifeless enclosure and unbounded void) then we confront some of the deepest problems of reading and criticism. Reading also has to operate between acknowledging the proper borders of a text (its self-sufficiency) and the text's capacity for future re-readings. If a text were not, at least in part, unassimilable then it would not require reading; but if it were not at least partly already translated into the present then it would not even allow an approach to reading.

Why must a text be read, and how does reading give life to the text? How do we judge certain readings, or failures to read, as accidental, parasitic, improper or unhistorical?

One of the ways in which modernity is often condemned has been to contrast the nightmarish and purely quantitative system of capitalist exchange with a world once defined qualitatively, where each being is defined according to its intrinsic or specific essence. It is possible to read Blake as a poet opposed to the overwhelming quantification of modernity, where individuals become nothing more than acts of force or will, and where the world becomes nothing more than blank and neutral raw material for appropriation. In this sense Blake would be anti-modern, and would be drawing on a long history of imagery that favors the organic and self-maintaining body over a world reduced to so much material devoid of form. Blake's ethics and aesthetics would be oriented towards returning technology, systems and differentiated units to the living hand and eye. Blake's poetry would be vitalist, with his entire poetic practice being oriented towards returning systems to 'life.' There is, however, a counter-vitalist imperative in Blake's work which lies both in his insistence on the eternal forms and infinities that open up from this world, and in the very body of his poetical work. Today, such an imperative deserves, more than ever, to be heard: the twenty-first century, despite its unprecedented destructiveness towards its own life, has fallen into a profound vitalist moralism. This vitalism includes not only the often-diagnosed biopolitical norms whereby governments ground policy on the management of health and population but also what is left of theory and philosophy – both of which indicate 'turns' towards life (Colebrook 2010).

Chapter 6

Life

The diagnosis of today's biopolitical normalization is now a familiar story. For Aristotle 'man' was defined primarily as a political social being of reason, who also possessed a bodily life; there was a distinction between *bios* and *zoe*, with the former being our proper form (achieved politically) and the latter being the 'mere life' that subtends that form. In modernity it is our bodily life or the needs of existence and evolution that can explain political formations (Foucault 1978). This general normalization of life accounts for contemporary 'biopolitics', where it is populations and bodily existence that become the material for political management. 'Life' in the strong sense allows all the beings and processes of the world to be referred back to a general logic or 'ratio.' Thus it is the same evolutionary theory that explains human beings, molluscs, and cultural processes. The vitalism referred to by Foucault's specifically modern concept of 'life' (which he argues emerged in the eighteenth century) would differ, then, from an earlier vitalism in which some rational power flowed through matter, granting matter specific forms and modes of becoming. Foucault includes historicism within the modern turn to a transcendental 'life' that would explain 'man's' particular empirical being. The development of cultures can now be explained as effects of general temporal processes, so that languages, economies, and even cultural forms no longer express a conscious human (or divine) intent so much as a broader logic of time. This is most evident in Marxist theories that would explain cultural production as expressions of economic relations, which are themselves required by the needs of life.

It was just such a shift in perception from a God who had once been an external or transcendent judge to God as the logic of nature that Blake also recognized. His attacks on modernity are double-edged in that he rejects the idea of 'man' as a tabula rasa and yet also insists upon the openness of the imagination. On the one hand Blake's poetry of energy does appear to place some vital force in opposition to derived systems, and yet he also regards that energy as *spirit,* as existing beyond 'Vegetative' life. Blake's energy or vitalism is therefore distinct from modern understandings of life as a substrate requiring formation through time; for Blake, life is subtended by Eternal forces: 'We who dwell on Earth can do nothing of ourselves; every thing is conducted by Spirits, no less than Digestion or Sleep' (J 3, K: 621; E: 145). His printing method will not only have the letters raised up from the plate, to indicate a form that is immanent in matter; he will also insist that even though God is immanent in human beings, each instance of that divinity is singular: 'God only Acts & Is, in existing beings or Men' (MHH, 16, E: 40; K: 155). Further, Blake will associate modernity both with the figure of Urizen who can only see the world as formless matter, and a God who can be deduced from the orderly and mathematical relations of the world. The 'single vision and Newtons sleep' that Blake berated combined a certain image of man as calculating reasoner with God as nothing more than a logical presupposition. Blake's target was, of course, the natural religion that insisted that God's existence could be proved from the being of the world. As Newton stated in the 'General Scholium' to the *Principia:* 'This most beautiful system of the sun, planets, and comets could only proceed from the counsel and dominion of an intelligent and powerful Being' (Newton 1934, 544). In 1727 Thomson declared that Newton 'from Motion's simple laws,/Could trace the secret hand of Providence,/ Wide-working from this universal frame' (Thomson 1836, 214). God is a logical condition inferred from the examination of nature. For Blake the deist sees human beings as finite, limited, and as part of the world. While pre-modern conceptions (such as Milton's) direct the self to an otherworldly God, the modern deist directs the self to the world. Both 'parties' accept that the world harbors a single logic. The bounded world of premodernity is oriented towards a transcendent God of reason, while the rational world of modern mechanistic science allows us to think of God as a divine watchmaker with 'life' as the single ground or ratio from which all events might be calculated.

Blake specifically identified the traditional conception of God with a bounded universe as opposed to a world as a collection of particulars:

> Then was the serpent temple form'd, image of infinite
> Shut up in finite revolutions, and man became an Angel;
> Heaven a mighty circle turning; God a tyrant crown'd.
>
> (*Europe* 10, 21–3, E: 63; K: 241)

This passage from *Europe* makes the connection between organized religion ('serpent temple') and the closure of the universe ('Shut up in finite revolutions'), human obedience to transcendence ('and man became an Angel'), and the law-giving, kingly character of God ('a tyrant crowned'). When Blake's God-figures are rule giving, punishing and enclosed in contemplation they recall Milton's God of ordering reason; when they are seated in the void or chaos and threateningly absent they are closer to the deist conception. In *The Book of Ahania* Fuzon's description of Urizen concentrates less on his rule bearing and ordering function than on emptiness and absence:

> Shall we worship this Demon of smoke,
> Said Fuzon, this abstract non-entity
> This cloudy God seated on waters
> Now seen, now obscur'd; King of sorrow?
>
> (*Ahania* 2, 10–13, E: 84; K: 249)

This concluding chapter will look at the ways in which Blake's poetry at a semantic level seems to repeat an anti-modern lament against modernity's disenchantment of the world, while at the same time Blake's poetry refuses to recreate a coherent mythology that would once again allow us to master the world. It is in this regard that Blake's work, both semantically and formally, challenges the normative image of life that has underpinned the ways in which we think about literary history and the history of ideas.

The often-stated idea that Blake inherited Milton's spirit of increasing internalization and apocalyptic revelation of the law, and therefore fulfilled the spirit of Milton's work against the letter, assumes that history (and particularly literary history) is a process of increasing recognition and humanization (Wittreich 1975, xv). There are aspects of this myth of ultimate unification and internalization in Blake, particularly in his unifying image of Albion as the one great body encompassing eternity. But there is a problem with reading Blake's work as an act of literary history, where literary history occurs as self-recognition and revivification. Not only does Blake frequently depict that ultimate human body of unity and eternity as possessing powers or openings to eternity that are beyond the comprehension of individuals, his illuminated books – as themselves material bodies – create singular differences that resist comprehension. It is possible therefore – and this will be the aim of the conclusion – to consider Blake as articulating and achieving a counter-vitalist aesthetic, in which it is *because* 'everything that lives is holy' and *because* 'deities reside in the human breast' that the living and the human always exceed recognition and recuperation. There is no single unifying totality within which specific beings are located; nor is there a single force that flows through and animates life, nor a final end towards which all beings develop. At the conclusion of Blake's great prophecies, *Milton* and *Jerusalem*, we may be given the eternal body of Albion, but that is a body or living being that is never at one with itself, never an autopoetic organism. Rather than a body in which each part finds its identity only in acting responsively for the aim of overall equilibrium, the redeemed body abandons self-righteousness and unity to allow for various durations, including literal distinction:

> ...& every Word & every Character
> Was Human according to the Expansion or Contraction, the Translucence or
> Opakeness of Nervous Fibres: such was the variation of Time & Space
> Which vary according as the Organs of Perception vary; & they walked
> To & fro in Eternity as One Man, reflecting each in each & clearly seen
> And seeing, according to fitness & order
>
> (J 98, 35–40, K: 746; E: 258)

The ambivalent figure of sexual difference so crucial for Blake's prophecies is exemplary of the tendency of his work as a whole. On the one hand there is a lament at fragmentation, separation, alienation, and chaos; on the other hand the figure of a single commanding body entirely at one with itself is also an image of nightmarish and rationalist enclosure. If the pathway to redemption is imagined by Blake as the opening out of the body from each of its multiple powers, the concluding figure of Albion incorporates a feminine that is always more than a reflection of the male. Blake's redeemed life is at once multiple, rather than binary – distinct powers rather than reason and its lesser counterpart – and univocal. It is this image of the body in which each 'member' opens to eternity that allows us to approach Blake's aesthetic method as haptic.

We might contrast the haptic, here, with the tactile. When the body is commanded by cognition, allowing the senses to be nothing more than mediators of a world to be mastered and quantified, then touch is located in the hand, which is an instrumental extension of the reasoning self. This is the body Blake presents in the character of Urizen, who both perceives the world through eyes reduced to chinks in a cavern, and who relates to the world as a chaos upon which form needs to be imposed. This is what John Protevi has referred to as the 'hylomorphism' of the Western tradition, where matter is devoid of form, and where the body requires command and control by the brain-centered self of reason, calculation, and cognition (Protevi 2001). By contrast, when the body's receptiveness is distributed in a divergent manner among the senses, with the eye, ear, skin, and taste *not* operating in accord, then we approach a haptic aesthetic. Blake both describes such a body and creates a form of counter-synaesthesia in his poetry. The counter-synaesthesia occurs when the engraved image 'accompanying' the poetry is at odds with the affect of the verse. Even at the moment of greatest epic despair and anguish Blake often couples the poetry with joyous bodies, and at moments of chaos and fragmentation still engraves bounded forms. In addition to performing a divergent series of affects, allowing the voice to become sonorous at moments of figural exactitude, and the visual figures to become abstract at moments when the poetry approaches prophetic declaration, Blake also describes a body of multiple durations within his poetry.

As an example we might think, in general, of *The Four Zoas* and its narration of an epic journey of the 'zoas' or living beings that make up the self or subject of the epic. *Milton* and *Jerusalem* both conclude with a seeming inclusion and incorporation of the separated feminine, but also signal an irreducible difference or non-comprehension of otherness within the self. Against the normative image of life, in which each being strives to maintain its own being – whether by striving towards transcendent form, or adapting to its environment – Blake writes about powers that are below and beyond the thresholds of the organism. He also produces a poetic and visual art that allows matter itself to shine by its own light. It is in this regard that we can read Blake as challenging a form of subjectivism that goes well beyond the notion of the modern subject and includes all forms of thought that would strive to ground single bodies and movements in an ultimate unity of life. Blake produces a poetry that challenges the idea of acting and purposive life, referring constantly to those minute particulars that bear a life or force that cannot be subsumed by human intentionality, nor rendered meaningful through an overall concept of self-furthering vitality. This should, I would argue, allow us to question the apocalyptic or theological notion of history as a gradual coming to presence of 'man' as a being liberated from imposed tutelage *and* the notion of history as a fall into fragmentation and technology from a world that was once lived in its proper and paradisiacal immediacy.

Blake's counter-vitalist aesthetic displaces the notion of life as bearing an intrinsic logos, where life tends towards realization, fulfilment, and self-recognition. Instead, it is possible to conceive of Blake's corpus as presenting the challenge of *madness*. If reading has been governed by theology, or the commitment to the notion that letter conceals a spirit or sense awaiting fulfillment in subsequent acts of reading, then madness is the absence of work, or the failure of elements to be subtended by a governing logic or an idea that governs matter.

Readings of Blake that have approached him through the insights of post-structuralism have tended to emphasize the ways in which his text allows for an *activation* of the reader's capacity for the creation of sense. Such readings have also emphasized the material letter's productive and creative potentialities. At the extreme there has been a reading of Blake's relation to Milton as apocalyptic and visionary, where the 'line of vision' presents a flourishing history of literary paternity with each poet bringing greater liberation and life to the preceding poet's corpus (Wittreich 1975A; Wittreich 1975B). Another way of reading Blake after the legacy of post-structuralism would be to take up the critical relation between life, techne, and time as articulated initially by Heidegger and later by Michel Foucault, Gilles Deleuze, and Bernard Stiegler. Here, the notion of a proper life or ultimate Being that then proliferates into beings but which is also always available for retrieval is set against the singularity of the text or technicity. For Heidegger and Foucault, in different ways, it is possible to consider the 'shining' of language – those aspects of the text that are not expressions of some preceding and self-present subject's manifesting sense but have their own rogue force.

At the same time as Foucault and Heidegger seem to repeat the more general observation in the history of ideas regarding a shift from a world conceived as bearing intrinsic essences to a world of uniform matter governed by internal physical processes, they also note both that this way of seeing history *and* the supposed radical break depend upon a deeper metaphysical commitment that they would both overcome. For Heidegger, 'the story of Descartes who came and doubted the world and then established the subject as the ground of knowledge' is nothing more than a 'bad novel'; according to Heidegger, Descartes is merely extending the tendency of metaphysics to organize the world and its differences according to some origin from which all differences might be explained (Heidegger 1968). For Heidegger, 'ontotheology' or the grounding of all beings on some ultimate and always present Being, does not end when the ground of all relations shifts from God to the subject. It is now 'man' who acts as the ground or *subjectum.* Heidegger's critique of humanism can be seen in many ways as both critical of, and in sympathy with, nineteenth-century arguments that were resistant to situating man as one more living being within the world.

Blake was highly critical of the 'natural man' who supposedly possessed some general nature that would explain and ground behavior, and he also explicitly rejected the Cartesian model of experience, where the mind is contained within a void of time and space and must somehow look outside itself to find a world from which it is distinct. The 'Newtonian voids' and the idea of a matter that bears no potentiality or life of its own are products of the closure of the mind within a space and time that are then seen as containers within which beings are located (as opposed to Blake's vision of each being bearing its own duration or infinite). In *Milton* Blake describes the being of finite humanity as man within chaos:

> There Chaos dwells & ancient Night & Og & Anak old:
> For every human heart has gates of brass & bars of adamant,
> Which few dare unbar because dread Og & Anak guard the gates
> Terrific! and each mortal brain is walld and moated round
> Within. (M 20[22], 33–37, E: 114; K: 502)

Here we might begin to question Blake's humanism, or the idea that man need only look within, or liberate himself, in order to achieve redemption. And we might also question the notion that Blake continues or expands upon a history of philosophy and ideas in which we move from a closed world of forms – with each being bearing its own law bestowed by God – to an 'open' world, where the form of the world is created or constructed by each self-fashioning man. Blake resists both the (supposedly pre-modern) notion of a world that possesses a logic emanating from a prior and transcendent creator and the (supposedly modern) notion of an open universe where the world has no law or logic other than that created by man as poet-god. The 'open' universe or 'Newtonian Voids' are delusions of a perception too enclosed within the body to discern the form of the stars:

> For the Chaotic Voids outside of the Stars are measured by
> The Stars, which are the boundaries of Kingdoms, Provinces
> And Empires of Chaos invisible to the Vegetable Man
> (M 37[41], 47–9, E: 138; K: 528)

The phrase 'Empires of Chaos' is typically Blakean in its valence. The first mention of 'chaotic voids' seems to suggest that what we perceive to be chaos is really ordered, but imperceptible to the 'Vegetable Man'. The second mention of 'Empires of Chaos' suggests that chaos in itself is perhaps not the evil, formless, nightmare that theology assumes it to be. Only a 'Vegetable Man' who sets goodness and order against what he cannot comprehend with his five senses regards chaos as an evil. The doctrine of worldly empiricism, which confines experience to *human* sense perception – and where the human is the man of reason governed by a central commanding intellect – is behind Blake's recurring motif of the limiting finitude of the natural man: 'when the five senses whelm'd/In deluge o'er the earth-born man; then turn'd the fluxile eyes/Into two stationary orbs, concentrating all things... ./and petrify'd against the infinite' (*Europe* 10, 10–15, E: 63; K: 241). A *transcendental empiricism* would release perception or experience from the body of the man of reason – where what is other than the self is devoid of real being – and would instead strive to think the experience or vibration of matters beyond the 'two stationary orbs.'

What Blake's poetry clearly suggests is that what we perceive to be nightmarish, chaotic and evil is symptomatic of a fallen vision in which we have always tried to imagine either that there is a Godly geometer who will give order to our world, or that we as rational beings will be able to command the formless voids within which we are located. In *There is No Natural Religion* the idea that the body limits human experience is rejected by Blake's assertion that the empiricist's touchstone, experience, should not be defined as merely experience of the senses: 'Mans perceptions are not bounded by the organs of perception' (NNR [b], E: 2; K: 97).

Blake's dual attack upon both Miltonic and enlightenment ideals of life as ultimately centered on a single logic is carried out in *The First Book of Urizen* where a continuity between pre-modern and modern thought can be identified in the valorization of selfhood. The values of a traditionally Platonic 'image of thought' – contemplation, attention to inward transcendence, the self-sufficiency of reason – are embodied in the figure of Urizen who is 'Self-closd,' 'A self-contemplating shadow,' and 'consum'd/Inwards, into a deep world within' (U 3–4, E: 70–72; K: 222–224). *The First Book of Urizen* is commonly interpreted as a critique of the Book of Genesis and the notion of a creation that emanates from a single and transcendent architectonic vision. Urizen's creation ends with nature 'self balanc'd' with a final description of Urizen's world as 'the pendulous earth' (U 28, 21, E: 83; K: 237). Such diction recalls the Miltonic emphasis upon earth's balancing in *Paradise Lost*.[1]

The Miltonic imagery of the self-balanced earth reinforced the sense of the world's internal order, its boundedness, its harmony and its spiritual centrality in the divine schema. Blake, on the other hand, figures the self-balanced earth negatively, seeing the free-standing globe awash in a sea of chaos as symptomatic of a structure of experience in which all that is beyond the bounds of the self is considered as fallen or as the 'dregs' that have failed to take on form and reason: 'And the salt ocean rolled englob'd' (U 28, 23, E: 83; K: 237). To see the world as balanced is to see it *within* something else, as ideally enclosed, and as grounded on a transcendent logic. For Blake, historical distinctions between an older unfallen/despotic world of order and a modern liberated/disenchanted world devoid of foundations belie the extent to which subjectivism has been adopted by both parties. In both cases an appeal is made to some preceding logic – God or reason – that would give form and order to matter. The older Miltonic cosmology passes over easily into the empiricism that sees the world in terms of a single ratio. *The First Book of Urizen* goes on to describe how the net of religion eventually causes human life to be 'bound down/To earth by their narrowing perceptions' (U 25, 46–7, E: 83; K: 236). While *Urizen* refers to the Old Testament God of self-contemplating creation as 'That solitary one in Immensity' (U 3, 43, E: 71; K: 223) the consequences of a world received through the senses by 'man' are analogous in their solipsism:

> For the ears of the inhabitants,
> Were wither'd, & deafen'd, & cold:
> And their eyes could not discern,
> Their brethren of other cities.
>
> (U 28, 15–18, E: 83; K: 236)

Urizen's power, the first line of *The First Book of Urizen* tells us, is 'assum'd.' Blake clearly identifies the myth of a self-enclosed, self-contemplating, solitary, and external deity with the assumption of power, or the subjection of divergent aspects of life and experience to a single point from which order supposedly emanates. Such a Urizenic world is clearly 'closed' insofar as the tyrant-God's creative powers and laws are external to the pendulous globe, and we might therefore read this section as critical of traditional theology's stress on a transcendent reason *and* on enlightenment theology's emphasis on the continuity between God and reason. The modern aspect of the Urizenic world – its 'voidness unfathomable' – may 'open' the world cosmologically (for the world no longer bears intrinsic forms or essences) but it equally 'closes' the embodied, empirical natural man within the sea of external time and space and its mathematical laws of weight and measure. Blake charts his way through this oscillation between closed order and open voids, not by the assertion of another ontology but through the creation of poetry as force, through rhetorical inversion and contradiction.

Evil Be Thou My Good

In *The Marriage of Heaven and Hell* Blake conducts a revaluation of values similar to that of Satan's 'Evil be thou my good' in Milton's *Paradise Lost.* By claiming that 'Good is the passive that obeys Reason' Blake provocatively devalues the angelic realm of heaven in favor of the energetic and interactive evil of hell. This metaphysical overturning directly concerns the style and logic of voice, and here we might take our cue from thinkers as diverse as Plato, Kant, and Habermas. Insofar as one engages in argument one makes a claim to truth. In the case of Plato's dialogues the sophists strive to articulate contingent and power-dependent moral positions, such as Thrasymachus's definition that 'justice is the advantage of the powerful' or 'justice is paying back what one owes.' In appealing to a definition, or aiming to secure what justice is, Thrasymachus opens a space of communication and dispute. Socrates will use the concept of justice – as what must be just in more than one case – to push Thrasymachus into contradiction: 'So if the powerful are mistaken about their interests, are their acts still just?' and 'Would you describe as just returning an axe you borrowed to a deranged man?' Plato's Socrates undermines the very possibility of a (Satanic) notion of justice as mere power or force, for any claim to value or right initiates a dialogue of justification. It makes no sense to claim that what I will is right, for I am immediately attributing a value of rightness to my will. I am, therefore, inaugurating an argument involving what is or is not the case. For both Socrates and Kant, then, evil is parasitic and derivative. On the Socratic model it is only a distortion of knowledge that corrupts the will; as soon as we know what is right we will – as rational beings – act for the good. And any assertion of right or justice, however sophistical, nevertheless depends upon a concept that cannot be reduced to force. For Kant, who abandons the possibility of human's knowing the good (for we can only know objects that are within this world of time and space) the evildoer is nevertheless inevitably already entwined in the moral law. One would only refer to a free will as evil; it would not make sense to refer to an inanimate or soul-less being as evil, for such a being could not have chosen otherwise. When a being, such as Milton's Satan, takes his own will as the sole ground of his action he at once situates himself as free and *capable* of morality, for his actions are those of his own making, at the same time as he refuses duty. He decides not to act in such a way that what he wills could be assented to by any will whatever; instead he makes a law or maxim of his own particularity. 'Evil be thou my good' is a definitively evil maxim in the Kantian sense. It at one and the same time acknowledges that we are beings capable of laws and maxims – *not* determined by our bodies or particular interests – and yet the maxim decides freely to choose the will or the negation of the moral law.

It is just that logic of sense, temporal coherence, the speech act and the moral self (who has an identity or being only insofar as he acts according to the maxims that he takes on as his own) that is overturned in the style of

Blake's poetry. At both the local and the epic level Blake embraces performative contradiction. If one were to remain committed to logic then it would not be possible for any thinking being to say that something is and that it is not. Further, it would make no sense to say that there is no truth. To do so would create a disjunction between the subject who speaks – who in speaking demands to be heard as making a legitimate claim – and the subject of the statement (the subject declaring the absence of truth). Blake does not resolve this problem so much as embrace it. How can we say, for example, that all laws are oppressive? Is this a law? How can we say that reason is the bound or limit of a more profound energy? Is this rational claim undermining itself by intimating a truth beyond itself? Blake's concept of energy, which appears to act as a foundational term as described, also operates in the very act of his poetry to undermine foundations. On the one hand there are voices of proverbial wisdom, prophetic declaration, universal despair and mastering knowledge, while at the same time such definitive voices are placed in relation. Energy, then, is both the (paradoxically) founding value of Blake's poetry that presents itself as the original force from which opposition emanates *and* the effect of relations among voices that undo the very possibility of foundation. Energy is seen as the primary and rightly governing life force that concepts of goodness and virtue had to usurp *because such concepts were weaker:* 'Those who restrain desire, do so because theirs is weak enough to be restrained; and the restrainer or reason usurps its place & governs the unwilling' (MHH 5, E: 34; K: 149). In a manner akin to Nietzsche's theory and dramaturgy of ressentiment, force becomes enslaved by weaker 'forces;' concepts of goodness and morality present themselves as other than force, as foundations for force. 'Goodness' is a force that denies the play of forces. In Blake, energy is enslaved or separated from its own potential by notions that limit energy. While Blake sees energy as primordial and goodness or reason as secondary, he still sees reason as essential to the continuation of the energy. There is no simple vitalist appeal to a single energy. There is no governing logic that precedes hierarchies, no term or field that would allow the material world to exist as *mere* matter outside form. Any sense of a grasped totality is the effect of taking a part of existence for the whole; outside that illusion there are only relations without ground:

> "Thus one portion of being, is the Prolific. the other, the Devouring: to the devourer it seems as if the producer was in his chains, but it is not so, he only takes portions of existence and fancies that the whole.

> But the Prolific would cease to be Prolific unless the Devourer as a sea recieved the excess of his delights"
>
> (MHH 16, E: 40; K: 155).

Blake's work prior to the prophetic books stressed the physical interaction of contraries. Because of Blake's view of the history of ethical and religious thought (where reason has enslaved its greater and threatening opposite, energy) his early works narrated the overthrow of Reason (Urizen) by the energetic Orc. Blake's theory of contraries at this early stage, though materialist, did not attribute symmetry to oppositions; reason or passivity has had to narrate a history of its primacy in order to enslave its greater opponent. Blake's programme is therefore corrective; energy must be given some dominating power to overcome the long period of reason's reign. Blake stresses that reason must remain as the bound or circumference of energy, even though he repeatedly attacks reason's value and doctrines. It often appears that Blake lays more emphasis on the destruction of reason's supremacy than the productive interaction of reason and energy. As Blake's career progresses he moves from a celebration of the figure of Orc, whose flames of terror destroy the limits of law, to more measured celebrations of bounds and limits – especially as figured in the artisanal image of Los. Without some binding form there can be no life and sense, even if life *as forming* must also have a necessarily destructive or form-annihilating power.

Blake's developing reservations about the resulting void of an Orcian annihilation of boundaries becomes clear in *The Book of Los*. Not only does he put forward the possibility of 'organiz'd' and intelligent flames of desire he also declares that, 'Truth has bounds. Error none' (BL 4, 30, E: 92; K: 258). This is in line both with his aesthetic theory and practice, and his poetic method. His figures are clearly bounded forms; his pages are not blank matter upon which poetry appears, but are themselves bounded, framed, and crafted forms; and his diction is highly idiosyncratic, creating proper names that require the mouth of habit to re-work at pronunciation and articulation (Bowlahoola, Entuthon Benython, Allamanda). Both the body described by Blake's poetry and the body required to read Blake's poetry are neither already formed as stable entities, nor without form in purely open or unbounded states. Instead, the body constantly creates lines, distinctions, borders and limits, and must overcome any already-given limit to do so. For Blake the condition for the possibility of creation is *not* to be a Miltonic God who is unaffected by encounters, but to be a body exposed to what is other than itself. This is the very condition of the haptic: the hand can only be an organ of touch, and the body can only be a locus of sensation if it constitutes itself as a limit between inner and outer. Against the idea, then, that there is a self who *then* uses a hand to touch the outside world, Blake's body begins with feelings that localize the self in space, a space that is intensive, for it is constituted only through the actions and relations of bodies.

When Los approaches the end of his fall he becomes incarnated in a body of 'finite inflexible organs' from which 'contemplative thoughts first ar[i]se;' he is thereafter referred to as 'the falling Mind' (BL 4, 40 & 49, E: 92; K: 258). Los becomes 'Mind' because the formation of 'finite, inflexible, organs' is the precondition for the dualism that disrupts the *original dispersion* of the imaginative self and necessitates an independent principle of 'mind.' To speak of original dispersion, here, is to set Blake's aesthetic of sounds, concepts, visual figures, and the material page against the idea of a world that is given to the centered eye of cognition that will then use its body to make its way in the world. Los's disembodied 'Mind' responds to the fall by 'Organizing itself' and attempting to create some form of resistance in the void: 'till the Vacuum/Became element, pliant to rise' (BL 4, 50–1, E: 92; K: 258). What Blake describes here is the coming into being of the sensuous: from an absence of sensation to the pliant. It is not that there is a world on the one hand and the body on the other. Rather, there is an emergence of perception and sensation that then gives the body its limits. The body of located organs – the eye that sees, the mouth that speaks, and the hand that touches and labors – emerges from a relation to matter that is not the body's own.

The description of Los's body, which follows the genesis from 'pliancy', is that of a biological and material body – a 'Fibrous form' constructed from various functioning parts (BL 5, 1, E: 93; K: 259). There is a coming into being of qualities from degree zero, the emergence of intensive quantities: from the vacuum of the void, to pliant elements, and then to the creation of form and chaos. Los needs to become an organized body before he discerns Urizen as 'a Form of impregnable strength' (BL 5, 19, E: 94; K: 259). Los responds to that form by taking the fires of light on his anvil and re-forming Urizen – anticipating Milton's molding of Urizen in *Milton* – depicting the ways in which the encounter or perception of forms elicits the need for re-formation. Los's efforts entail the expulsion of the chaotic sea of the external void: 'the Deeps fled/Away in redounding smoke' (BL 5, 43–4, E: 94; K: 260). But this could be just where Los fails; for he expels rather than incorporates the void, effecting a binary of expulsion rather than working with elements that are other than himself:

But no light, for the Deep fled away
On all sides, and left an unform'd
Dark vacuity; here Urizen lay

(BL 5, 48–50, E: 94; K: 260)

Los produces a finite and enclosed embodiment of Urizen, and then binds Urizen to the 'glowing illusion' of the 'self-balanc'd' sun. By doing so Urizen becomes the God in the sky of an ordered and centered cosmos. What results is 'a Human Illusion/In darkness and deep clouds involvd' (BL, 5: 56–7, E: 94; K: 260). Los has given Urizen a 'Form' but it is a fixed form based on the empirical body. The body is the container of the brain, and is set within a world that is radically alien and devoid of powers other than the potentiality to receive form. Urizen is both the effect of 'hylomorphic' creation – the imposition of form upon matter – and is himself a form within chaotic matter. Los binds Urizen to the sun, creating a formed center amidst 'Dark vacuity.'

Recent work in neuroscience and cognitive science has rejected the Cartesian notion of mind as an internal reason that calculates its relations to the world, and has instead argued that the human organism is nothing more than a self-regulating or autopoetic unity, managing its relation with the world only to maintain a state of 'homeostasis' (Damasio 2010). The organism develops certain perceptual mechanisms for maintaining that autopoiesis: we do not view the world as information or data to be processed. Instead, our relation to the world is vital and responsive: 'our world' is given first in complex bodily affections and is then registered or felt, and only subsequently known as a fixed and represented object. For humans this means that we might imagine (as Freud did) an original 'oceanic feeling' where there is no distinction between self and other (Freud 1930). For Freud, we abandon that primary continuity, form a sense of ourselves as a distinct ego, and then spend the rest of our lives managing how much stimulus from the outside world we require to live, without receiving so much external stimulus that we are no longer bounded selves. Such an intense influx of stimulus would be 'trauma.'

The Freudian model of the self is intrinsically and constitutively unhappy, for any involvement with the outside world is a compromise with the primary desire for life to remain within itself. More recent accounts of the self that follow Henri Bergson's notion of 'creative evolution,' and neuroscientific emphases on the emotions, along with the cognitive science of autopoiesis challenge this model of the bounded self that detaches itself from the world and then negotiates the degree of stimulus it receives. For Bergson, life – in contrast with Freud – does not follow a trajectory of returning to quiescence, but is instead primarily explosive (Bergson 1931). Life is the destruction of bounded forms, not for the sake of a return to a primary One, unity or primordial presence, but for the sake of ever new and more complex formations. The self, therefore, may produce mechanisms that allow it to master and manage the differences it encounters, but life in its proper and ultimate – and for Bergson, human – mode, is the creation of difference ever renewing itself. Experience or stimulus is not, then, a disruption of the self, nor a simple externality that the living being must encounter; for the self, or any living being, just *is* the encounters it undergoes. For the recent neuroscientists who have drawn upon this tradition of creative and affective life – a tradition that goes back to Spinoza – we should not see the outside world as external data to be known and mastered. Instead, the self or living body is a system of responses to the differences it encounters; some experiences disturb the body's equilibrium and we may then have a 'feeling of what happens' so that the brain registers some of its body's responses in the form of pleasure, pain, anger, happiness or disgust (Damasio 1999). In the beginning is the response, and the self is an effect of the brain's registration of those responses or emotions that are registered as feelings. Knowledge, or the perception of a world set over against the self that can be mastered mathematically is a late achievement, and one that might distract us from the true nature of life as affective, rather than cognitive.

For Bergson, the human being who has taken the path of cognition, rather than remaining at the level of immediate and responsive action, has the power to intuit once again what it might be not to *know* the world as disenchanted matter, but to feel the world in the mode of affective response (Bergson 1931, 284). At the lowest level we might imagine a tick, whose world consists of nothing more than a 'perception' of blood, uric acid, and skin. Such perception is not cognitive. The tick does not perceive a fleshy arm and then decide to act. The tick just *is* a response mechanism, orienting its movements affectively according to its specific environment (von Uexkull 2010, 51). As humans, we can represent and picture our world, and can imagine ourselves as distinct beings. But such 'representational' comportments are secondary and follow on from an originally responsive, affective and embodied relation to a world that is never mere data or information, but always *our world,* perceived as a horizon of possible responses. Organisms all aim at ongoing stability and predictable response mechanisms; the body is a self-maintaining and bounded system that is not placed within matter or chaos, but gives itself its world. One way to respond to this 'affective turn' is to see the autopoietic body – the body that is nothing other than its own responses – as the proper image of life to which we all ought to turn. Thus, we would overturn the Cartesian subject of knowledge and retrieve the body of passion and response, and this would then allow for a re-understanding of the world.

It might seem, at first, that we could place Blake and his criticism of Cartesian disengagement and disenchanted matter within this tradition, and it is certainly the case that Blake clearly refuses both the model of the man of reason and the ontology of the world as an alien and traumatically chaotic matter. But it is the response to this model that distinguishes Blake from the current theories of the self as affective. Whereas recent cognitive science, philosophy, and neuroscience return understanding to the self-maintaining body, Blake – like Bergson – takes a spiritualist path. We should not see the 'fall' into separation and selfhood as something that we might simply overcome, nor as something that does not allow us to see life differently. For Bergson, it is the intellect's power to detach itself from immediate action and response that allows it to achieve freedom: we are not simply responses to those encounters that affect us, but can delay our response – *not act* – and thereby open up more than one way in the world. Once we have established that delay, which for Bergson is the intellect, and which for Blake is the 'selfhood' or the fall of the self into spectre and emanation (reason and feeling), we can perceive a world that is not our own – a world that is not at one with our responsiveness. The fall into self-hood (for Blake) or intellect (for Bergson) is a fortunate fall or *felix culpa*: it is after the break with pure perception or immediate responsiveness that the self retreats into its own restrictive view of the world, but it is also from that detachment that it might regain the paradise of intuiting durations beyond its narrow range:

> Intelligence, by means of science, which is its work, will deliver up to us more and more completely the secret of physical operations; of life it brings us, and moreover only claims to bring us, a translation in terms of inertia. It goes all around life, taking from outside the greatest possible number of views of it, drawing it into itself instead of entering into it. But it is to the very inwardness of life that *intuition* leads us, – by intuition I mean instinct that has become disinterested, self-conscious, and capable of reflecting upon its object and of enlarging it indefinitely.
>
> That an effort of this kind is not impossible is proved by the existence in man of an aesthetic faculty along with normal perception. Our eye perceives the features of the living being, merely as assembled, not as mutually organized. The intention of life, the simple movement that runs through

> the lines, that binds them together and gives them significance, escapes it. This intention is just what the artist tries to regain, in placing himself back within the object by a kind of sympathy … (Bergson 1931, 186).

This yields a quite specific notion of creation and imagination. Perception is creative – and we can think here of Blake's call for enlarged and numerous senses – when it does not simply anticipate what is other than itself and map it according to habit and efficiency. Instead, perception responds not for the sake of self-maintenance, but for self-overcoming. The imagination is not some ultimate unifying power that would return us to the one underlying humanity that we might retrieve; it is not a return to the proper and originally productive self. The imagination is *destruction* of the self, not for the sake of return to an original presence, but for the sake of perceptions, feelings or responses beyond the organic, self-organizing, vital, homeostatic, and autopoietic body:

> South stood the Nerves of the Eye. East in Rivers of bliss the Nerves of the
> Expansive Nostrils West. flowd the Parent Sense the Tongue. North stood
> The labyrinthine Ear. Circumscribing & Circumcising the excrementitious
> Husk & Covering into Vacuum evaporating revealing the lineaments of
> Man
> Driving outward the Body of Death in an Eternal Death & Resurrection
> Awaking it to Life among the Flowers of Beulah rejoicing in Unity
> In the Four Senses in the Outline the Circumference & Form. for ever
> In Forgiveness of Sins which is Self Annihilation. it is the Covenant of
> Jehovah
> The Four Living Creatures Chariots of Humanity Divine Incomprehensible
> In beautiful Paradises expand These are the Four Rivers of Paradise
> And the Four Faces of Humanity fronting the Four Cardinal Points
> Of Heaven going forward irresistible from Eternity to Eternity
> And they conversed together in Visionary forms dramatic which bright
> Redounded from their tongues in thunderous majesty. in Visions
> In new Expanses… (J 98,17–31, K: 745; E: 257)

Blake does not only present what I will refer to as the distributed body within his poetry, he also formulates a distributed or haptic aesthetic, where the body is neither centered on cognition, nor oriented towards equilibrium or homeostasis. In order to understand how this works we can look at the dominant understanding of art put forward by contemporary neuroscience that emphasizes the body's self-maintaining tendencies, and the work of art's contribution to the self's way of managing its responses to its world. V. S. Ramachandran argues that we enjoy poetic metaphors, not because they enable knowledge of the world – 'love is like a rose' – but because the brain has certain perceptual response mechanisms, and that in certain cases visual and aural (or aural and olfactory, or tactile and visual) neural networks are contiguous or cross-modal. In the special case of persons known as synaesthetes, numbers are linked to specific colors or sounds; but this is just an intensification of a general synaesthesia in which certain adjacent areas of the brain trigger responses in other modes (Ramachandran and Hubbard 2003). Artists, Ramachandran suggests, are near synaesthetes, and we find pleasure in their metaphors because such linkings are not arbitrary, but tap into our neural networks. Ramachandran also forms more general rules for aesthetic pleasure, most of which are grounded in what he refers to as the 'aha' or 'peekaboo' effect, the joy we find in piecing together a pattern, or revealing a hidden order or figure (Ramachandran and Hirstein 1999). The enjoyment of art, then, is grounded in life and the organism's cognitive capacity to make sense of its own world. Art is not knowledge, nor is it representation. But art is a maximization of those neural tendencies that enable knowledge and representation. For Ramachandran the brain is neither a blank slate that is stamped with an impression of the world, nor a set of innate categories through which the world is presented. To this extent the modern adaptive self of neurology would be akin to Blake's self that is neither a brain open to receiving impressions, nor a body that has been determined by an original natural or evolutionary imperative. The self is a threshold that engages dynamically with what is not itself in order to continually form and reform its own borders.

The homeostatic nature of the body of recent neuro- and cognitive science yields an aesthetic theory that is oriented towards efficiency and stability, with pleasure being a maximization of the tendencies that allow us to make our way in the world. This, for Ramachandran, yields basic rules that explain how works of art *work*. His first explanatory device is 'peak shift effect.' Because we are geared, for evolutionary adaptation, to find women with large breasts and wide hips attractive, certain artworks will extend those features beyond any possible female body; but the viewer responds to the artwork's exaggeration of human tendencies that are extended to maximum effect. Ramachandran also explains the emergence of language and metaphor in a similar manner. Like other arguments in what is now referred to as 'cognitive archaeology' language is not fully arbitrary, as those of us trained in structuralism and post-structuralism were taught to believe. Certain sounds and movements of the mouth are connected with certain movements of the body and aural effects. When we exert effort we clench the teeth or grimace, and this is reflected in the words we use for violence. Such arguments recall a Rousseau-like argument that language begins with the impassioned cry that is an extension of the body.

There has always been, from theories of Adamic naming, to Rousseau's emphasis on a language that is continuous with the body's passion, an argument regarding language as an *extension* of life. Such an argument for an originally responsive language, a body of self-maintaining form, and a world that is an extension of the self's capacity for system and organization has also always been coupled with a moral (and vitalist) binary of good and evil. Once language becomes a detached technology or poem in its etymological sense (from *poiesis* as object detached from its creating praxis) we confront the evils of mechanism, a system that operates without intent, and without the spirit that gave birth to relations governing those relations. Given this theological commitment to flourishing vitality we might want to question the normative image of life that leads contemporary science to privilege examples of art that can be grounded on striving and purposive life. Life is (or ought to be) oriented towards self-realization; the organism's encounters with the world maximize and enhance its own potentiality, and those activities that seem to be counter-productive or 'beyond life' – such as art – can actually be explained by deeper, broader vitalist tendencies that go beyond consciousness.

The appeal to life as the ultimate ground that can explain all relations must always regard that which is not in accord with recognition and homeostasis as evil or, to use Foucault's less moral terminology, 'mad.' What Foucault sought to examine in his *History of Madness* was not some pure site of divine inspiration, but the ways in which culture approaches phenomena resistant to rationalization (Foucault 2006). Foucault's own work was, in part, influenced by a surrealist aesthetic that had already begun to consider the work of art's relation to mind, and the mind's potential to produce connections that were neither instrumental nor repeatable and meaningful. It was perhaps not surprising that Blake became one of the poets celebrated by Georges Bataille in his interrogation of literature and evil, where evil was celebrated as a flagrant and self-transcending disregard for (human and self-prohibiting) life (Bataille 1973). Such celebrations are not unfamiliar in Romanticism, and we can think of the ways in which Shelley, to name but one, presented the triumph of life as a mundane crushing of the spirit that would destroy the distinct and bounded individual for the sake of an infinite power that could also not be identified with an anthropomorphic and punishing deity: 'The world can hear not the sweet notes that move/The sphere whose light is melody to lovers.'

The anti-vitalism, evil or madness of Blake's work that I wish to consider here is distinct from that traditionally vitalist influx of force or energy that would be other than the self-preserving and bounded life of the organism. If we were to mark a distinction between pre-modern and modern forms of vitalism we could begin by saying that the vitalism of the seventeenth century was a spirit that imbued brute matter with a defining form or essence (Rogers 1996). The vitalism of Henri Bergson, by contrast, defines life as a creative energy that takes divergent paths and is impeded or rendered lazy by the organism's desire for self-preservation. For Bergson, as for many of the Romantics who preceded him and the modernists influenced by him, art would have to destroy the bounded, easy, and systemic forms taken on by an efficient and technologically mastered life, and would have to plunge back into the creative forces from which such systems and technologies emerge. In many ways we could read Blake as taking on a similarly critical attitude to the 'natural man', to 'single vision and Newton's sleep' and to the 'same dull round' that would quantify life and determine it in advance as so much manipulable matter. We could, in turn, celebrate Blake's madness as a form of inspiration or enthusiasm that would allow the true energy of life to flow into a world rendered rational and disenchanted.

The question of Blake's 'madness' has received some attention (Webster 1983; Youngquist 1989). What I wish to consider here is not the mental health of Blake, nor madness as a state of the psychophysical organism, but a corpus that resists the full attribution of intent and conscious will in accord with recognition and relations. Is it the case, as Jerome McGann has argued, that literature is best considered as social *act*? Arguing directly against French celebrations of the 'text', McGann insists that our approach to a text should not attend to the object that circulates in anthologies and that is detached from its original conditions of production; for we need to see even the most accidental disruptions of the communicable body of the poem as 'positively incoherent.' Blake's scored out lines in *Jerusalem* need to be understood as responses to the literary, social, and political context of his time, just as all future editions and decisions regarding Blake (or any poem) need to be understood as actions that play a role in social relations and reconfigurations. While such an approach can, of course, yield further insight and coherence to a corpus that might otherwise be too easily appropriated into some dominant idea of a general and ill-defined Romanticism, it nevertheless privileges once again a notion of the life of the text. Texts are acts; our response to a text should be to see its emergence as an act in a context of social action – where what one does is comprehensible only as a move in a game of possible responses and not as the expression of some singular and possibly ineffable vision. Considering the 'mad' aspects of Blake's poetry allows us to think beyond that normative image of life as self-realizing action.

First, there are elements in Blake's poetry that fail to act, or that resist connection. Far from this giving the reader a sense of liberating play, freedom, and creative textual production, they present a disturbingly dead or inassimilable element that disrupts any sense of literary history as increasing recognition and revelation. J. M. Bernstein has, following Adorno, captured this inactivity with the notion of art's 'a priori deadness' (Bernstein 2006, 213). Second, in addition to the singular and inassimilable moments of Blake's corpus, his work in general tends towards a 'haptic' aesthetic. The theme of the body that masters and synthesizes its world – the body of 'natural man' – is regarded critically within Blake's work, which privileges a body of divergent tendencies. In 'Night the Ninth' of *The Four Zoas* the 'regenerate' Albion accords each faculty of human existence its particular role and warns against the elevation of any particular function into a transcendent form:

Luvah & Vala henceforth you are Servants obey & live
You shall forget your former state return O Love in peace
Into your place the place of seed not in the brain or heart
If Gods combine against Man Setting their Dominion above
The Human Form Divine.

(FZ 9, p. 126, 6–10, E: 395; K: 366)

The 'Gods' Albion refers to are created when one of the states of the human soul (for example, reason or 'Urizen') is projected onto an external deity; Albion follows here by warning against the future elevation of any one state. Instead of contraries striving for domination Albion envisages harmonious interaction within the human form (which is not the bodily organism, but eternal):

In Enmity & war first weakend then in stern repentence
They must renew their brightness & their disorganizd functions
Again reorganize till they resume the image of the human
Cooperating in the bliss of Man obeying his Will
Servants to the infinite & Eternal of the Human form

(FZ 9 p. 126: 13–17, E: 395; K: 366)

Here, Albion is eternal not because he exists outside and independently of human life but because he is the form of every individual. When Blake introduces the human body into epic he does not give it a Platonic form that is transcendent in the traditional sense. Rather, Blake stresses that actual human being and all natural life are already eternal and infinite. In *Milton* it is Milton's *embodiment* not his existence in eternity that will awaken Albion:

> Now Albions sleeping Humanity began to turn upon his Couch;
> Feeling the electric flame of Miltons awful precipitate descent.
> Seest thou the little winged fly, smaller than a grain of sand?
> It has a heart like thee; a brain open to heaven & hell,
> Withinside wondrous & expansive; its gates are not clos'd,
> I hope thine are not: hence it clothes itself in rich array;
> Hence thou art cloth'd with human beauty O thou mortal man.
> Seek not thy heavenly father then beyond the skies:
> There Chaos dwells & ancient Night …
>
> (M 20[22], 25–33, E: 114; K: 502)

After Albion is roused by the descent of Milton, Blake reiterates the potential for even the most minute aspects of creation to reveal heaven and hell. If the body's 'gates are not clos'd' it too will disclose eternity. The fallen or vegetable body is the body of the empiricists: a body that can be perceived and analyzed as a material thing. This biological body is the province of Tirzah and natural religion:

> To Natural Religion! to Tirzah the Daughter of Rahab the Holy!
> She ties the knot of nervous fibres, into a white brain!
> She ties the knot of bloody veins, into a red hot heart!
>
> (M 19 [21], 54–56, E: 113; K: 501)

Blake's body, on the other hand, is a form; it is inextricably intertwined with the imagination. Blake stresses the embodiment of the imagination in order to counter the Platonic/Miltonic tradition of the otherworldly character of genius but he also stresses the imaginative character of the body in order to disavow the physicalism of the empiricists. The vegetable body is finite and excluded from eternity: 'These are the Visions of Eternity …/But we see only as it were the hem of their garments/When with our vegetable eyes we view these wond'rous Visions' (M 26[28],10–12, E: 123; K: 512). Although Blake emphasizes the importance of eternity and the immortality of the imagination, the passage to Golgonooza can only be reached by the redemption of the mortal body, which can be neither mortified nor subordinated. The body of natural science, the vegetable polypus, must be passed through in order to achieve vision:

For Golgonooza cannot be seen till having passd the Polypus
It is viewed on all sides round by a Four-fold Vision
Or till you become Mortal and Vegetable in Sexuality
Then you behold its mighty Spires & Domes of ivory & gold
(M 35 [39], 22–25, E: 135; K: 525)

Consequently, within the same plate of *Milton* Blake speaks of both deliverance from the body and the glory of the body. The first reference, to deliverance, employs the neo-Platonic imagery of the descent of souls to the body through the south and north gates:

The Souls descending to the Body, wail on the right hand
Of Los; & those deliverd from the Body, on the left hand
(M, 26[28]: 16–17, E: 123; K: 512)

Blake goes on to state that these souls are 'With neither lineament nor form but like to watry clouds.' After they are clothed, fed, and housed (given material and bodily needs) they become generated bodies with 'inward form:'

And every Generated Body in its inward form,
Is a garden of delight & a building of magnificence,
Built by the Sons of Los in Bowlahoola & Allamanda
And the herbs & flowers & furniture & beds & chambers
Continually woven in the Looms of Enitharmons Daughters
In bright Cathedrons golden Dome with care & love & tears
(M 26[28], 35–39, E: 123; K: 512)

The 'inward form' of the generated body is built by Los's sons; it is a product of time and imagination. The dwelling of the body is provided by space – Enitharmon's daughters – and human feeling ('care & love & tears'). Similarly, the form that Milton creates for Urizen is an artistic sculptural form of clay, a product of invention:

Silent they met, and silent strove among the streams, of Arnon
Even to Mahanaim, when with the cold hand Urizen stoop'd down
And took up water from the icy river Jordan: pouring on
To Milton's brain the icy fluid from his broad cold palm.
But Milton took of the red clay of Succoth, moulding it with care
Between his palms: and filling up the furrows of many years

Beginning at the feet of Urizen, and on the bones
Creating new flesh on the Demon cold, and building him,
As with new clay a Human form in the Valley of Beth Peor
(M 19[21], 6–14, E: 112; K: 500)

Urizen's act of 'baptism' uses formless water whereas Milton picks up malleable clay. By pouring icy fluid on Milton's brain Urizen hopes to numb Milton's own mental powers; Blake's figure of reason paralyses or freezes the individual imagination. This episode of *Milton* provides an allegory for Blake's response to his precursor poet. By giving Urizen a clay form, Milton is embodying reason, giving it a Human form. He is also bringing Urizen into present time: 'filling up the furrows of many years.' He is providing it with limits and circumscribing it such that he can now walk around it: 'as the sculptor silent stands before/His forming image; he walks round it patient laboring' (M 20[22], 8–9, E: 114; K: 502).

This notion of inward form might be liked to Raymond Ruyer's 'transcendental forms' which always unfold from embodied life, but exceed any single body by being the forms towards which anybody tends to reach individuation (Ruyer 1958). Blake is neither a poet of the body, nor spirit, so much as a laborer at the thresholds of the two – working to bring out the forms of matter. In his invocation to *Milton* Blake adopts an image of corporeal inspiration. Milton's invocation to Book Three of *Paradise Lost* summoned eternal and primordial light to 'Shine inward, and the mind through all her powers/Irradiate' (PL.3.52–53). Blake calls the Daughters of Beulah who are associated with 'soft sexual delusions' and describes the physical course of inspiration:

... Come into my hand
By your mild power; descending down the Nerves of my right arm
From out the Portals of my Brain, where by your ministry
The Eternal Great Humanity Divine. Planted his Paradise
(M 2, 5–8, E: 96; K: 481)

Although Blake describes the bodily nature of this visitation he also recalls Milton's 'paradise within.' At the same time that Blake is answering Milton's spiritual invocation by including the body, he is also spiritualizing the body with the visitation of the 'Eternal Great Humanity Divine.' Once again, this reinforces Blake's particular non-individualist humanism. Without the immanence of this divine form the body is still the vessel of nerves and brain and incapable of vision. Later the poet laments:

O how can I with my gross tongue that cleaveth to the dust,
Tell of the Four-fold Man, in starry numbers fitly orderd
Or how can I with my cold hand of clay! But thou O Lord
Do with me as thou wilt! for I am nothing, and vanity.

(M 20 [22], 15–18, E: 114; K: 502)

After Milton has turned his back on the 'Heavens builded on cruelty' the seven angels instruct him in the possibility of a human form that is not another Satanic individualism but is based on 'brotherhood.' The angels themselves insist that they are not individuals but supra-individual states:

We are not Individuals but States: Combinations of Individuals
We were Angels of the Divine Presence: & were Druids in Annandale
Compelld to combine into Form by Satan, the Spectre of Albion
Who made himself a God &, destroyed the Human Form Divine.
But the Divine Humanity & Mercy gave us a Human Form
Because we were combind in Freedom & holy
Brotherhood

(M 32[35], 10–16, E: 131; K: 521)

The angels go on to affirm the primacy of imagination. Not a state, the imagination is the spirit of humanity, which is not a psychophysical humanity, but eternal and therefore set against the alienated abstractions of reason and memory:

The Imagination is not a State: it is the Human Existence itself
Affection or Love becomes a State, when divided from Imagination
The Memory is a State always, & the Reason is a State
Created to be Annihilated & a new Ratio Created
Whatever can be Created can be Annihilated Forms cannot
The Oak is cut down by the Ax, the Lamb falls by the Knife
But their Forms Eternal Exist, For-ever. Amen Halle[l]ujah

(M 32[35], 32–36, E: 132; K: 522)

There is a double sense in which 'Reason is a State': at the level of the human body, reason is a faculty that centers the body in upon itself, creating a relation to the world of an inside viewing an outside. Reason is also a state politically, for there can only be an external, transcendent imposed political body with the idea of a general 'ratio' that discloses the world's proper order. Against this 'ratio' Blake uses the word 'form' in a manner of reversed Platonism. Blake locates these eternal forms not in an otherworldly sphere but in the imagination. When these forms are detached from the imagination or interpreted statically (as in a naïve Platonism) they become states. If the imagination is the ground for all being, it is nevertheless an immanent transcendence or 'transcendence in immanance'; it is transcendent only to individuals, but not to Blake's humanity. In *Jerusalem* the primordiality of imagination is repeatedly stressed: 'For All Things Exist in the Human Imagination' (J, 69: 25, E: 223; K: 707). By contrast, Blake regards satanic 'inwardness' as 'opacity' because it obstructs divine vision and grounds self-righteousness. A self-annihilating figure of inwardness is the imagination, where what appears transcendent and eternal is made human. This type of inwardness is individuated, but not individual; it is not self-enclosed in the manner of the Urizenic inwardness of the Lambeth prophecies, but it does move to intensified distinction rather than generality. It expands to include heaven, earth, and humanity. Unlike Satanic opacity this inwardness is translucent:

> What is Above is Within, for every-thing in Eternity is translucent:
> The Circumference is Within: Without, is formed the Selfish Center
> And the Circumference still expands going forward to Eternity.
> And the Center has Eternal States! these States we now explore.
> . . .
> For all are Men in Eternity. Rivers Mountains Cities Villages,
> All are Human & when you enter into their Bosoms you walk
> In Heavens & Earths; as in your own Bosom you bear your Heaven
> And Earth, and all you behold, tho it appears Without it is Within
> In your Imagination of which this World of Mortality is but a Shadow.
> (J 71, 6–19, E: 225; K: 709)

The imagination is the ground and condition of all existence, but is not solely a human imagination (or, at least, the human for Blake is not the human species); the imagination, as human, is also Christ or the Lamb of God. At the beginning of *Milton* the 'Divine Vision' is identified with the 'Living Form' of the 'Human Imagination/Which is the Divine Body of the Lord Jesus' (M 3, 3–4, E: 96; K: 482). For Blake the imagination is Jesus and the 'Divine Humanity;' the figure of Christ unites humanity with the eternal spirit of inspiration. Here, again, there is a doubleness in Blake's humanism: humanity is at once the ground of all creative form and yet is also not human in the bounded sense of psychophysical man. Later in *Milton* the Bard reiterates the identification between humanity, the imagination, and divinity: 'According to the inspiration of the Poetic Genius/Who is the eternal all-protecting Divine Humanity/To whom be Glory & Power & Dominion Evermore Amen' (M 14[15], 1–3, E: 108; K: 495). This is at once reactively theological – man as fragment of an expressive divine – and radically immanent, for the theological is not an external ground but that which is disclosed from *this life.* The consequence of this coupling of imagination with the divine humanity of Christ is that religion and faith no longer manifest themselves in the worship of external deities but in the active creation and exercise of the imagination. To Milton's static and rational theology Blake opposes a dynamic aesthetics that lacks any *ethos* or proper place. In the 'To the Christians' section of *Jerusalem* Blake declares that true religion entails the flourishing of human creativity: 'I know of no other Christianity and of no other Gospel than the liberty both of body & mind to exercise the Divine Arts of Imagination' (J 77, E: 231; K: 716–17). The imagination is the eternal and plural – 'Divine Arts' – ground against which all natural being is secondary: 'Imagination the real & eternal World of which this Vegetable Universe is but a faint shadow & in which we shall live in our Eternal or Imaginative Bodies, when these Vegetable Mortal Bodies are no more' (J 77: E: 231; K: 717). Although the Imagination is eternal it creates a temporal world. In *Jerusalem* Blake describes this constitutive function of the imagination. The 'Visionary forms dramatic' are human but precede and condition all individual existence, and create Time and Space:

> In new Expanses, creating exemplars of Memory and of Intellect
> Creating Space, Creating Time according to the wonders Divine
> Of Human Imagination, throughout all the Three Regions immense
> Of Childhood, Manhood & Old Age[;] & the all tremendous unfathomable Non Ens
> Of Death was seen in regenerations terrific or complacent varying
> According to the subject of discourse
>
> (J 98, 30–40, E: 258; K: 746)

The 'unfathomable Non Ens,' as Blake refers to this noumenal or not yet actualized world, must be regenerated into human meaning. Originally 'Man anciently containd in his mighty limbs all things in Heaven & Earth' (J 27, E: 171; K: 649). The present fallen condition is a consequence of forgetting that all being is originally human – but this is not to say individual, for the 'human' in Blake lies beyond natural man. Hence, *Jerusalem* ends by reiterating the necessity for 'humanizing' all aspects of being, which is also to open the human to durations beyond itself. Human 'Forms' include

'Tree Metal Earth.' All being is humanized, brought into the sphere of temporality and made immanent to life:

> All Human Forms identified even Tree Metal Earth & Stone. all
> Human Forms identified, living going forth & returning wearied
> Into the Planetary lives of Years Months Days & Hours reposing
> And then Awaking into his Bosom in the Life of Immortality.
>
> (J 99, 1–4, E: 258; K: 747)

Conclusion

There has always been a proto-anti-capitalist and anti-technological ethic, well before the advent of late capitalism or modernity proper. It is possible to see the general (or 'logocentric') resistance to detached systems and technology as an anticipation of an anti-digital aesthetic: while we may need to have a language of differentiated terms or units to master and represent the world, it should always be possible in principle to trace the genesis of those fixed terms from a continuous, animating, and flowing life. Blake also – most famously in *The Marriage of Heaven and Hell* – posits the emergence of language and the relations of the world from animating spirit, and then laments the fall of that active naming into system:

> The ancient Poets animated all sensible objects with Gods or Geniuses, calling them by the names and adorning them with the properties of woods, rivers, mountains, lakes, cities, nations, and whatever their enlarged & numerous senses could percieve (MHH 11, E: 38; K: 153).

What renders this passage more complex than might first appear is the original notion of the poets animating the world with 'enlarged and *numerous* senses,' suggesting both that the attribution of sense and spirit does not emerge from a single origin, *and* that the perception of the world is plural. Blake does, on the one hand, aim to return all life, systems and spirits to the body. The soul is not some distinct Cartesian ghost in the machine, nor an image of a transcendent divinity lodged within the human breast. Instead Blake seems to define soul and body as contraries: the body itself is not fallen – and Blake sees the notion of a merely physical body as an illusion – nor is the spirit some force that would ideally be liberated from matter. Blake would also seem to be in accord with contemporary, post-Spinozist notions of the mind as 'an idea of the body': 'the body or outward form of Man is derived from the Poetic Genius' (ARO, E: 1; K: 98). In the beginning are action, affect, relation, and creation; as the body registers certain responses it forms a 'map' or sense of itself as embodied. But Blake also provides a diagnosis and genealogy of the mind as distinct from body, and of the mind that somehow has to perceive the world as an alien substance to be mastered. All this would seem to place Blake in line with the trajectory of apocalyptic poetry, in which a world that begins as alien and external is finally recognized as one's own, as a projection of the poetic imagination.

However, and on the other hand, alongside Blake's images of recognition, internalization, and retrieval, and alongside his narratives of an originary animation there is also a far more complex poetic method in which both voice and image operate in conflict with that seemingly Blakean insistence on an original and retrievable animation. The most significant way in which Blake's poetry challenges the ethics of vitalism is in its mode of language, and in its use of figuration, both of which can be considered haptic and analogical. In order for language to be propositional and to refer it needs to be digital: marking the world out in equivalent units of measure. A language divides the sound spectrum into phonemes, and the visual and experiential plenum into concepts, and then allows for a certain grammar of combinations. Such a language is digital not only in its distribution of terms into units that can then be recombined, it also presupposes a certain comportment of the hand. The hand, mastered by the eye, which surveys the world and folds it around its efficient point of view, becomes a digit: a counting and marking tool that allows time to be rendered in the form of so many extended units. The voice that accompanies this surveying, judging eye of 'man' – an eye that sees in the here and now what would be true for any eye whatever in a quantified time and space – is a voice of communication and reason. If one speaks one already makes a claim to be understood, and if one makes a claim then one already appeals to the possible assent of others.

It would make no sense, or be a performative contradiction, to speak without striving for consensus and referential truth: that would be a form of saying and not-saying (Habermas 1992, 80; Apel 1998, 141). Blake's poetry, both as it describes and performs itself, is just such a poetry of performative contradiction, and this because it is haptic rather than digital, or radically digital. Let us say that a simple digitalism presupposes a concept of life as vital striving: living beings are not mere matter but work to maintain and preserve themselves. 'Man' does not merely respond immediately and intensively to the differences that confront him. Rather, he posits a world over and against his own body, and allows that world to take on some uniformity through time; concepts allow him to measure this world now, in terms of the past and future. The eye becomes a way of seeing the world as so much measurable space, and the hand a tool for measuring. For all his talk of energy Blake never regards energy as a quantity – that which would allow us to compare and weigh one being with another. For Blake, energy appears in intensive rather than extensive quantities: an increase in energy – such as love – becomes rage or jealousy at certain thresholds. There is not a general field of force that can be measured as the same through time according to a common unit, for each exertion of force produces certain relations or resistances that have their own light, speed, intensity, and duration.

It is in this sense that I would situate Blake as a counter-vitalist poet. Whereas vitalism is the commitment to a life that maintains, masters, and preserves itself, Blake's poetry describes the ways in which organisms are imprisoned by their desire for 'selfhood.' Liberation occurs with self-annihilation: not an organism that allows itself to receive a certain amount of stimulus to live through time and endure, but an influx of experience so intense that judgment, recognition, and self-consciousness fall away.

Consequently Blake frequently employs images of centers opening towards vision: 'Wonder siezd all in Eternity! to behold the Divine Vision. open/The Center into an Expanse, & the Center rolled out into an Expanse' (J 57, 17–18, E: 207; K: 689). Eno's ameliatory function in *The Four Zoas* involves opening out centers to reveal eternity: 'She also took an atom of space & opend its center/Into Infinitude' (FZ 1, p. 9, 12, E: 305; K: 270). In *Milton* the fall of the zoas is depicted as a fall into the center: 'All fell towards the Center sinking downward in dire Ruin' (M, 34[38]: 39, E: 134; K: 524). There are, then, two modes of immanence: one in which the turn inward reduces everything to the same system, a system of quantified individualism, and another in which the interior opens out to eternity, to other modes of individuation. Each entity has its own particular identity, not because it is bestowed by God or some ratio, but because the world is formed and created in minute particularity: 'every Class is determinate/But not by Natural but by Spiritual power alone (M 26[28], 39–40, E: 124; K: 512). Blake's railing against commerce in his *Public Address* is therefore part of a broader invective against a single axiom:

> Commerce Cannot endure Individual Merit its insatiable Maw must be fed by What all can do Equally well at least it is so in England as I have found to my Cost these Forty Years
>
> Commerce is so far from being beneficial to Arts or to Empire that it is destructive of both as all their History shews for the above Reason of Individual Merit being its Great hatred.
>
> (E: 573–74; K: 593–94)

In *The Four Zoas* the fallen universe is described as a world where market or generalized value triumphs: 'The Horse is of more value than the Man' (FZ, p.15, 1, E: 309; K: 275). Blake – in opposition to generality – constantly insists on the intrinsic character of entities. Unlike 'Bacon, Newton & Locke,' Blake relies upon a notion of an *eternal* imagination that endows each entity with its particular essence. In the Satanic world 'every thing is fixd Opake without Internal light' (M 10[11], 20, E: 104; K: 491). The competitive modern individual sees his own identity as excluding the will of others and this because he assumes the transposed or internalized form of a law-giving deity 'making to himself Laws from his own identity.' As a result, 'man's' world loses its own character; it becomes the chaos over which he must rule tyrannically (M 11[12], 10, E: 104; K: 491). The fall of the Eternal Man in *The Four Zoas* is accordingly described as a loss of definition: 'The Mans exteriors are become indefinite' (FZ 1, p. 22, 40, K: 279). In 'Night the Second' Albion gives up his power to Urizen, 'the great Work master' (recalling Milton's great Work-Master [PL.3.696]) whose fallen universe is an abyss of 'Non Existence,' 'Voidness' and 'indefinite space' (FZ 2, p. 24, 1–5, E: 314; K: 280). Once power has been handed to the centered 'Nobodaddy' or reasoning God, form is lost and chaos ensues. In an unfallen world, however, authority is decentered and 'Every thing in Eternity shines by its own Internal light' (M 10 [11], 16, E: 104; K: 491). Blake repeats this idea in *Jerusalem:*

> In Great Eternity, every particular Form gives forth or Emanates
> Its own peculiar Light, & the Form is the Divine Vision
> And the Light is his Garment This is Jerusalem in every Man
>
> (J 54, 1–3, E: 203; K: 684)

When nature is seen imaginatively and when it is recognized that 'every Natural Effect has a Spiritual Cause' (M 26[28], 43, E: 124; K: 513) nature has a redemptive function. The epistemological doubt that characterized the Cartesian turn is based on the premise of an independent and alien world.[1] I can only question my senses and their ability to know the world if I have already posited an independently existing world. This problem of doubt has no relevance for Blake who identifies the appearing world with the world *per se:*

> I assert for My self that I do not behold the Outward Creation & that to me it is hindrance & not Action it is As the Dirt upon my feet No part of Me. What it will be Questiond When the Sun rises do you not see a

> round Disk of fire somewhat like a Guinea O no no I see an Innumerable company of the Heavenly host crying Holy Holy Holy is the Lord God Almighty I question not my Corporeal or Vegetative Eye any more than I would question a Window concerning a Sight I look thro it & not with it.
> (VLJ p. 95, E: 565–66; K: 617)

While the female figure of Vala represents nature and its renewal in *The Four Zoas,* she is also important in the process of reunification because of her femininity. Although she is the alienated 'female will' of *The Four Zoas,* the process of reintegrating the feminine is central to the narrative of this and Blake's later prophecies. The horror of the 'Spectres of the Dead' in 'Night the Seventh' is a consequence of their being without their female counterparts. This isolation of the masculine precludes the possibility of vision: 'Each Male formd without a counterpart without a concentering vision' (FZ 7, p. 87, 30, E: 369; K: 330). Vala as a representation of alienated female will and independent nature is joined by the redemptive female figure of Jerusalem. The emergence of Jerusalem occurs after Enitharmon (or the separated female emanation) has woven bodies for the spectres; this process is described as 'humanising', so that humanity is distinct from 'man.' (FZ 8, p. 101, 46, E: 374; K: 344). It is only after the embodiment of the male spectral self that the retrieval of the female emanation can occur. Los and Enitharmon together create a form for human life, 'a Vast family wondrous in beauty & love' (FZ 8, p.103, 37, E: 376; K: 345). Immediately after this Enitharmon names and acknowledges Jerusalem:

> And Enitharmon namd the Female Jerusa[le]m the holy
> Wondring she saw the Lamb of God within Jerusalems Veil
> The divine Vision seen within the inmost deep recess
> Of fair Jerusalems bosom in a gently beaming fire
> Then sang the Sons of Eden round the Lamb of God & said
> Glory Glory Glory to the holy Lamb of God
> Who now beginneth to put off the dark Satanic body
> Now we behold redemption Now we know that life Eternal
> Depends alone upon the Universal hand & not in us
> Is aught but death In individual weakness sorrow & pain
> (FZ 8, p.104, 1–10, E: 376; K: 346)

With the appearance of Jerusalem, the body is no longer dark and Satanic, but a created and imaginative body woven by Enitharmon.[2] More importantly, the atomization of the individual self is overcome with the recognition of the transcendence of the 'Universal hand.' Jerusalem, the agent of this moment of redemption becomes the figure against whom a war of sexual difference is conducted. The blocking of the infinite occurs as a 'hermaphroditic' enclosure of the feminine, almost in the manner of a counter-birth:

> The war roard round Jerusalems Gates it took a hideous form
> Seen in the aggregate a Vast Hermaphroditic form
> Heavd like an Earthquake labring with convulsive groans
> Intolerable at length an awful wonder burst
> From the Hermaphroditic bosom Satan he was namd
> Son of Perdition terrible his form dishumanizd monstrous
> A male without a female counterpart a howling fiend
> Fo[r]lorn of Eden & repugnant to the forms of life
> Yet hiding the shadowy female Vala in an ark Curtains
> (FZ 8, p. 104, 19–28, E: 377; K: 347)

Blake uses the figure of Satan elsewhere (for example, the 'Bard's Song' of *Milton*) to represent the impulse towards an annihilation of distinction and particularity. Here, Satan as a 'Hermaphroditic form' is a symptom of the primary loss of difference – the difference of sex. He becomes the warlike 'female hid within male' by concealing Vala. It is as though the female, through being veiled, becomes that which is both nightmarishly other and that which promises itself (as veiled) as the apocalyptic end. Satan the accuser protects and maintains Vala as an alienated femininity, which in turn expresses itself in external nature and idolatry. The hermaphroditic character of Satan is associated with a 'dishumanizd' form. But the mystery this Satanically-produced Vala encourages is overcome when the Lamb of God descends through Jerusalem's gates (FZ 8, p. 104, 30–35, E: 378; K: 347–48). Vala herself is later redeemed in 'Night the Ninth.' As Albion awakes he gives Luvah and Vala their rightful place in the human form (FZ 9, p. 126, 5–10, E: 395; K: 366). After this has been achieved Vala, united with Luvah, emerges from a pastoral landscape and acknowledges to Luvah the vegetative sleep that has consumed her past:

> Come forth O Vala from the grass & from the silent Dew
> Rise from the dews of death for the Eternal Man is Risen
> She rises among flowers & looks toward the Eastern clearness
> She walks yea runs her feet are wingd on the tops of the bending grass
> Her garments rejoice in the vocal wind & her hair glistens with dew

She answerd thus Whose voice is this in the voice of the nourishing air
In the spirit of the morning awaking the Soul from its grassy bed
Where dost thou dwell for it is thee I seek & but for thee
I must have slept Eternally nor have felt the dew of thy morning
(FZ 9, pp. 126–27, 31–37 &1–2, E: 395–96; K: 367)

Vala's overcoming of her own selfhood prefigures the conclusion of 'Night the Ninth' where the importance of the recognition of others, rather than individualism, is proclaimed by the Eternals:

In families we see our shadows born. & thence we know
That Man subsists by Brotherhood & Universal Love
We fall on one anothers necks more closely we embrace
Not for ourselves but for the Eternal family we live
Man liveth not by Self alone but in his brothers face
Each shall behold the Eternal Father & love & joy abound
(FZ 9, p. 133, 21–26, E: 402; K: 374)

Blake's counter-vitalism, expressed in his insistence on liberation from the organism that maintains itself, is not only described in his calls to perceive eternity in the smallest moments of the present; it also inflects his poetic and visual techniques. If the hand were to liberate itself from digital mastery, then it could either become completely manual, producing splashes on the page, or gouging the plate violently – both of which do occur in Blake – or it could become haptic. Here, the eye that views the canvas would *feel* the resistance of matter. Matter would not be the passive vehicle infused with some forming life-power or logic; each matter would bear its own intrinsic force or potentiality that the hand would encounter. In *All Religions are One* Blake stresses the 'genius' of all things – using genius in its original sense of indwelling spirit – and claims that this genius determines form: 'the forms of all things are derived from their Genius' (ARO, E:1; K:98). This, indeed, is what we see in Blake's engravings.

Figuration is destroyed: we do not see, for example, the human form as it has been traced out by the history of art. The lines that compose the human form have to be wrested from the resistance of the engraved plate, with the color also taking on its own force. The forms are given in line, the color in overlaid tints and washes. The eye does not see through the painting to the world it figures, but feels the emergence of figure itself. Whereas the stipples and hatches of Blake's time used the smallest lines and marks to produce shades and tones, Blake either uses bold outlines that play the dynamism and fluidity of his leaping bodies against the weight of the material upon which they are engraved; or, he uses fine lines to produce shadows that flout the representation of light as an illumination of the scene. Halos, shadows, and luminosities are distributed across the page, so that the finest of lines can sometimes be seen as shading, sometimes as line itself. The eye is also divided between the functions of reading and viewing, between comprehension and apprehension. Far from using line and light to produce a point of view that implies a position of spectatorship, the eye is assaulted by the autonomy of artistic techniques.

For Blake, the historicizing vision in which fragmentation, dissension, damage, and loss are recuperated and restored as moments of one life can occur only with a blindness to the minute particulars and openings to eternity that are not one's own. It is the limited voice of *Songs of Experience* who 'Present, Past & Future, sees' (K: 210; E: 18), from a single, commanding and located point of view. Redemption occurs with the opening up of divergent times, either through the perception of a vortex, which in the present appears as a point within time, but then expands to include pasts and futures that are not those of the present (K: 497; E: 109), or through the pulsation of an artery: 'Every Time less than a pulsation of the artery/Is equal in its period & value to Six Thousand Years' (K: 516; E: 127). Far from imagining a divine life in which all the swerves of evil serve only to bring forth goodness, Blake is a poet of the singular. There is not a general medium of life or energy that flows through living beings. Each pulsation has its own consciousness or apocalyptic potential. This is given most clearly in his image of the body.

Blake presents life as one gigantic body, but the nature of his body is not that of a lived body – a body in which each limb plays its part in some coherent and mindful unity. Instead, the body is no longer a vehicle through which the self makes its way in the world, but harbours its own distinct, divergent and hidden times:

> … for man cannot know
> What passes in his members till periods of Space & Time
> Reveal the secrets of Eternity: for more extensive
> Than any other earthly things are Man's earthly lineaments
> (M 21, 8–11, K: 503; E: 115).

Blake's human projection does not produce the universe as unified *mind,* nor the vital as a force that *acts*; instead inspiration occurs in *Milton* through a body that is never fully intentional. When 'this Vegetable World appear'd on my left Foot/As a bright sandal form'd immortal of precious stones' (M 21, 12–13), the eternity that opens is given through body parts and things, through contingent connections that are not thought or represented but felt.

Blake's claim for minute particulars produces both a poetry that resists the centered economy of traditional thinking – a system of relations emanating from a divine reason – and that also remains resistant to a single economy of flowing energy without bound or limit. Instead, Blake constantly depicts the opening up of systems of relations and forces from singular points: at what threshold does a body fall into despair, rage, rebellion, guilt, accusation, violence or submission? The body is neither a being with a proper form towards which it ought to develop (with that proper form emanating from the divine life that is being); nor is the body a mere mechanism occurring as nothing more than a neutral energy or force. Each body is a potentiality for relations, and becomes what it is through encounters.

An increase in quantity may simply produce a difference in degree but – at singular points – a quantity passes a threshold and becomes something else – opening a new line of becoming (Smith 2010). At a certain singular point the desire for liberation becomes repressive, redounding on the body that the desire for freedom originally defined. At a singular point the love for another body becomes possessive and repressively jealous and violent. Blake's poetry is therefore a poetry *about* intensive time and space, at the same time as it produces temporal intensities. Extended time is a time that at each moment bears the same measure: clock time is extended time, for an hour is always an hour. Intensive time operates differently at each of its moments and can change its nature at certain thresholds or singular points; a year is not always a year, for 1789 changed the very way in which time would progress, be perceived and be lived. An hour can be like any other, but can also be that hour of pain or subjection that finally prompts a body to rebel.

Blake presents moments of break or rupture that were neither intended, nor anticipated, but which free time from all measure. Presented *within* the poetry this is a radically futural time: not the 'same dull round' in which the world as it is merely plays itself through time, but a time in which change, becoming and difference are no longer the difference *of* any being that is already given. For Blake, the capacity to see eternity in a grain of sand is to grasp a time that is not a unified medium or container, but a time that can produce change and events that are not those of man as the measure of all things. Not only does Blake's poetry present and describe such 'openings to eternity,' his formal method also challenges a historicizing vision of time as a medium of recognition. The most radical historical moments in Blake's poetry are the untimely: both the described scenes of the unintended, unwitnessed and ineffectual ruptures, *and* those points of inscription that resist sense and comprehension.

History therefore needs to be rethought in relation to Blake's poetry. How might we think historically if we do not regard time as the medium within which we locate texts? First, we might see the ways in which a text is a singular point that *gives time.* Two centuries of Blake criticism have followed from the working through of those moments in his poetry that are resistant to synthesis; with criticism having to repeat, master, narrativize, and trace the geneses of the inassimilable. Our very doctrine of what it is to read has unfolded from Blake, with works such as Northrop Frye's *Anatomy of Criticism,* Harold Bloom's *Anxiety of Influence* and Jerome McGann's *Social Values and Poetic Acts* defining literature and literary history in general through, in part, the use of Blake. But if Blake's work has called for historical work it has done so precisely because it is not yet historical, because it presents itself as material requiring temporal labor.

Images and lines from Blake's work circulate in and constitute our present, but often in ways that diverge radically from the original force of their emergence. Phrases such as 'I must create a system or be enslaved by another man's', the proverbs of hell from *The Marriage of Heaven and Hell,* and the hymn 'Jerusalem' are all fragments of Blake's corpus that operate with an effect that cannot be reduced either to their original condition or brought to presence. Like some of Milton's more famous lines – 'Better to reign in hell than serve in heaven' – the poetic work has a potential to produce relations that cannot be referred back to the potentiality of an act that foresees some end or form. This is a potentiality or time of becoming that is not oriented to a proper actuality. Many of the circulating lines and images of Blake's work present themselves less as social acts whose force we might read, than as matter that stands alone, without sense or relation, and that seem to present themselves as potentiality for sense without that sense being given.

In addition to challenging the ways in which we understand history, either as an unfolding progress or as humanly constituted synthesis, we can also see the ways in which Blake's poetry both works within and challenges the historical imperative of recognition. Blake's work is at once prophetic in its attempt to rework literary history (and the Miltonic debt in particular), at the same time as it is counter-prophetic in its production of moments of sacrifice, forgiveness, and divergence that present 'time in its pure state:' not time as a sequence through which we live and measure the world, but time as *the capacity for material to produce duration.* Blake's works constantly present the act of mastering material – molding a body for Urizen out of clay, writing by corrosives to destroy the complacency of the present, weaving a textile to protect the present from the nightmare of chaos – but they also present directly the potentiality of matter to stand alone. This is why Blake's image of writing is not that of an *extension* of thought or the brain; writing is not a simple vehicle. In fact, Blake overturns the Cartesian cogito, in which the being of self follows from thinking (at the same time as his thought and poetry are hyper-Cartesian in the recognition of a hyperbolic thought that cannot be contained within the experienced present). In *Jerusalem* Blake's 'I hear… Therefore I print,' follows not from the activation of the mind, but from the Ear, which (like the brain for Blake) is not transparent to the self, but harbours unfathomed depths: 'Even from the depths of Hell his voice I hear/Within the unfathom'd caverns of my Ear./ Therefore I print' (J 3, 7–9, K: 621; E: 145). Blake does celebrate a capacity of looking inwards, but the self neither finds its own being, nor discovers a divine conscience that would be the law of the world in general. Instead, each self is composed of multiple times. The figure of the body allows Blake to demonstrate that the life that is most proximate, our own bodily being, is not known to us, not mastered by us, and holds the potential to open up divergent futures: 'We who dwell on Earth can do nothing of ourselves; everything is conducted by Spirits, no less than Digestion or Sleep' (J 3, K: 621). Writing is not then a direct conveyance of the spirit of life, for life is composed of divergent and multiple spirits, with writing itself having its own force. The act of writing works with, and succumbs to, the resistance of matter. We can see this in the way Blake's engraved poems often have to adapt to the form of their material substrate – producing line breaks when the end of the plate is reached – and bearing the traces of a thought that is not in command of itself (so that erasures remain as scars in the text).

That notion of time *in its pure state* refers to durations that are not yet synthesized according to a continuing measure, and instead open out to the singular, the inactive, and the non-intended. This mode of time is, I would argue, both a theme within Blake's poetry and a problem that is brought to the fore in the material object of Blake's work. If we consider matter, not as the potential through which the forming power comes to itself, and if we consider the *text* not as that through which the act takes place, then we are forced to confront the poem not as a living body that harbors life, but as a corpse: a body that requires ritual and working through.

The poem is essentially unhistorical in its singularity; for it is the constant interpretation of the poem, and its continual re-reading, that is evidence not of its ongoing life, but of its resistance to full actualization. There is always a dead, unthought, singular, not yet synthesized element that haunts the present. If that were not the case, then we would no longer be impelled to read. It is also in this sense that the poem is intrinsically sexual, presenting a difference that is both desired and unreadable: a difference that has also detached itself from all production and fruition. Difference is *sexual* not when two bodies couple for organic or biological continuity but when there is a desire that goes beyond bodily survival and interest (Grosz 2004). Woman or the feminine occurs as sexual difference when some otherness is given that is beyond the subject's own reflexivity and recognition. Against the notion of the feminine or matter as being nothing more than the potential for form and actuality (a concept Blake regards as fallen – the feminine void outside existence), we can see Blake's poetry as bringing matter in its own right to its full sexual dimension. Matter becomes sexual when it is no longer in the service of some general expansive and productive life, but creates its own differences and relations – or behaves perversely.

If logocentrism has been grounded on an image of the man of onto-theology – a being who departs from himself only to father his own sense and give form to his own world – then it is the notion of the feminine – as that matter which acts as a law unto itself, resisting the forming and historical sense – that characterizes the literary. As Deleuze writes in his book on Foucault, we can imagine a language that no longer acts as the communicational medium for 'man': language not as medium for self recognition, but language in its own being or 'stammering' (Deleuze 2006C, 105). Language is not a material vehicle for sense but is better thought of as materiality (De Man 2005). It is this materiality that is both presented in Blake's poetry – in all his descriptions of bodies and body parts that have their own times and vortices – and that is evidenced in the materiality *of* Blake's poetry.

Not only is Blake's visual art haptic rather than digital or manual, being neither the mastery of the hand by the surveying eye, nor the insubordination of the hand; his poetry is haptic rather than sonorous. Just as the visual dimension of Blake's work allows the viewing eye to 'feel' the scars and surfaces of the text, so the verbal dimension of Blake's corpus draws the ideality or spirit of sense into its relation with the felt materiality of sounds. Blake's words are not so many units in a conventional grammar or diction. Blake uses neologisms, composite mythologies, and idiosyncratic prosody to present sound not as the ordering of the world, nor as expression of a natural logic, but as a force in its own right. We feel the coming into form of each sound, rather than sounds composed into an overall rhythm or rhyme scheme. Most importantly, though, although there is a mutational or genetic quality to the sound – such that we can sense the coming into form of our everyday phonemes – this haptic aesthetic challenges the extensionist conception of language. Language is not, as Rousseau or contemporary cognitive archaeology would have it – an *extension* of the immediate human cry: the sounds that we deploy to express ourselves have their own material force and autonomous and singular variability. Sound is technical and machinic, operating beyond the organism's intentionality. Blake's poetry is neither sound divorced from sense (vocal), nor the pure formality of sense (abstract), but it does allow one to *hear* the forming of sense. Blake's aesthetic is one of allowing the analog differences of variation to become audible within the digital system of phonemes.

If the voice were to become fully insubordinate then we might have a purely sonorous or musical poetry (such as the poetry of e.e. cummings), but again Blake produces a play between the voice that speaks in terms of sense – commanding, proposing, prophesying, and judging – and a voice that becomes sensible. This is not voice becoming musically sonorous, but haptic. Indeed, Blake does not allow the voice to become pure sound, nor does he foreground rhythm, assonance, rhyme or meter.[3] The sound of Blake's poetry is not that of music (rhythm, meter, rhyme, assonance) but the sound of *semantic intonation* and variation. Urizen is a variant of horizon/Ur-reason; Urthona is earth-owner; Theotormon of theological torment; Nobodaddy is both nobody's daddy and a near-nonsense word; Tharmus is possibly 'thymos'. Other names – Enitharmon, Orc, Ahania, Thel – might suggest origins, but their genealogy (as in all language) is undecidable. Further, Blake's poetry often *sounds* as though it is clear, declarative, and assertoric, even if there is no clarity of reference or sense. There is a prosody in meaningful speech – a rising inflection for a question, a deepening of pitch for a command, an increase of volume for a warning. This differs from music, which may bear its own semantic system (so that it happens to be the case that we associate minor keys with sadness or imperfect cadences with hymn tunes). Blake's poetry is haptic in presenting the resistance of verbal material, both in its tonal and phonemic variability. In his use of highly idiosyncratic and almost clumsy or inarticulable names, such as the following passage from *Milton,* he couples the declarative and sonorous force of prophecy with semantic vagueness:

To measure Time and Space to mortal Men, every morning.
Bowlahoola & Allamanda are placed on each side
Of that Pulsation & that Globule, terrible their power.

But Rintrah & Palamabron govern over Day & Night
In Allamanda & Entuthon Benython where Souls wail: (M 29, 25–28, K: 517; E: 127)

One can also think here of Blake's epic lists of names, which unlike Milton's similarly lengthy taxonomies of (say) the fallen angels, cannot be referred back to a single origin and instead tend to proliferate in an incantatory manner. It is as though we have the sound and grammar of prophecy and message – *that there is prophecy* – without the sense or meaning of that prophetic tone.

The Male is a Furnace of beryll; the Female is a golden Loom;
I behold them and their rushing fires overwhelm my Soul;
In Londons darkness; and my tears fall day and night,
Upon the Emanations of Albions Sons! the Daughters of Albion
Names anciently rememberd, but now contemn'd as fictions:
Although in every bosom they controll our Vegetative powers.
These are united into Tirzah and her Sisters. on Mount Gilead.
Cambel & Gwendolen & Conwenna & Cordella & Ignoge.
And these united into Rahab in the Covering Cherub on Euphrates
Gwiniverra & Gwinefred. & Gonorill & Sabrina beautiful.
Estrild, Mehetabel & Ragan, lovely Daughters of Albion.
They are the beautiful Emanations of the Twelve Sons of Albion
(J 5, 40–45, K: 624; E: 148)

In the fifth plate of *Jerusalem* Blake lists the emanations of Albion 'who control our Vegetative powers.' Tellingly, here, Blake presents those female figures who stand for the projection of the natural world as alien and as a negation of the mind's controlling reason; those figures of Rahab and Tirzah cover over the real names of the beautiful emanations. It is as though language as we know it gives a fallen, because referential, view of the world. By contrast those names only 'anciently rememberd' hark back to a list of female powers that we can now only imagine as objects. It is a mistake, I would argue, to include Blake within a Cabbalistic and neo-Platonist tradition of returning fragmentation to one body and one undifferentiated ground. For every reference in his poetry to the eternal man, Blake also refers to the multiple powers – each opening to the infinite – that compose that man. Each pulsation of the artery is not part of a system striving for ongoing life, but itself a form of bodily being, or ensouled matter, that is irreducible to any center of intent or cognition.

The Cabbalistic and Adamic idea of recalling and restoring an original and pre-linguistic sense is both undone and reinforced by Blake's poetic method: undone, because the idea of an original language is far from evident in Blake's proliferating and recalcitrant names, where words start to shine by themselves (literally, as illuminations). Blake's poetry suggests that there was a time when words were powers themselves, multiplying energetically and prolifically, not yet fettered by the need for mastery. Blake's doctrine of the 'enlarged and numerous senses' explicitly sees form, not as the means by which the eye masters a scene – where form would be the ordering of matter. On the contrary, form is intuited only when the eye is no longer enclosed within the organism of the 'natural man.' In his annotations to *The Works of Sir Joshua Reynolds* Blake makes this point clearly: 'All Forms are Perfect in the Poets Mind. but these are not Abstracted nor Compounded from Nature but are from Imagination' (E: 648; K: 459). Whereas the tradition of Platonic metaphysics saw Reason as the correct faculty for apprehending forms, because forms were logical and independent, Blake located the capacity for intuiting forms in the Imagination:

> This is my Opinion but Forms must be apprehended by Sense or the Eye of Imagination
> Man is All Imagination God is man & exists in us & we in him
> What Jesus came to Remove was the Heathen or Platonic Philosophy which blinds the Eye of Imagination The Real Man
>
> (Annotations to Berkeley's *Siris*, E: 664; K: 775)

What is at issue here is more than simply the shift of a capacity from one faculty to another. Blake assigns the forms to the *creative,* rather than receptive, aspect of human existence. In doing so the character of forms changes. Forms are constituted and dwell within a faculty of human being that is not only the primary faculty ('Man is All Imagination') but also a faculty that Blake identifies with divinity. In *Milton* Blake describes the imagination as 'the Divine Body of the Lord Jesus' (M 3, 4, E: 96; K: 482). But whereas divinity had traditionally been transcendent, Blake's imagination is thoroughly human. Blake locates the apprehension of forms in an immanent, though divine, faculty of human being. Furthermore, by involving *sense* in the perception of forms Blake sets himself against the Platonic–Christian denigration of sense experience. Blake's 'Sense,' however, is not the sensation of the natural or biological body; nor is sense the functional meaning produced by a body located within the world. 'Sense [is] the Eye of the Imagination.' Blake is able to establish a notion of *sense perception* that anticipates Deleuze's transcendental empiricism. Sense emerges from sensations, but sensations are not located within psychophysical or isolated bodies: sensations are inhuman powers or forces that may or may not be actualized. Blake's conception of the spiritual body overcomes the dichotomy between the sense of the soul and the incarnated body; the faculty of Imagination perceives and constitutes a 'human form divine,' which *is* the spiritual body. The body is therefore already involved with the imagination or creative faculty and can participate in the world of 'forms.' The Platonic distinction, then, between the realm of the forms and the realm of the material world becomes untenable, for the correctly perceived world is already 'formed.' In answer to Berkeley's definition of the Platonic soul Blake responds: 'The Natural Body is an Obstruction to the Soul or *Spiritual Body*' (E: 664; K: 775, emphasis added). There is neither a reduction of life to the natural body, nor some separate substance of spirit; the body is a spiritual body. The sense that apprehends forms is the sense of the spiritual body, not the body limited by natural science. Blake's poetry is Christian in just this abandonment of the self to a divinity that is in bodies themselves:

> This is what Christian painting had already discovered in the religious sentiment: a properly pictorial atheism, where one could adhere literally to the idea that God must not be represented. With God – but also with Christ, the Virgin, and even Hell – lines, colors, movements are freed from the demands of representation. The Figures are lifted up, or doubled over, or contorted, freed from all figuration. They no longer have anything to represent or narrate, since in this domain they are content to refer to the existing code of the Church. Thus, in themselves, they no longer have to do with anything but "sensations" – celestial, infernal, or terrestrial sensations. Everything is made to pass through the code; the religious sentiment is painted in all the colors of the world. One must not say, "If God does not exist everything is permitted." It is just the opposite. For with God, everything is permitted. It is with God that everything is permitted, not only morally, since acts of violence and infamies always find a holy justification, but aesthetically, in a much more important manner, because the divine figures are wrought by a free creative work, by a fantasy in which everything is permitted (Deleuze 2005, 7).

Far from being the expression of a logic or metaphysics, by allowing matters to stand alone and shine by their inner light, Blake sacrifices the position of judgment and unity for the sake of a divinity, which if it resides in the human breast is still wondrous and *in*human in its resistance to cognition.

Blake's doctrine of forms is connected with both his ontology and his aesthetics. Blake insistently asserts the particular identity of things in response to modern science's drive to uniformity, which he sees as the denial of form. Accordingly, in his fine art, Blake stresses the importance of bounding lines that will emphasize particularity and difference. Blake values 'form' above 'tints:' 'In a work of Art it is not fine tints that are required but Fine Forms, fine Tints without, are loathsom Fine Tints without Fine Forms are always the Subterfuge of the Blockhead' (*Public Address*, E: 571; K: 591). In 'Night the Seventh' of *The Four Zoas* Los begins the process of universal redemption by giving form to Urizen's chaos. In doing so he uses line:

And first he drew a line upon the walls of shining heaven
And Enitharmon tincturd it with beams of blushing love
It remaind permanent a lovely form inspird divinely human
Dividing into just proportions Los unwearied labourd
The immortal lines upon the heavens with sighs of love
(FZ, p. 98[90], 35–39, E: 371; K: 332)

Robert Essick has carefully described the ways in which the reproduced copy C of Blake's *Jerusalem* looks as though it is distorted by accidental and clumsy splashes, while the rarely seen original allows the eye to discern fine tonal gradations that are intentional. The minutiae lost in mass reproduction allow the plates to take on an ad hoc quality, so that the intentional act is lost both in dissemination and through the process of time (for as Essick also notes, the unavoidable fading of plates emphasizes the bold outline and diminishes the finer lines and stipples.) Blake's work is peculiarly subject to the time of matter. The very conditions that set his artistry outside mass production, the unique individuality of each of his plates, were the same conditions that tied his art, not to a formal language that could be repeated and circulated regardless of the tokens used, but to materials that could act with a 'life' of their own, deadening the intuition of differences that were so important for Blake. This resisting matter that Blake's poetry so positively allows to stand alone – in his embrace of the ways in which the materials guide his hand and contribute to his figures – also works against Blake.

In this regard Blake's corpus brings the paradox of the archive to the fore. The condition for a poem living on is that it take on some body and submit to the forms of matter. But those very forms that allow for its maintenance through time also destroy continuous time: the poem depends upon the matter on which the text is engraved (the paper, plates, color, and ink), and requires the forms that matter dictates (only some modes of line and light are possible within Blake's techniques for transmission). Blake's humanity within which all deities reside is not, therefore, a humanity that creates itself from itself and constitutes its own time. It is a humanity that will be exposed to an incarnation that it cannot master.

Humanity, for Blake, is redeemed not by mastering time and matter, but by self-annihilation: destroying the point of view that would fold the world around its own practical, efficient, and lawful body. Matter must not be redeemed – rendered spiritual – but allowed to be, in its own duration. But this is not as easy or straightforwardly redemptive as it sounds. The conditions for allowing matter to be, discerning its own time and spirit, are also the same conditions that humanize and master matter. This can be explained more concretely in terms of Blake's sexual politics.

Modernist aesthetics had maintained the Romanticist tradition of affirming the feminine as the figure of an unbounded life and plenitude that might re-vivify a language enslaved to function, technology, and mastery. In the modernist tradition inflected by Blake's poetry we can think of Yeats' 'Leda and the Swan,' where an act of rape must precede creation: a violent and disruptive overtaking of female fertility inaugurates a force that is liberated from all worldly and already formed matter: 'How can those terrified vague fingers push/The feathered glory from her loosening thighs? … A shudder in the loins engenders there/The broken wall, the burning roof and tower/And Agamemnon dead.' We can also think of D.H. Lawrence's sexual metaphysics, in which a sexuality that is no longer human – no longer oriented to maintaining the organic life of man – liberates time from ongoing history, creating an apocalyptic event. Suggestions of rape or masculine force overcoming the inertia of matter are not far from Lawrence's sexual imagery. It is only when bodily force or energy takes over, and not the 'sex in the head' of intention, that time can be lived creatively. Modernism often renders explicit a notion of self-fathering that has marked the history of poetry; creation overcomes or dominates the resistance of matter or otherness and creates from itself in a godlike manner. Blake also used images of violence and rape to figure the overcoming of resistance as a preamble to revolution, as though poetry were a prophetic break with chronological time. Such is Blake's insistence on the necessity for breaking the rules of chastity and morality that the 'Preludium' to *America* depicts the rape of the 'shadowy daughter of Urthona.' Prior to being raped the 'shadowy' female lacks both voice and identity; when she is seized by Orc her resistance is not that of a subject but of an impersonal objectivity. Referring to Urthona's womb, the voice declares that 'It joy'd':

> The hairy shoulders rend the links, free are the wrists of fire;
> Round the terrific loins he siez'd the panting struggling womb;
> It joy'd: she put aside her clouds & smiled her first-born smile;
> (*America* 2, 2–4, E: 52; K: 196)

It is Blake's insistence on the value of excess and the destruction of bounds to the creative imagination that in his earlier works often implied a valorisation of violence. It is this aspect of Blake's poetry as animation – as antithetical to inertia and resistance – that has provided the rubric for reading his later work. Matter or the feminine is not in itself evil, but becomes so when it is detached from the forming energizing power, becoming a tyrannical mystery or desired but unobtainable 'harlot.' The original poetic impulse that animates the world should therefore destroy all that which has become enslaved to system. Poetry is not, then, a creative activity within the world, but life itself. This world exists in its distinction only because the powers of perception give form, life, and spirit. Perception is, or should be, active and bodily. But if the poetic and creative power of perception is lost and we receive the world as so much external matter then we fall into despair, judgment, accusation, guilt, and terror.

There are two ways, however, in which the doors of perception might be cleansed. The first, as I have suggested, is in accord with a tradition of rationalist, vitalist, and masculinist poetics. Matter in itself is devoid of life and can only be animated by an active forming power. In Blake's poetry, this ethic expresses itself as a journey from the feminine as terrifying and external nature, to the feminine as the emanation or contrary of one's being – the deflection required by life to recognize itself. Poetry would, then, be an expression of life, a giving of body to the spirit, and would be presented in all Blake's images of molding, engraving, and weaving. However, there is also a resistance to the norms of reflection and self-fathering in Blake's poetry. If his early poetry celebrated the young, male, destructive, and fiery body of Orc that would tear down all law and system, his later poetry is aware of the ways in which that violent desire to overcome all resistance and contrariety creates a satanic self-enclosure. One way of thinking this other Blake is to retrieve the radical Christianity of his work, not Christianity as a religion that might make its way in the world, but Christianity as a problem of incarnation.

In *Milton* Blake presents the earlier poet taking up his female emanations, recognizing his own Satanic (accusing, moralizing) tendencies, and also realizing that his redemption requires recognition of what cannot be reduced to law, principle, and mind. The 'real' human Milton is a walking body (M 20, 13), while the Milton of mind has to mold a clay body for Urizen (or the reasoning power [M 20 10–12]). However, that very process of *recognizing* the feminine and corporeality reduces sexual otherness to the medium of the subject's own redemption. One might say that sexual difference discloses the problem of language per se: in referring to what is other than itself the sign can only do so by way of incorporation. Difference is referred to by way of being reduced. The way beyond this closure of difference, language, and desire is pursued by Blake through several paths. The first is the dramatic nature of his poetry, where voices of redemption and salvation fall back into accusation, becoming the very tyranny they overthrow. The second is through performative contradiction: Blake's poems at one and the same time condemn the voice of morality, principle, law, accusation, and mastery, at the same time as they judge the world to be suffering *from* morality.

In his early poetry Blake tackles this necessary duplicity of voice by setting innocence alongside experience. The problem with the voice of innocence is that in *this* world, as it is, the commitment to an unfallen, redeemed, divine, and blissful life precludes any action that would lead to change or revolution. The problem with the voice of experience is that while it recognizes the suffering that should prompt us to act, it does so in such a despairing and distant manner that it can see no way – other than judgment or condemnation – for the world to change. The truly new can only emerge beyond the *states* of innocence and experience. If 'The Imagination is not a State: it is the Human Existence itself' (M 32[35], 33, E: 132; K: 522), then it cannot be given in any voice or figure but only in the relations among figures.[4] Blake's poetry struggles between remaining above and beyond the states, figures, or matters of life – prophetically distanced from the voices he masters – and sacrificing poetry to the force of matter itself, allowing voices, rhythms, names, myths, and figures to take over the imagination. Reading Blake is therefore similarly poised between the vital and the inert, between the commitment to making sense of the work by returning it to its animating intent, and allowing that work to exist as it is in itself, bearing a time that can never be brought to presence. On the one hand Blake's poetry is that of the man of onto-theology, who differs from himself only to recognize himself and all that appears as other as an emanation of his own life. On the other hand, Blake's is a poetry of sexual difference, in which the medium through which the self is reflected and knows itself is never the self's own; the feminine is neither man's complement nor mirror – neither a void from which existence is formed nor the self's other half.

Finally, it is in this regard that Blake's poetry is poised between Christianity and theology. As *Christian*, Blake's poetry renounces the sense and meaning of this 'vegetative' world and yet strives to express the divine *in matter* – to give matter itself its own spirit, life, and time. The body as expressed in Christian art is not the image of mastery, activity, and progressive time, but is a force or power that opens up times not our own. As *theological* Blake's poetry strives to regard the divinity of worldly bodies as signs of the ultimate humanity of all existence. We can take the phrase that 'all deities reside in the human breast' in two mutually exclusive (or contrary) senses. To say that all divinity is *human* is to say that the spiritual is of our own making, that we animate the world, and that there is nothing that cannot be redeemed, internalized, and recognized as an expression of the one ultimately human life. To say that the human breast harbors *deities* is to suggest that there are eternities, vortices, and powers in the human which are not those of mind, and which open up lines of time not our own. Criticism, insofar as it reads poetry, must work with both these senses.

There is, ultimately, a theology of all reading, or a sense that the text expresses a life of which we are also expressions; without that intimation of the meaning of life we would remain within ourselves. At the same time, the poem stands alone, as a material and created thing, detached from the life that gave it being. Without that sense of the distance, separateness, and *death* of the poem, reading would not be able to think beyond its own life.

Notes

Preface

[1] 'For if geometry is not part of painting, there are nonetheless properly pictorial uses of geometry. We called one of these uses 'digital,' not in direct reference to the hand, but in reference to the basic units of a code. Once again, these basic units or elementary visual forms are indeed aesthetic and not mathematic, inasmuch as they have completely internalized the manual movement that produces them. They still form a code of painting, however, and turn painting into a code. It is in this sense, close to abstract painting, that we must understand Sérusier's saying: 'Synthesis consists in reducing all forms to the smallest number of forms of which we are capable of thinking – straight lines, some angles, arcs of the circle and the ellipse.' Synthesis is thus an analytic of elements. When Cézanne, on the contrary, urges the painter to 'treat nature through the cylinder, the sphere, the cone, putting the whole in perspective,' one has the impression that abstract painters would be wrong to see this as a blessing – not only because Cézanne puts the emphasis on volumes, except the cube, but above all because he suggests a completely different use of geometry than that of a code of painting. The cylinder is this stovepipe (emerging from the tinsmith's hands) or this man (whose arms do not matter...). Following current terminology, we could say that Cézanne creates an 'analogical use of geometry, and not a digital use.' (Deleuze 2005, 79).

[2] 'Now this merely subjective (aesthetic) judging of the object, or of the representation through which the object is given, precedes the pleasure in it, and is the ground of this pleasure in the harmony of the faculties of cognition; but on that universality of the subjective conditions of the judging of objects alone is this universal subjective validity of satisfaction, which we combine with the representation of the object that we call beautiful, grounded.

That being able to communicate one's mind, even if only with regard to the faculties of cognition, carries a pleasure with it, could easily be established (empirically and psychologically) from the natural tendency of human beings to sociability. But that is not enough for our purposes. When we call something beautiful, the pleasure that we feel is expected of everyone else in the judgment of taste as necessary, just as if it were to be regarded as a property of the object that is determined in it in accordance with concepts; but beauty is nothing by itself, without relation to the feeling of the subject' (Kant 2001, 103.)

[3] 'If capitalism is the universal truth, it is so in the sense that makes capitalism *the negative* of all social formations. It is the thing, the unnameable, the generalized decoding of flows that reveals *a contrario* the secret of all these formations, coding the flows, and even overcoding them, rather than letting anything escape coding. Primitive societies are not outside history; rather, it is capitalism that is at the end of history, it is capitalism that results from a long history of contingencies and accidents, and that brings on this end' (Deleuze and Guattari 2004A, 168).

[4] Josephine A. McQuail (2000) argues that Blake is a mystic, and that his vision of integration should be interpreted as the reincorporation of male/forming and female/receptive principles – the separation of the latter constituting evil.

Chapter 2

[1] 'Since no utterance can be isolated completely from this dialogic matrix, each utterance, as a response, has its source in the discourse of others. These references in Blake's writings to other figures, in statements and in addresses, indicate a profound realization of the dialogic nature of discourse' (Jones 1994, 3).

Chapter 3

[1] There is some dispute whether bodies, organisms or phenotypes are nothing more than vehicles for genes to become actualised, but the 'selfish gene' motif does suggest that embodied life is nothing more than a temporary medium allowing genes to survive and compete. For an intelligent critique of this problem see Mader 2010.

[2] This logic of Christ's sacrifice as the reversal of humanity's overvaluing of itself is made most clear in Milton's *Paradise Lost* where 'one greater man' will be the means through which life may regain its proper trajectory towards divinity. In his book on the painting of Francis Bacon, Deleuze (2005) argues for a becoming-secular of Christian aesthetics that occurs in the imperative to paint the body of Christ, to make the matter of paint itself expressive of spirit. In this sense one could regard contemporary and seemingly secular theories of immanence – where life itself bears its own creative, fruitful, and self-expressive qualities as post-Christian or onto-theological precisely insofar as it is life now, rather than God, that is the ultimate expansive power that knows no outside, finitude or negation.

Chapter 6

[1] For example: "The pendulous round Earth with ballanc't air" (PL.4.1000), "Upon her Center pois'd" (PL.5.579), "This pendant World" (PL. 2. 1052) and "And Earth self-ballanc't on her Center hung" (PL. 7. 242).

Conclusion

[1] Harold Bloom, writing of *There is No Natural Religion*, points out that Blake's reaction to Cartesian doubt was to endow the natural world with as much truth and meaning as possible: 'As Descartes had resolved to doubt whatever could be doubted, so Blake in reaction resolved to find an image of truth in everything it was possible to believe.' (Bloom 1963, 24).

[2] Morton D. Paley has argued that Blake's theory of creation-as-emanation in *The Four Zoas* forces him to see the body as fallen despite his avowed valorisation of the body elsewhere. The figure of weaving, or the garment, is therefore introduced to overcome this difficulty by placing an intermediary between the spiritual and natural levels of being: 'In introducing the figure of the garment, Blake makes it possible for us to view the body as a buffer zone between the drives and appetites which constitute man as mere spectre and Beulah, the potential earthly paradise within.' (Paley 1973, 126).

[3] Paul Mann (1986) has argued that Blake's language approaches the 'semiotic' function. Following Julia Kristeva, there is a position between the undifferentiated flux of pre-Oedipal plenitude, and the orderly and lawful difference of language. The semiotic is disclosed in language that is close to the body: cries, laughter, pulsations, and infant musicality.

[4] According to Tilottama Rajan, 'the synthesis of the two contrary states is unembodied by any specific poem in the collection, and remains something that must be brought into being in our own minds' (Rajan, 1994, 40).

Works Cited

Abrams, Meyer Howard. 1963. 'English Romanticism: The Spirit of the Age.' In *Romanticism Reconsidered: Selected Papers from the English Institute*. Ed. Northrop Frye. New York: Columbia University Press, pp. 26–72.

Agamben, Giorgio. 1998. *Homo Sacer: Sovereign Power and Bare Life*. Trans. Daniel Heller-Roazen. Stanford: Stanford University Press.

Agamben, Giorgio. 1999. *The Man without Content*. Trans. Georgia Albert. Stanford: Stanford University Press.

Apel, Karl-Otto. 1998. *From a Transcendental-Semiotic Point of View*. Ed. Marianna Papastephanou. Manchester: Manchester University Press.

Badiou, Alain. 2011. 'The Democratic Emblem.' In *Democracy in What State*. Eds. Giorgio Agamben, et al. Trans. William McCuaig. New York: Columbia University Press, pp. 6–16.

Bataille, Georges. 1973. *Literature and Evil*. Trans. Alastair Hamilton. London: Calder and Boyars.

Benjamin, Walter. 2008. *The Work of Art in the Age of Mechanical Reproduction*, Penguin Great Ideas Series. Trans. J. A. Underwood. Harmondsworth: Penguin.

Benn Michaels, Walter and Steven Knapp. 1982. 'Against Theory.' *Critical Inquiry*. 8.4(Summer): 723–742.

Bergson, Henri. 2004. *Matter and Memory*. New York: Dover.

—. 1931. *Creative Evolution*. Trans. Arthur Mitchell. New York: H. Holt and Company.

Bernstein, J. M. 2006. *Against Voluptuous Bodies: Late Modernism and the Meaning of Painting*. Stanford: Stanford University Press.

Blake, William. *The William Blake Archive*. Eds. Morris Eaves, Robert N. Essick, and Joseph Viscomi. 10 May 2011 <http://www.blakearchive.org/> .

Bloom, Harold. 1963. *Blake's Apocalypse: A Study in Poetic Argument*. New York: Doubleday.

Bloom, Howard K. 2000. *The Global Brain: The Evolution of Mass Mind from the Big Bang to the 21st Century*. New York: Wiley.

Byers, Damian. 2002. *Intentionality and Transcendence: Closure and Openness in Husserl's Phenomenology*. Madison: University of Wisconsin Press.

Capra, Fritjof. 1996. *The Web of Life: A New Scientific Understanding of Living Systems*. New York: Anchor Books.

Colebrook, Claire. 2008. *Milton, Evil and Literary History*. London: Continuum.

—. 2010. *Deleuze and the Meaning of Life*. London: Continuum.

—. 2011. 'Matter Without Bodies.' *Derrida Today*. 4.1: 1–20.

Collingwood, Robin George. 1976. *The Idea of Nature.* Oxford: Oxford University Press.
Damasio, Antonio. 1999. *The Feeling of What Happens: Body and Emotion in the Making of Consciousness.* New York: Harcourt Brace.
—. 2010. *Self Comes to Mind: Constructing the Conscious Brain.* New York: Pantheon Books.
De Man, Paul. 1976. 'Political Allegory in Rousseau.' *Critical Inquiry.* 2.4(Summer): 649–675.
—. 1986. *Resistance to Theory.* Minneapolis: University of Minnesota Press.
Deleuze, Gilles. 2004a. *The Logic of Sense.* London: Continuum.
—. 2004b. *Difference and Repetition.* Trans. Paul Patton. London: Continuum.
—. 2005. *Francis Bacon: The Logic of Sensation.* Trans. Daniel W. Smith. London: Continuum.
—. 2006a. *Nietzsche and Philosophy.* London: Continuum.
—. 2006b. *The Fold: Leibniz and the Baroque.* Trans. Tom Conley. London: Continuum.
—. 2006c. *Foucault.* Trans. Sean Hand. London: Continuum.
Deleuze, Gilles and Claire Parnet. 2007. *Dialogues II.* 2nd Edition. New York: Columbia.
Deleuze, Gilles and Félix Guattari. 1994. *What Is Philosophy?* London: Verso.
—. 2004a. *Anti-Oedipus: Capitalism and Schizophrenia.* London: Continuum.
—. 2004b. *A Thousand Plateaus: Capitalism and Schizophrenia.* Trans. Brian Massumi. London: Continuum.
Derrida, Jacques. 1987. '*Geschlecht II*: Heidegger's Hand.' *Deconstruction and Philosophy: The Texts of Jacques Derrida.* Ed. John Sallis. Trans. John P. Leavey, Jr. Chicago: University of Chicago Press, pp. 161–196.
—. 1989. 'Biodegradables Seven Diary Fragments.' Trans. Peggy Kamuf. *Critical Inquiry.* 15.4(Summer): 812–873.
—. 1993. 'Of an Apocalyptic Tone Newly Adopted in Philosophy.' In *Raising the Tone of Philosophy: Late Essays by Immanuel Kant, Transformative Critique by Jacques Derrida.* Ed. Peter Fenves. Baltimore: Johns Hopkins University Press.
—. 2004. *Dissemination.* Trans. Barbara Johnson. London: Continuum.
Detienne, Marcel. 1996. *The Masters of Truth in Ancient Greece.* Trans. Janet Lloyd. Cambridge: MIT Press.
Dimock, Wai-chee. 2003. 'Nonbiological Clock: Literary History against Newtonian Mechanics.' *The South Atlantic Quarterly.* 102.1(Winter): 153–177.
Eagleton, Terry. 2008. *Literary Theory: An Introduction.* Minneapolis: University of Minnesota Press.
Fish, Stanley. 2001. *How Milton Works.* Cambridge, MA: Belknap Press of Harvard University Press.
Foucault, Michel. 1978. *The History of Sexuality.* Volume 1. Trans. Robert Hurley. New York: Pantheon Books.
—. 1979. *Discipline and Punish: The Birth of the Prison.* Trans. Alan Sheridan. New York: Vintage Books.
—. 2006. *History of Madness.* Trans. Jean Khalfa. London: Routledge.
Freud, Sigmund. 1930. *Civilization and Its Discontents.* Trans. Jean Riviere. New York: J. Cape and H. Smith.
Gilson, Etienne. 1983. *The Christian Philosophy of Thomas Aquinas.* Virginia: Octagon.
Goldmann, Lucien. 1975. *Towards a Sociology of the Novel.* Trans. Alan Sheridan. London: Tavistock.

Goode, Michael. 2006. 'Blakespotting.' *PMLA*. 121.3: 769–786.
Grosz, Elizabeth. 2004. *The Nick of Time: Politics, Evolution, and the Untimely*. Durham: Duke University Press.
Habermas, Jurgen. 1973. *Theory and Practice.* Trans. John Viertel. Boston: Beacon Press.
Haberman, Jurgen. 1992. *Moral Consciousness and Communicative Action.* Trans. Christian Lenhardt and Shierry Weber Nicholsen. Cambridge: MIT Press.
—. *Justification and Application: Remarks on Discourse Ethics.* Trans. Ciaran P. Cronin. Cambridge: MIT Press.
Hartman, Geoffrey. 1970. 'Romanticism and Anti-Self-Consciousness.' *Beyond Formalism: Literary Essays 1958–1970.* New Haven: Yale University Press, pp. 298–310.
Hayles, N. Katherine. 2007. 'Hyper and Deep Attention: The Generational Divide in Cognitive Modes.' *Profession.* 13: 187–199.
Hegel, Georg W.F. 2009. *The Phenomenology of Spirit.* Trans. J. B. Baillie. Digireads.com
Heidegger, Martin. 1968. *What Is a Thing?* Trans. W. B. Barton, Jr. and Vera Deutsch. Chicago: H. Regnery Co.
—. 1977. *The Question Concerning Technology, and Other Essays.* Trans. William Lovitt. New York: Harper & Row.
—. 1996. *Being and Time.* Trans. Joan Stambaugh. Albany: State University of New York Press.
—. 1998a. 'Plato's Doctrine of Truth.' In *Pathmarks.* Ed. William McNeill. Cambridge: Cambridge University Press, pp. 155–182.
—. 1998b. 'Letter on "Humanism." ' In *Pathmarks.* Ed. William McNeill. Cambridge: Cambridge University Press, pp. 239–276.
Husserl, Edmund. 2006. *The Basic Problems of Phenomenology: From the Lectures, Winter Semester, 1910–1911.* Trans. Ingo Farin and James G. Hart. Dordrecht: Springer.
Jones, John J. 1994. '"Self-Annihilation" and Dialogue in Blake's Creative Process: Urizen, Milton, Jerusalem.' *Modern Language Studies.* 24.2(Spring): 3–10.
Kant, Immanuel. 1998. *Critique of Pure Reason.* Trans. and Eds. Paul Guyer and Allen W. Wood. Cambridge: Cambridge University Press.
—. 2001. *Critique of the Power of Judgment: The Cambridge Edition of the Works of Immanuel Kant in Translation.* Eds. Paul Guyer and Eric Matthews. Trans. Eric Matthews. Cambridge: Cambridge University Press.
—. 2007. 'Anthopology from a Practical Point of View.' In *Anthropology, History and Education.* Eds. Gunther Zoller and Robert B. Louden. Trans. Robert B. Louden. Cambridge: Cambridge University Press.
Lacoue-Labarthe, Philipe and Jean-Luc Nancy. 1988. *The Literary Absolute: The Theory of Literature in German Romanticism.* Trans. Philip Barnard and Cheryl Lester. Albany: State University of New York Press.
Lovelock, James. 1979. *Gaia, A New Look at Life on Earth.* Oxford: Oxford University Press.
Lyotard, Jean-Francois. 1993. *The Postmodern Explained: Correspondence, 1982–1985.* Trans. Julian Pefanis and Morgan Thomas. Minneapolis: University of Minnesota Press.
—. 1994. *Lessons on the Analytic of the Sublime: Kant's Critique of Judgment.* Trans. Elizabeth Rottenberg. Stanford: Stanford University Press.
Mader, Mary Beth. 2010. 'Foucault's 'Metabody.' *Journal of Bioethical Inquiry.* 7.2: 187–203.

Mann, Paul. '*The Book of Urizen* and the Horizon of the Book.' In *Unnam'd Forms: Blake and Textuality*. Eds. Nelson Hilton and Thomas A. Vogler. Berkeley: University of California Press, pp. 49–68.

McGann, Jerome J. 1983. *The Romantic Ideology: A Critical Investigation*. Chicago: University of Chicago Press.

—. 1988. *Social Values and Poetic Acts: A Historical Judgment of Literary Work*. Cambridge: Harvard University Press.

McQuail, Josephine. 2000. 'Passion and Mysticism in William Blake.' *Modern Language Studies*. 30.1 (Spring): 121–134.

Mee, Jon. 1992. *Dangerous Enthusiasm: William Blake and the Culture of Radicalism in the 1790s*. Oxford: Clarendon Press.

Milton, John. 2008. *Areopagitica: A Defense of Free Speech*. Rockville: Arc Manor.

Mohanty, Jitendranath. 1976.*Edmund Husserl's Theory of Meaning*. The Hague: Martinus Nijhoff.

Nancy, Jean-Luc. 2003. *A Finite Thinking*. Ed. Simon Sparks. Stanford: Stanford University Press.

Newton, Isaac. 1934. *Sir Isaac Newton's Mathematical Principles of Natural Philosophy and His System of the World*. Trans. Andrew Motte (1729). Rev. and Ed. Florian Cajori. Berkeley: University of California Press.

Otto, Peter. 1991. *Constructive Vision and Visionary Deconstruction: Los, Eternity, and the Productions of Time in the Later Poetry of William Blake*. Oxford: Clarendon Press.

Paley, Morton D. 1973. 'The Figure of the Garment in the Four Zoas, Milton and Jerusalem.' *Blake's Sublime Allegory: Essays on the Four Zoas, Milton, Jerusalem*. Eds. Stuart Curran and Joseph Wittreich. Madison: University of Wisconsin Press.

Pirsig, Robert M. 1974. *Zen and the Art of Motorcycle Maintenance: An Inquiry into Values*. New York: Morrow.

Protevi, John. 2001. *Political Physics: Deleuze, Derrida and the Body Politic*. London: Athlone.

Rajan, Tillotima. 1994. 'The Other Reading: Transactional Epic in Milton, Blake, and Wordsworth.' *Milton, the Metaphysicals and Romanticism*. Eds. Lisa Low and Anthony John Harding. Cambridge: Cambridge University Press, pp. 20–46.

Ramachandran, V. S. and Edward M. Hubbard. 2003. 'The Phenomenology of Synaesthesia.' *Journal of Consciousness Studies*. 10.8: 49–57.

Ramachandran, V. S. and Hirstein, William. 1999. 'The science of art: A neurological theory of aesthetic experience.' *Journal of Consciousness Studies*. 6: 15–51.

Rawls, John. 1972. *A Theory of Justice*. Oxford: Clarendon Press.

Rogers, John. 1996. *The Matter of Revolution: Science, Poetry, and Politics in the Age of Milton*. Ithaca: Cornell University Press.

Ruyer, Raymond. 1958. *La genese des formes vivantes*. Paris: Flammarion.

Smith, Daniel W. 2003. 'Mathematics and the Theory of Multiplicities: Badiou and Deleuze Revisited.' *The Southern Journal of Philosophy*. 41.3: 411–449.

Stempel, Daniel. 1981. 'Blake, Foucault and the Classical Episteme.' *PMLA*. 96.3: 388–407.

Stiegler, Bernard. 1998. *Technics and Time 1: The Fault of Epimetheus*. Stanford: Stanford University Press.

Stiegler, Bernard. 2010. *For a New Critique f Political Economy*. Trans. Daniel Ross. Cambridge: Polity.

Taylor, Mark. 2007. *After God.* Chicago: University of Chicago Press.
Thompson, Evan. 2007. *Mind in Life: Biology, Phenomenology, and the Sciences of Mind.* Cambridge, MA: Belknap Press of Harvard University Press.
Thomson, James. 1836. 'To the Memory of Sir Isaac Newton.' *The Poetical Works of James Thomson.* Volume 2. London.
Villa, Dana R. 1996. *Arendt and Heidegger: The Fate of the Political.* Princeton: Princeton University Press.
Viscomi, Joseph. 1993. *Blake and the Idea of the Book.* Princeton: Princeton University Press.
Von Uexküll, Jakob. 2010. *A Foray into the Worlds of Animals and Humans: With a Theory of Meaning.* Trans. Joseph D. O'Neil. Minneapolis: University of Minnesota Press.
Webster, Brenda S. 1983. *Blake's Prophetic Psychology.* Athens: University of Georgia Press.
Whitehead, Alfred North. 1978. *Process and Reality: An Essay in Cosmology.* Eds. David Ray Griffin and Donald W. Sherburne. New York: Free Press.
Wittreich, Joseph Anthony. Ed. 1975a. *Milton and the Line of Vision.* University of Wisconsin Press.
—. 1975b. *Angel of Apocalypse: Blake's Idea of Milton.* Madison: University of Wisconsin Press.
Youngquist, Paul. 1989. *Madness and Blake's Myth.* University Park: Penn State University Press.

Index

Continuum Literary Studies Series
Also available in the series:

Active Reading by Ben Knights and Chris Thurgar-Dawson
Adapting Detective Fiction by Neil McCaw
Beckett's Books by Matthew Feldman
Beckett and Death edited by Steve Barfield, Matthew Feldman, and Philip Tew
Beckett and Decay by Katherine White
Beckett and Phenomenology edited by Matthew Feldman and Ulrika Maude
Canonizing Hypertext by Astrid Ensslin
Character and Satire in Postwar Fiction by Ian Gregson
Coleridge and German Philosophy by Paul Hamilton
Contemporary Fiction and Christianity by Andrew Tate
Ecstasy and Understanding edited by Adrian Grafe
English Fiction in the 1930s by Chris Hopkins
Fictions of Globalization by James Annesley
The Imagination of Evil by Mary Evans
Joyce and Company by David Pierce
London Narratives by Lawrence Phillips
Masculinity in Fiction and Film by Brian Baker
The Measureless Past of Joyce, Deleuze and Derrida by Ruben Borg
Milton, Evil and Literary History by Claire Colebrook
Modernism and the Post-Colonial by Peter Childs
Novels of the Contemporary Extreme edited by Alain-Phillipe Durand and Naomi Mandel
The Palimpsest by Sarah Dillon
Post-War British Women Novelists and the Canon by Nick Turner
Postmodern Fiction and the Break-Up of Fiction by Hywel Dix
Seeking Meaning for Goethe's Faust by J. M. van der Laan
Sexuality and the Erotic in the Fiction of Joseph Conrad by Jeremy Hawthorn
Such Deliberate Disguises: The Art of Phillip Larkin by Richard Palmer
Women's Fiction 1945-2000 by Deborah Philips

Blake, Deleuzian Aesthetics, and the Digital